POLITICS AND RELIGION

Steve Bruce

KU-525-766

polity

First published in 2003 by Polity Press in association with Blackwell Publishing Ltd

Editorial office:
Polity Press
65 Bridge Street
Cambridge CB2 1UR, UK

Marketing and production:
Blackwell Publishing Ltd
108 Cowley Road
Oxford OX4 1JF, UK

Distributed in the USA by
Blackwell Publishing Inc.
350 Main Street
Malden, MA 02148, USA

A catalogue record for this book is available from the British Library.

Library of Congress Cataloging-in-Publication Data

Bruce, Steve, 1954–
Politics and religion / Steve Bruce.
        p. cm.
Includes bibliographical references and index.
ISBN 0-7456-2819-2 (hb: alk. paper)—ISBN 0-7456-2820-6 (pbk.: alk. paper)
1.   Religion and politics. I. Title.
BL65.P7 B78 2003
322'.1—dc21   2002015363

Typeset in 10.5 on 12 pt Palatino
by Kolam Information Services Pvt. Ltd, Pondicherry, India
Printed and bound in Great Britain by MPG Books, Bodmin, Cornwall

For further information on Polity, visit our website: www.polity.co.uk

CONTENTS

DETAILED CONTENTS

PREFACE

It has its moments of originality, but this book is intended as an introduction to a very large and somewhat neglected topic. Social scientists interested in politics have generally not given much attention to religion and much sociology of religion ignores politics entirely. Because I have covered a lot of ground, some of the examples have had to be treated in a rather cursory manner. This may offend the experts, but I have used extensive endnotes to point the interested reader to the sources where the omitted detail can be found.

A number of principles have informed the selection of illustrations for the general analytical points I want to make. Some are little gems that, like a magpie with baubles, I have hoarded for years, just because they fascinated me. For example, I have long wanted an excuse to tell the story of the Moscow Cathedral that became an open-air swimming pool, just because it is a great story. Most illustrations have been chosen for the slightly more principled reason that they make the necessary point in a reasonably economical manner. For example, in discussing the ways in which empires tried to manage peoples of diverse religious cultures, I chose to concentrate on the Ottoman Empire and the British Raj because, as well as being interesting in their own right, they allow me to introduce countries and states that later illustrate other points.

A point about method: I hope it will be clear that I am not taking sides. Much writing on religion and politics is partisan. As well as analysing connections, it wants to score points. Adherents are often concerned to alter the moral record so that their faith is credited with social virtues and avoids the blame for social evils. A liberal

Muslim may simply assert that Pakistan, Saudi Arabia and the like are 'unIslamic'. Doubtless my own preferences occasionally intrude, but I have tried to maintain a tone of religious neutrality throughout. I am certainly not doing any 'really'; as in 'Is Saudi Arabia "really" Muslim?' Except where there is some compelling evidence to justify doing something else, I take claimed identities at something like face value. The Ayatollah Khomeini claimed he was a Muslim. Millions of Muslims think he was a Muslim. Of course I might want to add that many Muslims disagreed with him, but it is not my business to decide who is a true Muslim. Likewise I assume that people who regularly attend church and say in surveys that they are Christians are actually Christians. Or rather, to put it the other way round, I am not qualified to decide who 'really' has the ear of God.

There are no universally accepted rules for rendering Arabic and Chinese into English. I have tried to be consistent in my own text but I have not altered spellings in things I have quoted.

ACKNOWLEDGEMENTS

I would like to thank Sophie Ahmad of Polity Press for suggesting I write the book. I would also like to thank the Economic and Social Research Council, which funded the Scottish survey mentioned briefly in chapter 4, and my colleague Tony Glendinning, who assisted greatly with the analysis of the data it produced. As have most of my books, this has been copy-edited by the meticulous Hilary Walford and is all the better for it.

Finally I would like to thank David Martin for years of encouragement. Critics who think I exaggerate the secularization of liberal democracies often cite David Martin against me. My impression of our relationship is very different. I have always taken his insistence on setting the questions that sociologists ask of religion in their proper historical, geographical and political contexts as a model to us all. I was honoured that he examined my doctoral thesis in 1980 and, though I am sure this book would have been considerably more erudite if he had written it, I hope that he will see something of his own spirit in it.

Steve Bruce

I

RELIGION

Introduction

Religion in the comfortable societies of the modern industrial world is now largely a private and domestic matter. The radicals of the French Revolution may have wanted, in a phrase popularized by Diderot, to strangle the nobility with the guts of the priests.[1] The English Methodists may have wanted to break the power of the established Church of England with the Great Reform Act of 1832. But by the late 1960s most Western Europeans would have thought there was little of interest to say about the impact of religion on politics. What we believed about the supernatural was a personal matter, its reach largely confined to the private sphere of home and hearth. Most democracies were formally secular. They accorded few privileges to their dominant churches and inflicted few disabilities on the followers of minority creeds. Modern bureaucracies managed national systems of education, social control and social welfare that paid little attention to religious affiliation and claimed little by way of divine approval. Elites might pay lip service to some God and great state ceremonies might be graced by clergy, but piety and theological rectitude played very little part in government policies. Regional peripheries tended to be more traditionally religious than cosmopolitan centres, but that was treated, along with thick accents, as proof of quaint backwardness. In most Western societies active participation in organized religion was in decline. If the Christian churches were politically active, it was usually in some worthy cause that was not especially religious:

the plight of the homeless or the needs of immigrants. They were ignored by governments when they criticized public policy and they were ignored even by their own members when they criticized morals.

It was easy then to suppose that the bond between religion and politics was a fit subject only for historians. This casual lack of interest could be given theoretical justification. Although Marxism was less of an influence on Western social science than its critics supposed, there was among sociologists and political scientists of all schools a general consensus that religion was no longer very important. Like nationalism, religion was thought to have been superseded as a source of identity and motivation by social class. And, where nationalism was active (in Africa, for example), it was then largely secular.

The world looks very different at the start of the twenty-first century. Partly because of events and partly because of a change in perspective, religion is now back on the agenda of the political commentator. We have become aware of just how powerful a role religion still plays in ethnic and national identity. Between 1945 and 1960 just over half the world's civil wars were to some large degree informed by religio-ethnic identity. Between 1960 and 1990, with the collapse of the Soviet Empire, the proportion rose to three-quarters.[2] While we may argue over just what part of the conflict in Azerbaijan or Palestine or Indonesia or Nigeria results from religious affiliation or ideology, we cannot doubt that many of those involved in such struggles explain and justify their causes by reference to their religion. The Iranian revolution of 1979 changed 'fundamentalism' from a unit in the currency of Protestant theological argument into a universal (if sloppily used) unit of political analysis. At the same time, Iran's Great Satan, the United States, was affected by its own fundamentalist movements when the Moral Majority, Christian Voice and other conservative Christian pressure groups became active in electoral politics.

And then came 11 September 2001.

Some illustrations

This book has three related aims. It describes a large variety of ways in which religion and politics interact. It explains some of the general features of that array of links. And it attempts to draw out of those general features some very abstract propositions about the sorts of political regimes and movements that are associated with different religions. By way of advertising the text, I will begin with a few illustrations of the salience of religion for politics.

For centuries the Muslim Ottoman Empire spread far into Europe, an entity conventionally defined by its Christian culture. At one point Muslim armies stood at the gates of Vienna. And yet, at the end of that long period of interaction, Turkey, the successor to the Ottoman Empire, remained far more alien to the West than did Russia. The key difference was not economic integration or levels of social development. In 1900 Omsk or Kiev was little more like the industrial cities of England or France than was Istanbul. The difference was religion. One reason why the British government declined the Bolshevik suggestion that it give a refuge to the Romanovs was that it feared that the Czar's presence might stimulate revolution in Britain. Unlikely as that may seem now, such concern was partly fuelled by the remarkable resemblance between the last Russian Czar, Nicholas II, and the British monarch George V. They could easily have passed for brothers; they were actually cousins. Such integration of ruling houses from either end of Europe was possible because the Russians were Christians. One cannot imagine a child of Queen Victoria marrying a Turk.

One very simple way of recognizing the divisive and defining power of religion is to contrast it with that other common boundary-marker: language. A Jewish family might raise its children to speak Yiddish and English. A Saudi family might teach its children Arabic and English. Bi-lingualism is commonplace, but very very few families will raise their children to adhere simultaneously to two competing religions.

It is not just in the great divisions – Muslim versus Christian or Jew versus Muslim – that religion bonds with ethnic or national identity. Where people are not divided by confession, they may call into play smaller differences. In legitimating their territorial disputes, Georgians and Abkhazians, both Christian peoples, now argue about which became Christian first.[3] In the fourteenth century the Scots and the English similarly contended for their political rights by asserting that the Christian Church in one land was older than that in the other.[4] Contemporary Ukrainian nationalists who share the Orthodox Christianity of their Russian neighbours insist that their church is an independent entity, not a satellite of the Russian Church.[5]

Even within stable liberal democracies of the West, the combination of religion and ethnicity has been a potent force. Until the 1960s it was rare for a Scottish Catholic descended from Irish immigrants to marry a Presbyterian Scot. As those divisions softened, they were replaced by new lines as large numbers of Muslims and Hindus migrated to the West: Indians, Pakistanis and Bangladeshis in Britain and Turks in France and Germany.

Where religion was not a force because of its close ties with ethnic or national identity, it often remained powerful because of indirect links through social class. Although the values promoted by the Roman Catholic Church normally fit more easily with the political right, Catholics in Britain, Australia, New Zealand and the United States have tended to support the political party most closely associated with the labour movement because the history of Irish and South European migration to these countries meant that Catholics entered the labour market at the bottom. In all four settings they prospered but the traditional ties with the left were slow to be eroded.

Even once religion ceases to be closely associated with other major cleavages such as socio-economic class, it can still be a potent political force in struggles over moral issues such as divorce, gender roles, homosexuality and abortion. In the United States in the 1980s, television evangelists led powerful political pressure groups. In Britain's parliamentary elections of 1997 the Pro-Life Alliance fielded candidates on an anti-abortion ticket.

Caution about method

In one sense it is now obvious that religion matters. But it is always possible to argue that, like the coloured shirts of rival football teams, it is merely a group identifier with no particular content. As satirized by Jonathan Swift in *Gulliver's Travels*, religious identity may be no more significant than the argument between those who crack their boiled eggs at the big end and those who crack them at the little end.

Another way to erase religion from the equation is not to deny that it is there but to suppose that it is a 'constant', that it appears on both sides and so can be discounted without changing the analysis. Everyone claims divine approval. All states mobilize for war by first enlisting God as their recruiting sergeant. Hence there is much God-talk about, but the real causes of political action lie elsewhere. Religion is merely rhetorical window dressing.

Clearly there is much truth to both of these points, but this book would not have been written if I thought they exhausted the topic.

It is my contention that religion matters for politics, first, because there are important differences between secular and religious politics and, second, because the major religions differ in the sorts of politics they promote and legitimate. However, before I embark on a detailed study of what those differences might be, I want to enter a number of cautions about this project.

The mix-and-match wardrobe

First, we need to be mindful of the political flexibility of religious traditions. Whatever the links between religion and politics, they will not be the invariable relationships that are the goal of the natural sciences. Without much thought, we can quickly cite many examples of the same religious tradition being claimed as the source of inspiration for quite contradictory political agendas. Leading figures in the Catholic Church in Latin America in the 1970s could be found supporting right-wing military regimes such as Pinochet's Chile and radical movements such as the Sandinistas in Nicaragua. In Germany in the 1930s, leading Lutherans could be found supporting, tolerating and vigorously opposing Hitler.

This apparent flexibility might be a consequence of taking too large a unit. If we look closely at South American Catholicism or German Lutheranism, we might identify important subdivisions that do have consistent connections to a particular political posture. But, even when we change the order of magnification, we still find people drawing on what is apparently the same stock of religious ideas to come to very different conclusions about what God requires of us. Jerry Falwell and Bob Jones III were both influential independent fundamentalist Baptists in the United States in the 1980s. From his base in Lynchburg, Virginia, where he ran the Liberty Baptist University, televangelist Falwell concluded that America had become so secular that fundamentalists had to become actively involved in pressure group politics and he founded the Moral Majority, one of the most significant elements of the early 'New Christian Right'. From his base in Greenville, South Carolina, where he ran the university founded by his grandfather, Bob Jones III judged that Falwell's movement 'holds more potential for hastening the coming of the anti-Christ and building the ecumenical church than anything to come down the pike in a long time'.[6] That is, he was against it. While Falwell wanted conservative Protestants to mobilize to regain the social and political prominence they had enjoyed a century earlier, the Jones coterie argued for the classic pietist retreat programme: the world is so bad we should remain aloof and concentrate on personal salvation. Falwell thought the Jones position a neglect of responsibility; Jones believed that Falwell was repeating the Catholic error of supposing that good works would buy salvation.

People sufficiently interested in theology could acquaint themselves with the distinction between Arminian and Calvinist views of salvation. Joseph Arminius (1560–1609) believed that Christ had died to redeem the sins of all of us and that we could all be saved if we believed that and acted accordingly. John Calvin believed that our salvation destinies had already been determined by God before our birth. Christ had died only for the sins of the chosen ones, the elect. These medieval differences had generated two competing tones in modern Protestantism: one democratic and active; the other elitist and fatalistic. We could then argue that the Falwell and Jones positions followed in some regular way from the fact that the former was on the Arminian side of the debate while the Bob Jones University had traditionally been more Calvinist. If we can all be saved, it is perhaps worth reforming the world. If only a small elect has been chosen for salvation, then it would be better preserving its purity in splendid isolation.

But even this degree of refinement does not readily permit us to trace unvarying connections between religious ideas and political postures. Though he did not think that social reform would deliver salvation, Calvin assisted the religious leaders of Geneva to impose what they believed was a religiously mandated social order on its inhabitants. And one can find revival preachers of the Arminian stamp who were active in reshaping the world (through, for example, the anti-slavery movement and the temperance crusades) and others who blithely ignored the world while they preached personal salvation.

The mystical Sufi branch of Islam has proved similarly capable of producing quite different responses to the world. To modern Westerners, Sufism is the acceptable pacifist, spiritual and introverted face of Islam: the occasional philosophy of rock guitarists and a far cry from the puritanical fundamentalism of Iran. But Sufism also produced the whirling dervish fighters of the Mahdi in Sudan in the nineteenth century, Sufis were at the heart of Algerian resistance to French colonial rule, and the Sanusi Sufis fought vigorously against Italian imperial ambitions in Libya.

I do not want to labour the point, but I will add a final example that shows that, even within one very narrow strand of one small religion, clerics can reason themselves from the same texts to entirely different views of what is required in a situation of political choice. In 1993 Yasser Arafat, chairman of the Palestine Liberation Organization, and the Israeli prime minister Yitzhak Rabin signed the Oslo Accords – agreements in which the Israelis gave the Palestinians political autonomy in return for the Palestinians accepting the existence of the State of Israel: a trade of land for peace. Equally Orthodox rabbis disagreed about the propriety of the scheme. Some argued that Rabin was a *rodef* (one who threatens the life of a Jew) and a *moyser* (one who hands Jews to their enemies). Others countered that Rabin's compromise would save Jewish lives. Some argued that Rabin had offended against the vital principle of *lo tichonem* – the requirement to strike down the enemies of Israel. Others said that this was irrelevant because it applied only to idolaters; Muslims, because they share parts of the same religious heritage, were not regarded as idolaters by the early rabbinic authorities. Rabin narrowly carried the day with all but the most conservative rabbis but was assassinated by a student from the ultra-Orthodox Bar Ilan University who justified his action by saying: 'My whole life I learned Jewish law.'[7]

The point is a simple one. Religious principles can bear a variety of interpretations or, as R. Scott Appleby put it: 'Religious traditions can adapt to their environments without eroding continuity with the sacred past because the past is capacious.'[8] However, as I will argue along the way and in the conclusion, this is not the same as saying that there are no significant differences between religions. A possibly useful metaphor is that of the 'mix-and-match' suit collection sold by major clothes shops. As well as the three-piece suit in the same material, there is a second jacket, waistcoat and trousers of identical cut but contrasting material. Instead of just two suits there are six combinations that 'go together' far more than any randomly selected three items of clothing.

The limits to comparison

We must also be cautious of the evidence for drawing conclusions about the political consequences of religion. Social science depends on the quasi-experimental method of the selective comparison. We choose cases that seem similar in every respect except for the two things that interest us: what we want to explain and what we think is the explanation. For example, if we want to consider whether Islam has a particular tendency to produce despots, we might compare the regimes of Muslim Pakistan and Hindu India. India and Pakistan share a common history. They were part of British India until 1948, when the north-east and north-west, where Muslims were in a majority, were granted their own state. Except for brief periods, Pakistan has been ruled by military dictators. Apart from Indira Gandhi's brief imposition of emergency powers in the 1970s, India has been a democracy. With so much else about the two countries being similar, it is tempting to suppose that the religious tradition explains the difference: Islam produces dictatorship and Hinduism encourages democracy. To give another example: at first sight there is a strong coincidence of Catholicism and fascism in twentieth-century Europe. Italy, Spain, Portugal, Austria, Croatia and Slovenia are all Catholic states.

There are at least two problems with such comparisons. First, we may make too much of a pattern that is perhaps the result of accident. Consider again the fascism example. Let us suppose that Britain and France and the USA had intervened in the Spanish Civil War on the Republican side as actively as Italy and Germany supported the Falangists. The Republican government would not have had to rely so heavily on the Soviet Union, Franco might have lost the war, Spain would have remained a democracy, and Germany and Italy might have been more reluctant to press on with the actions that brought fascism to Austria, Croatia and Slovenia. Imagine that Winston Churchill had died as a young man during his South African adventures and that appeasers and collaborators such as Lord Halifax had taken power in Britain in 1939. It may seem obvious to us now that Britain was incorruptibly anti-fascist, but that is not how it looked to many contemporaries. For some time George Orwell thought a right-wing coup possible and some of the early Home Guard units were raised by socialists anxious to avert such a possibility.[9] With only a few changes to the historical record, the listing by religion of European states as democracies and dictatorships would have looked very different and then the assertion that Catholicism encourages an underlying predisposition to dictatorship would look very much less convincing.

This leads me to my second caution. Compared to the natural sciences, the social sciences are perpetually short of comparable cases from which to generalize. The biologist developing theories about the reproductive behaviour of drosophila has the defence of extraordinarily large numbers of cases: he can breed millions of his tiny flies. The social scientist trying to draw conclusions about the links between religious cultures and political regimes has very few examples on which to draw. A repeated concern of this book is the relative influence of religious culture and material circumstances. In order to see whether Christianity and Islam generally produce different sorts of regimes, we need, as the natural scientist would put it, to 'control for' other causal factors. It is quite possible that religious culture is neither here nor there and that what determines the political complexion of any state is something material. The wealth of a nation, the levels of education and literacy of its citizens, the existence of effective welfare systems, the stability of its borders – all these and other mundane considerations may sensibly be proposed as having much greater effect on the likelihood of a stable democracy than the religious affiliations of a people. If the real world was as accommodating as material that can be generated in a laboratory, we would have a plethora of stable wealthy Islamic states to compare with the stable wealthy Christian ones. Then we could with more confidence 'control for' mundane considerations and draw sensible conclusions about the impact of religious values and beliefs. But we cannot breed the social equivalent of drosophila; we must deal with the world as it is. We are confined to drawing out our abstract patterns from a very limited number of cases.

Defining politics and religion

Politics, Kenneth Minogue says, 'used to refer merely to the actions of monarchs, parliaments, and ministers, and to the activities of the politically committed who helped or hindered their accession to authority. Everything else was social or private life.'[10] He notes that as governments have expanded their reach almost everything has come to be regarded as political. He might have added that many pressure groups have collaborated in this by campaigning to have some private matter recognized as a public cause. Although the boundaries around the subject matter will not be drawn very tight, I will generally confine myself to the nature and actions of states and governments, to political parties, to the actions of groups intended to influence governments, and to the basic liberties that, these days, states are supposed to protect. As the above examples show, I draw my cases widely, but much of the book is concerned with relatively modern politics. In part this is because it is only in complex societies that religion and politics are sufficiently separate for us to talk about the way one affects the other. It also reflects the novelty of some of the variables. We cannot ask how the religion of Russian serfs of the sixteenth century affected their political preferences because serfs were not supposed to have preferences and, if they did, no one recorded them.

Having suggested what I mean by politics, I might as well define religion. I mean 'beliefs, actions and institutions that assume the existence of supernatural entities with powers of judgement and action'. So as not to exclude the more philosophical forms of Buddhism and Hinduism, that definition can be broadened slightly to include impersonal powers or processes possessed of moral purpose. However, I might add that such extension is probably unnecessary. Tiny numbers of Westerners are attracted by the idea of karma as a spiritual force that offers a God-free accounting system in which the nature of our rebirths ensures we get our just desserts, but most Buddhists and Hindus have their Gods.

Religion standing apart

This may seem obvious, but it is worth explaining here why religion may act as an autonomous force in politics. A good place to start is with the famous description offered by Marx of religion as the opiate of the masses.[11] It is undoubtedly true that religion is often socially conservative. By binding a people together under a shared God, a common cosmology and a common morality, religion creates order and stability and its rituals create social cohesion. By promising to the pious poor rewards in the next life, it reconciles them to their fate in this one and thus discourages them from rebelling against their condition. This is especially so if it adds that those rewards are to be gained by cheerful acceptance of present hardships. Hierarchical societies are usually buttressed by religious cultures that allocate differing religious obligations to different 'castes' or 'stations' and promise that either rebirth in a more elevated position or eternal salvation in heaven will be delivered only to those who faithfully perform the ritual obligations of their position. Before the introduction of Christianity, Hutus and Tutsis in Rwanda shared a common God – Imana – whose agent on earth was the Tutsi king. The subordinate Hutus were taught that to revolt against the king was to offend Imana.[12] The Japanese religion of Shinto was so firmly associated with support for the Emperor and the social order over which he presided that in 1936 the Catholic Church decided that Japanese Catholics could take part in Shinto ceremonies because these were civil rites 'of filial reverence toward the Imperial family and to the heroes of the country'.[13] The King of Morocco makes much of his title of Amir al-mu'minin (Commander of the Faithful). The Saud family stresses its control over the holy sites of Mecca and Medina. The Jordanian royal family reminds its people that it is descended from the

Prophet. After the reforms of Peter the Great, the priests of the Russian Orthodox Church were required to swear by Almighty God 'that I resolve and am in duty bound, to be a faithful, good, and obedient slave and subject to my natural and true Tsar and Sovereign' and also promised to 'defend unsparingly all the powers, rights and prerogatives belonging to the High Autocracy of his Majesty'.[14] This was not just hot air: priests were required to report any treasonous or rebellious sentiments expressed in the confessional.

But to stop with the Marxist dictum is to see only half the picture and much of this book is concerned with the other half: religion as inspiration to radicalism and rebellion. Religion is a potential threat to any political or social order because it claims an authority higher than any available in this world. Religion offers the possibility of challenging princes and potentates. Jahangir, the fourth emperor in the House of Babur (1569–1627), had the fifth Sikh Guru Arjun killed by torture, partly because he was polite to Jahangir's rebellious son (and thus treacherous) but largely because he rejected Jahangir's authority by insisting 'that God is the only true king'.[15] Oliver Cromwell wrote in his diary of his feelings the night before a crucial battle in the English Civil War: 'I could not (riding about my own business) but smile in praises to God in assurance of victory, because God would, by all things which are not, bring to naught things that are. Of which I had great assurance, and God did it.'[16] It is the supposed power to 'bring to naught things that are' that challenges the status quo.

Some religious radicals are thoroughly aware of the implications of their dissent and consciously promote political change. The 'liberation theology' of radical priests in Latin America in the 1960s was as much a political as a religious movement. Some dissenters honestly disdain any this-worldly purpose, but nonetheless their insistence on serving a higher master is seen by others as a challenge. In the late seventeenth century Margaret Fell, a leading Lancashire Quaker (and later wife of George Fox), repeatedly petitioned the king to protest her loyalty and seek relief from persecution.[17] She failed to appreciate the threat that she and her fellows posed to the status quo. It was not just that they refused to recognize the legitimacy of the established Church of England (and, more practically, to pay their tithes to the church). As one element of their general insistence that we are all equal in the eyes of God, Quaker males, like Winstanley's Diggers[18] before them, refused to doff their hats to their social superiors. In a wonderfully simple but potent act of defiance, they took to wearing hats with extravagantly wide brims, just so that everyone would know they would not bare their heads to show their subordinate status. They may have thought themselves loyal citizens, but that simple act of not removing a hat symbolized a repeated affront to the entire hierarchical nature of British society in the eighteenth century.

There is a further and very general sense in which religion is always inherently disruptive: zealots do not deal from the same pack as ordinary people. I do not mean that they are irrational in their reasoning; the point is that they have extra reasons. True believers do not weigh possible courses of action in the same way as people whose political calculations are made with purely secular criteria. Most observers believe that the 1997 Belfast agreement offers the Protestants of Northern Ireland who wish to remain part of the United Kingdom the best possible accommodation with the rising power of Irish nationalists. Yet, rather than accept it, Reverend Ian Paisley and his Democratic Unionist Party seek to bring down the devolved assembly and renegotiate the agreement. It seems obvious that, under new elections, the Irish Republican party Sinn Fein will increase its vote (and hence its negotiating power) at the expense of more moderate nationalists. It is also clear that the British and Irish governments have no intention of supporting anything Ian Paisley might find acceptable. If he were to confine his reasoning to purely mundane matters, Paisley would come to the same conclusion as his liberal unionist rivals and sue for a settlement. He does not because he has a trump card: God. He genuinely believes that God may reward those who are faithful to him, as he did for the Children of Israel. Paisley's uncompromising politics is underpinned by the hope that God will send showers of revival rain on the barren fields of Ulster.

Divine inspiration, the sense that one is doing God's will and will be rewarded for it with far greater riches than the mundane world can offer, can lead people to acts of extraordinary bravery and folly. In Uganda in late 1987, Alice Lakwena, a 27-year-old Acholi woman who believed herself divinely possessed, promised the followers of her Holy Spirit Movement that they would be invulnerable.[19] Though a tiny, ragged and ill-equipped band, the HSM offered (literally and metaphorically) spirited resistance to the government troops of Yoweri Museveni. Just before Osama Bin Laden's suicide pilots carried out the attacks on the World Trade Center, two young men, one from Morocco and one from Tunis, blew themselves to pieces in order to kill Ahmad Shah Massood, the leader of the Northern Alliance in Afghanistan. Since Islamic militants used the technique to attack well-defended US and French barracks in the Lebanon in the 1980s, the suicide bomb has become a popular way for the weak but radically inspired to attack the powerful. It is not unknown for such actions to be inspired by secular causes. For example, ten Irish Republicans starved themselves to death in prison in Northern Ireland in 1981. But such martyrdom is much more likely when the volunteer believes that his death will be rewarded with eternal bliss.

Even if naive of radical implications, religion may have profound political effects because it relativizes all human institutions and hierarchies. The Christian missionaries who took Protestantism to Korea in the late nineteenth century did not deliberately threaten the social order; on the contrary, most were careful to insert their faith into the fabric of Confucianism and punctilious about respecting local sensitivities. Nonetheless, the radical potential was there: 'the imported faith held that parents should be revered only in a way compatible with the commands of God.' As one early Protestant convert said of a vital social-class distinction: 'God did not make one man a yangban and another a sangnam. Men have made that distinction. God made all men equal.'[20] Missionary work in India was even more radical in its impact. Although effort was often concentrated on converting high-caste Indians, large numbers of lower-caste and outcaste Hindus were attracted to Christianity precisely because it rejected the caste structure.

Outline

The following chapters consider a very wide variety of links between religion and politics. I begin by considering the problems that religious diversity poses for empires. In chapter 3 I explore the links between religion and nationalism. The next three chapters concentrate on aspects of the relationship between religion and politics in modern democracies. Chapter 4 examines the links between religion and party politics. Chapter 5 deals with protests and moral regulation: the attempts by religious people to use the power of the state to impose religiously inspired norms and values. Chapter 6 reverses the question and looks at the various ways in which modern states attempt to control religion, especially new religious movements.

The final chapter draws together the implications of the detailed examples to address the key question. Interesting though it is, it is not enough to produce example after example to demonstrate that religion and politics are frequently associated. The real challenge is to draw out from such associations underlying causal connections. The ultimate goal of this study is to see if, and to what extent, religions differ in the sorts of regimes and movements they encourage.

2

EMPIRE

Introduction

In most times and places religion is social. A people share a common religion and they acquire it, as they acquire their language, at birth. Correctly worshipping the God or Gods is a mark of membership of a community and conformity is required. It is also a mark of loyalty, so that, on the rare occasions that rulers and ruled differ in their faith, one or other will change. Strange to say, this seems one of the few battles the common people win. When the Huguenot prince Henry was offered the throne of France in 1589, it was on the condition that he renounced the Protestant heresy and became a Catholic. When the new Balkan kingdom of Romania appointed a Catholic German prince to its throne, it was on the condition that Carol I converted to Orthodoxy.

The desire for uniformity may seem strange to the modern mind, accustomed as we are to the principle of personal preference. To understand the role of religion in politics we need to set aside the relativism that we now unthinkingly apply to most clashes of culture. Religions that suppose that the deity can appear in a variety of shapes – Hinduism and Buddhism, for example – have less need for uniformity, though they can still be hostile to those who believe otherwise. The monotheistic religions of the Middle East – Judaism, Christianity and Islam – suppose that there is one truth about the one true God and that those who refuse to accept this are badly mistaken.

This supposition creates important problems of inter-communal politics. How will a people of one religion deal with those of another? In particular, how does a political regime that encompasses a variety of religions balance the competing imperatives of uniformity and peace? Expansionist monarchs may well be interested in spreading their faith across their subject peoples, either because they are personally committed to it or because they see it as useful for social cohesion. But they have to calculate cost. The Russian emperors alternated between supporting and restraining the spread of the Russian Orthodox Church. 'The missionary activities of the Church were even restricted in newly conquered Tatar territories in the sixteenth and seventeenth centuries.'[1] In the 1770s Catherine the Great took the surprisingly modern view that Russia's hold on the Steppes would be strengthened if she positively encouraged rather than undermined local Islamic institutions. To that end she sent Tatar Muslim preachers to the region. The plan backfired: instead of playing their allotted part, the Tatars fuelled anti-Russian sentiments.[2] Whatever the imperial policy, it is always mediated by local implementation. General Konstantine Von Kaufman, who was the Russian governor general of Turkistan from 1866 to 1882, did not mind Islam, but he feared competing sources of authority. So he banned Orthodox preachers and permitted Muslims to worship unhindered, but he deliberately undermined the standing of Muslim clerics.

In this chapter I will consider the attitudes to religion in the Ottoman and the British empires. These two examples have been chosen because they are interesting in their own right and because the brief histories allow me to introduce many of the nations, states and ethnic groups that will be discussed again subsequently.

The Ottoman Empire

The dynasty that created the Muslim Ottoman Empire in the fifteenth century ruled over lands in Anatolia (what is now modern Turkey) from the late thirteenth century. It spread rapidly into Europe and in 1453 took Constantinople, which had since the sixth century been the centre of the Eastern or Byzantine Christian Empire. At its largest in the sixteenth century, Ottoman rule stretched from the Persian Gulf to Morocco in the south and from the Crimea to Vienna in the north. The failure to capture Vienna in 1683 marked the turning point in its fortunes. The growing European powers alternately encouraged secessions in the Balkans and, for fear of each other's ambitions, bolstered the failing empire, until, after it had backed the losing side in the First World War, it was dismembered. It ended formally on 1 November 1922 when the Turkish Grand National Assembly abolished the Sultanate and Mehmet VI, the last Sultan, sailed into exile on a British warship.

To understand the politics of the Ottoman Empire we must begin with two observations. First, and in contrast to Christianity, Islam was from its foundation a political religion. Second, unlike the British Empire, which was based on a powerful and coherent nation state, the Ottoman Empire was essentially a pre-nationalist formation.

Islam, like Christianity, is a founded religion. It dates from the religious experience of a seventh-century Meccan merchant Muhammad, who believed that he had been chosen as a prophet 'to bring a divine message to humankind about the existence of a unique, all-powerful God, a warning of an impending doomsday and judgement, and an encouragement to live a virtuous life'.[3] When the citizens of Mecca became concerned about his increasing influence, he and his followers moved to Yathrib (later renamed Medina). There Muhammad rose to become the social, religious and political leader of a powerful community. Three times the Meccans attacked Medina and were repulsed. With each battle Muhammad became stronger and in 630 AD Mecca surrendered to the Prophet.

Under the title of 'Caliph', the leaders of Islam after Muhammad combined the roles of prophet and king, of spiritual and political leader. Over the next twenty-four years, as Islam grew and spread across the Arab world, there were three such leaders. However, the lack of an agreed method for selecting the Caliph guaranteed trouble and it came when the fourth Caliph – Ali, son-in-law of the Prophet – was assassinated. His son Hassan made an ineffectual claim to succeed and then retired from politics. Nineteen years later, Hassan's brother Hussayn tried to succeed to the Caliphate but gained little support. With a small band of followers, mostly members of the Prophet's family, he was killed at Kerbela and in the manner of his death established martyrdom as a central theme in Shi'ite Islam.

As Islam grew and evolved it became divided into innumerable competing traditions and sects. Some, like the varieties of Christianity, were based on particular interpretations of religious principles. Other divisions resulted from disagreements about the legitimacy of successors to the Prophet's political leadership. The majority of Muslims, the Sunnis, accept the legitimacy of the Umayyad dynasty. The minority Shi'ite strand insists that the proper succession should be traced through Ali, Hassan and the martyr Hussayn. The Shi'ites are further divided according to which of the subsequent Imams (or leaders) they accept.

The spread of Islam ensured that its initial political unity would fragment and powerful leaders set up their own kingdoms, each claiming to be the true Caliphate. In the eleventh century, for example, Egypt was ruled by the Fatimids, who were Ismaili Shi'ites.

The basis of legitimacy in the Islamic state was always religious. The state existed to defend and promote the interests of the faithful. The 'heathen' were forcefully converted or driven out. As followers of the Old Testament, Jews and Christians were accorded a superior position and tolerated. The shariah, the law under which Muslims lived, was part of their religion, and clearly it could not apply to Christians or Jews, so they were allowed to live under their own laws, managed by their own leaders. This was the basis of the millet system, which Roux economically describes as 'hierarchized pluralism'.[4] The various millets were given a degree of autonomy, but Muslims enjoyed a number of privileges. Their religion was embodied in the highest levels of government and, although all people were subject first to the laws of their own millet, in any dispute between Muslims and others, Islamic law prevailed.

The vast size of the empire, and the enormous varieties of linguistic, ethnic and religious groups within it, make it very hard to generalize about conditions. It would certainly be a mistake to suppose, as later Europeans did, that Islamic rulers uniformly imposed harsh burdens on their non-Muslim subjects or were accepted as legitimate only by Muslims. What is forgotten is that Christians did not then form a single population with common interests. Before the rise of the effective modern state, the social unit that provided the effective conditions of life for most people was tiny. A regime that gave advantages to one town or small area might be unacceptable to another that was, by our standards, close by. When the predecessors to the Ottomans, the Seljukid Sultans, extended their influence over the territories of the former Byzantine Empire, their rule was often welcomed by pockets of non-Greek Christians, who had returned to them possessions that had been confiscated by the Byzantines.

War against the unsubjected infidel did not exclude protection of the infidel subject, nor did it even exclude profitable commercial exchanges between one raid and the next. In these circumstances indigenous Christians came to seek an understanding with the Turcomans more willingly than the protection of the Byzantine government, which was often haughty and inefficient, and was accompanied by high taxation. History is full of these little exchanges between neighbours, who subsequently turn up as allies against their respective rulers.[5]

Their willingness to make local alliances and accommodations does not mean that the sultans were not committed Muslims. It merely reflects the weakness of pre-modern administration. Where they were able, they vigorously promoted Islam. For example, in the second half of the eighteenth century there were forced mass conversions in the Rhodope mountains and in the Razgrad district of north-east Bulgaria.

The religious foundations of the Ottoman Empire are clear from the organization of the two crucial links between the ordinary people and the primitive pre-modern state: military service and taxation. What the modern state regards as burdens properly laid against all citizens, the Ottoman regime construed in religious terms. The faithful were expected to serve the Caliph or his subordinate lords as part of their holy obligation to *jihad* or the active promotion of Islam. Christians were exempted from conscription but forced to pay a substantial tax in lieu. From our standpoint, military service might seem a burden rather than a privilege, but service in arms was one of the main routes to political advancement and the booty acquired in war one of the main sources of wealth. And the basis of taxation was different. Muslims supported the state, such as it was, as part of their *zakat* or religiously mandated alms giving, while non-Muslims were subject to often punitive tax farming.[6]

Christians were expected to accept a number of prohibitions that reflected their subordinate status:

> in theory they could not bear firearms, wear conspicuous or rich clothes, or don the color green, sacred to the Muslims. They were supposed to dismount when passing a Muslim on horseback; their houses could not be richer than or overlook those of their Muslim neighbors. Christian churches could not have bells or belltowers; new churches were not built, but old ones could be repaired. Despite the fact that by the nineteenth century many of these measures were no longer enforced, the Christian remained in a distinct and recognized inferior position. It was perhaps this aspect of Ottoman rule that was most resented by the subject population.[7]

The theocratic nature of the Ottoman state is well illustrated by the *devshirme* levy. Every five years or so in the Balkans, one of every four young men aged between 10 and 20 had to be given into Ottoman service. They were converted to Islam, educated and pressed either into civil administration or into military service as members of the janissary corps.[8]

But, unlike the later British Empire, which deployed a very large number of British officials to administer its possessions abroad, the Ottoman Empire depended heavily on certain groups of foreigners for its government. 'By the end of the eighteenth century it was clear that among the Balkan people the Greeks occupied the most favorable place.'[9] The Christian millet was run by the Orthodox Church, through the office of the Patriarch of Constantinople, which was consistently controlled by Greeks. Serbian and Bulgarian structures were demoted or abolished, so that Greek officials by the end of the eighteenth century controlled about eight million Christians, a quarter of the empire's population. Phanariote Greeks (so-called after a district of Constantinople where many of the families lived) also occupied many of the most senior administrative offices in the empire.

The Balkan secessions

It is difficult to summarize two centuries of an enormous empire, but the basic fact of the Ottoman Empire was decline in the face of more powerful forces. The empire lacked a decent administration and a loyal army. In the Balkans, the janissaries acted like bandits and resisted attempts by the centre to control them for a long time before the corps was eventually abolished. From the start of the nineteenth century, the empire was so obviously falling behind the West European powers that it was able to maintain its possessions (or lose them only slowly) only by constantly forming and changing alliances with Britain, Russia and France, playing one off against the other. As well as constant trouble from its Balkan possessions, the empire was threatened with other schisms. Egypt gradually became such a power that, in the 1830s, under Mehemet Pasha, it went to war with the empire and won. Only the intervention of the European powers to preserve the status quo prevented the complete loss of that component and the settlement gave Britain considerable influence in Egypt.

In the nineteenth century all the Balkan components of the empire successfully broke away to form autonomous nation states.[10] Greece began its war of independence in 1821 and was established as an independent kingdom under British, Russian and

French protection in 1832. Serbia became completely independent in 1878. In the same year Bulgaria was granted the status of an autonomous principality that accepted Ottoman overlordship, a link finally broken in 1909.

It would be anachronistic to impute too strong a sense of collective identity to these Balkan peoples prior to their struggles for autonomy. Most of the rebellions were initiated by local notables whose interests were often thoroughly practical and mundane and they were fomented by the European powers for their own interests. But the secessionist movements were able to draw on Christian resentments over Muslim rule and they also played on proto-national grievances over Greek domination of the Christian millet. As well as seeking freedom from Ottoman sovereignty, the secessionists usually also sought autonomy for their mother-tongue strand of Orthodox Christianity.

It is worth noting a theme that characterizes the end of British imperial rule: an escalation of local hostilities. The weakening of imperial Muslim control did not necessarily mean greater freedom for religious minorities. As noted, the centre was often unable to impose itself effectively. This was as true of the Greek Patriachate's control over the fringes of the Christian people of the empire as of the Muslim Sultan's ability to dominate his non-Muslim subjects. The gradual replacement of this loosely articulated imperial system by more homogenous local regimes meant that the people who formed a majority of that new unit were able to impose themselves more effectively on their minorities. As Muslim rule was pushed back, shorter-range and more intense rivalries could come into play. For example, for a period between 1716 and 1791, the Austrian Hapsburg monarchy was able to control what eventually won its autonomy as the kingdom of Serbia and it created a new source of conflict by allowing Catholic church officials to evangelize the Orthodox Serbs – something the Ottomans, with their great physical and ideological distance from their subjects, had rarely tried.

As the basis on which the local notables justified their claims to autonomy was the supposed religious and ethnic distinctiveness of their people, the logic of their campaign required them to impose a uniform culture. In some places this was done without great conflict. But the greed of the secessionists often created new tensions. To make their autonomous units as powerful as possible, the local leaders (encouraged in this by their external backers for their own reasons) sought to encompass the largest possible area and the greatest number of people they could control, which meant that the new units often included alienated ethnic and linguistic minorities. Where the logic of empire could tolerate such internal variation, the homogenizing ethos of nineteenth-century national-ism meant that these people had to be converted to the new dom-inant culture. As Serbia, Greece and Romania gained autonomy, they subordinated their own 'national' parts of the Christian Church to their emerging nation states and, on the Russian model, made the church a government department that contributed both in ideology and structure to strengthening the state.

The failure of reform

Faced with the growing evidence of its decline in wealth and power relative to Britain, France, the Austro–Hungarian Empire and Russia, the empire tried to reform. The nineteenth century saw a whole series of changes to the structure and ethos of the empire that were collectively known as the *Tanzimat* (or 'ordering'). Impressed by the productive capacity, the efficiency and the mili-tary might of the European powers, Ottoman officials tried to implement a wide range of modernizing changes. A new model army corps was created and the janissaries supressed. Tentative steps were taken to create a secular system of education. Bureau-cratic reforms aimed at curbing the powers and corruption of local officials were introduced.

But reform was compromised by the very basis of the empire. The empire had succeeded as an embodiment of the community of the faithful, a universalizing religious entity, which tolerated very large groups of non-Muslims but dealt with them as distinct col-lectivities, in a discriminatory manner, through the millet system. This was effective when the demands that the state tried to make on its subjects were minimal and could be implemented through local intermediaries, but it meant that there was little that bound indi-vidual non-Muslim subjects to the empire (other than the passing thought that its rule was less harsh than some alternatives). There was certainly no sense of belonging to a single entity or being bound in some heroic cause. Even those subjects who were Muslims, and thus might accept in principle that they owed loyalty to the Sultan/Caliph as the protector of the faithful, were in prac-tice distanced from the empire by local loyalties (among which were divergent strands of Islam).

In a belated attempt to consolidate the empire by creating some popular sense of belonging, the Tanzimat removed some of the most obvious sources of inequity. The poll tax on non-Muslims was abolished, as was the restriction on the right to bear arms.[11] However, such good intentions were often subverted by the empire's inability either to impose its good intentions on the local powers or to prevent European states encouraging secessions. A small example will illustrate the former difficulty. The Laramans were Kosovans who had originally been Roman Catholics but who had converted to Islam in the eighteenth century. In the middle of the nineteenth century, as though sensing which way the geopolitical wind was blowing, many converted back to Christianity. While the empire's millet system allowed the toleration of peoples who had never been Muslims, the empire's commitment to Islam did not readily permit the notion of individual choice and it certainly never encouraged those who had the true faith to give it up. It was only in 1844 that the law punishing apostasy by death was repealed. The compromise for the Laramans was that reversion was permitted but only with the express agreement of the local imperial governor. In 1845 twenty-five Kosovan families were refused permission to revert to Catholicism and were sent to prison in Constantinople. There they secured the necessary permission to change faiths, but when they returned to Kosovo they were again imprisoned and sent into exile in Anatolia. Many died in the harsh winter conditions and it was only after considerable political pressure from a number of European countries that the survivors were allowed home.[12]

The Young Ottoman Society (formed in 1865) sought to adopt aspects of Western civilization – science, education, technology, economic advance – without losing the basic unity of the empire. But the tension at the heart of this programme was clear in the reforms of 1876. All citizens were declared equal and the creation of an independent judiciary was announced, but at the same time the primacy of Islam was reasserted and Sultan Adbul Hamid II made a symbolic claim to the old basis of Ottoman legitimacy by declaring himself Caliph or spiritual leader.

The old model of a vast theocracy accommodating internal diversity through a structure of millets had failed to create a unit coherent enough to withstand internal fragmentation and external conquest. The Tanzimat had failed to increase internal cohesion by setting all subjects on an equal footing. As the empire decayed and shrank, so its remaining people became less tolerant. The unforgiving drive for conformity of the new nationalism was exhibited in massacres of Turks in many parts of the Balkans and it was increasingly reciprocated within the heartlands of the empire. Large numbers of Christians were massacred by Turks in 1860, 1876, 1895 and 1915. Under the cover of the First World War, as many as a million Armenians were killed by Turks or died in forced migration. Hundreds of thousands of Assyrian Christians, living as a semi-autonomous people under their leader Patriarch Mar Shiman, were driven out of their homeland in south-eastern Turkey and into Iran.[13]

The British Raj

The empire created by the British was quite unlike that of the Ottomans in that it was a very long way from home, both geographically and culturally. Controlling foreign peoples may have given some Britons occasion to think about their own polity, but they began that thinking from the strong position of a stable nation state, the identity of which was not in doubt. Hence the question of how to manage people of a very different religion, although it provoked soul searching, was not, as it was for the Ottoman Turks, compounded by considerations of how the British defined and ruled themselves.

The other great difference was that, once the American colonies had declared their independence, the British homeland was vastly more prosperous and better administered than the foreign territories it conquered. In the nineteenth century, the Ottoman Empire was perpetually threatened by secessionist movements in territories that were richer and more cohesive than its centre and were aided by superior powers. In contrast, the British had a much freer hand to determine how they would deal with the peoples they conquered. The considerable autonomy permitted to peripheral territories and to the non-Muslim millets was a matter of necessity for the Ottomans. There could be sporadic and brutal impositions on this or that group, but the empire's lack of a strong central administration meant that a concerted attempt to convert all its subject peoples to Islam was rarely a possibility. Thus, while Justin McCarthy praises the tolerance of the empire, it is more realistic to see this as a necessity than a virtue.[14] The British could at least contemplate the idea that they had both the opportunity and the obligation to convert their subjects to the true faith.

It simplifies, of course, but the attitude of the British to the religious culture of the peoples of their empire shows a swing from toleration to missionary zeal and back to toleration in a relatively short period. To be more precise, two positions initially competed: 'Leave as much alone as is compatible with basic decency and efficient control' and 'Convert the heathen to the true faith'. The non-interventionist view finally won out, in part because experience of the mission field changed the missionaries. Both positions are expressed in the opening sentences of the declaration that Victoria made to her Indian subjects when she was crowned empress in 1858: 'Firmly relying ourselves on the truth of Christianity, and acknowledging with gratitude the solace of religion, we disclaim alike the right and desire to impose our convictions on any of our subjects.'[15] The second part of the sentence was written by civil servants and reflects the professional imperial administrator's desire for a quiet life. Victoria herself added the first sentence as a declaration of her personal commitment to evangelical Protestantism.

The change in status of India was a response to the Indian Mutiny, or 'First War of Indian Independence', as some Indian nationalists would have it; the War of Religious Insensitivity might be a better title. There were many pressing and enduring grievances involved, but the proximate cause of the Sepoy rebellion pretty well illustrates British attitudes to religion. Indian troops were issued with cartridges that were greased with a mixture of pork fat and lard. As Muslims regard the pig as unclean and Hindus regard the cow as sacred, greater offence could not have been more universally given had that been the intention. Instead of accepting their mistake, British officers punished the soldiers (who they supposed could not really care *that* much). A cavalry regiment mutinied in support and northern India was in revolt.[16]

From their first involvement in India in the seventeenth century, the officers of the East India Company had taken the view that their primary concern was trade and disclaimed any great interest in trying to change religious culture in (or much else about) those parts of India they came to control. As the Ottomans did, the British sought to work with existing political divisions and through local agents. After he retired, the first governor general of the East India Company in Bengal, Warren Hastings, was somewhat implausibly charged with unnatural interference in Indian affairs, but, unlike his successors, he was interested enough in Indian culture to learn Urdu and Persian. He appointed the Oxford oriental scholar William Jones to a judgeship in Bengal. He opposed as 'wanton tyranny' the suggestion that Bengalis should be governed by English common law and proposed instead that they be governed 'according to their own ideas, manners and prejudices'.[17] He employed Hindu and Muslim clerics to collate and codify Hindu and Muslim local law and had the results translated into English. These codes were then interpreted by British and Bengali judges sitting together. Hastings's own religion seems to have been the diffuse deism that was then popular with the ruling classes. The attitude of many of that generation was well expressed by William Jones when he said: 'I hold the doctrine of the Hindus concerning the future state to be incomparably more rational, more pious and more likely to deter men from vice than the horrid opinions inculcated by Christians of punishments without end.'[18]

The Scots Presbyterian Robert Dundas, who, as President of the Board of Control, oversaw the operations of the Company on behalf of the British government, said in 1808 that we had 'virtually contracted an obligation... to support... those establishments which have immemorially been held in reverence and deemed sacred by their subjects'.[19] The Governor of Bombay in 1826, John Malcolm, said: 'The most important of the lessons we can derive from past experience is to be slow and cautious in every procedure which has a tendency to collision with the habits and prejudices of our native subjects.'[20] William Wilberforce and the British evangelicals hated this laissez-faire attitude. Prime Minister William Gladstone (himself an evangelical) was horrified when he discovered that for forty years the Company had been managing Hindu festivals such as that at Jagganath (the origins of our word 'Juggernaut'). The Company's position was pragmatic. Very large numbers of people gathered for religious festivals. The Company had a responsibility to manage large public gatherings so as to reduce the dangers of accidents. In so doing it was not promoting a heathen religion; it was merely maintaining good order.

Strange as it may seem now, the argument over whether it was right for Christians to evangelize the pagans was not between committed Christians on the one side and the religiously indifferent on the other. Even those who had no doubt at all about the correctness of the Christian faith and its superiority over Islam or Hinduism or Buddhism could have reservations about missionary work (though they were the opposite of modern reservations). In 1796 the General Assembly of the Church of Scotland was invited to endorse the recent foundation of the Glasgow and Edinburgh Missionary Societies. The majority declined to do so and they declined on the grounds that trying to convert the heathen was 'highly preposterous, in so far as it anticipates, nay, reverses, the order of nature. Men must be polished and refined in their manners before they can be properly enlightened in religious truths. Philosophy and learning must, in the nature of things, take the precedence.' The Moderates were also concerned that evangelizing the heathen would disrupt social relations; hence missionary societies were 'highly dangerous in their tendency to the good order of society at large'.[21] That sentiment reflected the fear of anarchy generated by the French Revolution. With increased distance from those events, British Christians became less anxious about the social consequences of giving subordinate peoples ideas above their station and the evangelicals eventually won the argument. In 1824 the Church of Scotland reversed its position. With its blessing, Alexander Duff arrived in Calcutta in 1830 and founded a Christian college that in little over a decade would grow to have 900 students.

At the same time as churches were becoming more active in missionary work, the second pincer of the evangelical attack, pressure on the government, was also working. In 1813, when it faced opposition in Parliament to having its charter renewed, the East India Company agreed to pay for a Church of England bishop and three archdeacons to work in India. In 1838 it was prohibited from managing native religious ceremonies. Restrictions on missionary work were removed. What had originally been intended as a religious establishment for the benefit of British civil servants was gradually expanded through missionary recruitment and became a state-funded Church of India. Because many of those who had pressed Parliament for the right to promote Christianity in India were not members of the Church of England, the government extended funding to dissenting Protestant clergy and also to Roman Catholic priests.

Contrary to the view we now have of Christian missionaries as uncritical promoters of Western civilization, most evangelicals were only too well aware of the defects of the West; after all, as we will see in chapter 5, Wilberforce and his 'Clapham Sect' spent much of their time trying to reform industrial urban Britain.[22] But they naturally took the view that social vices resulted from insufficient Christian piety. By way of rather tasteless advertising for mission work, some evangelicals were at pains to point out that Christian converts had not been involved in the Mutiny. The author of a 1920s promotional review of missionary work began by noting that Christendom could be criticized for 'its drunkenness and prostitution, its white slave trade, its war spirit, its mad race for riches and pleasure', and adds: 'We are not concerned to deny these charges, nor do we hold a brief for the defence of western civilization.' But this is a just a preliminary to asserting that: 'The vital element of difference between Christendom and the heathen world lies in this, that in the former the powerful leaven of the gospel is at work...In Christendom the Gospel is at war with vice and wickedness in every form; in heathenism abominable evils are wrought under the sanction of religion.'[23]

It was largely the experience of working in the mission field that softened the attitude of evangelicals. Alexander Duff said: 'We need to be wary how we thrust upon our Eastern converts anything that is solely of ourselves and not of Christ, for it is their own Christ they must find.'[24] One leading ideologue of missions went so far as to consider the idea of replacing the Old Testament in his Bible with selections of Hindu scriptures, a clever idea that flattered the Indians by accepting that Hinduism could be as good a preparation for accepting the true faith of the New Testament as the religion of the ancient Jews while nonetheless presenting Christianity as trumping Hinduism. When J. W. Farquhar's *Crown of Hinduism* was published in 1915, it was regarded as dangerously avant-garde because it found virtues in Hinduism and described it not as a damnable heresy but as an incomplete perception of the truth.[25]

Christian missionaries could not remain indifferent to the social and material conditions of the heathen. Inevitably they were drawn into providing education, medical help, trade networks, technical expertise and social work. Such peripheral good works may have been promoted initially in the entirely instrumental spirit of creating a fertile field for the preaching of the gospel by proving that the Christian God could deliver, but they developed their own impetus and came to be viewed as virtuous in their own right.

Two things happened in that process. First, merely by educating Indians, missionaries reduced the social distance between them and the objects of their evangelical activity and came to think better of them: hence the increasing appeal of Farquhar's respectful approach to Hinduism. Second, the educational work took on a life of its own. It was necessary to 'raise up the Hindoo' so that they could appreciate the true religion. To win their confidence (especially of high-caste Hindus, who thought themselves second to none) the conversionist ethos had to be toned down. Educating became an end in itself. Indians gradually ceased to be viewed as the objects of Christian endeavour and became partners in a collaborative enterprise that outgrew its evangelistic roots. The dominant view of the 1930s can be summarized as follows:

> The task of the missionary today ... is to see the best in other religions, to help the adherents of those religions to discover, or rediscover, all that is best in their own traditions, to cooperate with the most active and vigorous elements in the other traditions in social

reform and in the purification of religious expression. The aim should not be conversion...Cooperation is to replace aggression.[26]

The end result of a century of Christian missionary activity was a return to a position very similar to the pragmatic laissez-faire of the East India Company.

In practice the missionary impetus had never been strong enough to counter the local administrator's imperative to manage effectively. Whatever waves the likes of Wilberforce and Gladstone made in London were very faint ripples by the time they reached the outposts of the empire. Where there was a strong local religious culture, the imperial civil servants worked with it. In the Sudan the British applied the Indian Penal Code of 1837 and later the Indian Civil Procedure Code – laws that Hastings would have approved. In criminal matters secular law was applied, but in private matters (which included marriage, divorce and inheritance) the shariah or Islamic law was applied to the Sudanese Muslims. Indeed, the British not only permitted the application of the shariah; they also improved it. So that it could have the same status and formality as secular law, they codified the shariah and they trained Islamic jurists.[27]

In a recent attempt to improve our estimations of the Ottoman Empire, McCarthy has been highly critical of the British for continuing the millet system in those parts of the Ottoman Empire they managed after the First World War on a mandate from the League of Nations: 'The Ottoman Mecelle legal code remained as the law of personal relationships. Islamic pious foundations remained under control of religious hierarchies in the mandates long after being taken over by the state elsewhere.'[28] It is hard to resist the impression that for some critics the empire is damned if it did and damned if it didn't. When the British impose their culture, they are criticized for orientalism and imperialism; when they do not, they are criticized for not pressing on with the more progressive reforms of the final days of the Ottoman Empire.

Common humanity

The modern view is that indigenous cultures should be respected and that missionary activity is unacceptable, because it involves the ideological representatives of powerful nations imposing themselves on the weak. As the quotation from the Church of Scotland's initial rejection of foreign missions shows, however, opposition to conversion can as easily be based on disdain as on respect.

It was not just Scottish Presbyterians who worried that converting the natives to Christianity would give them ideas above their station. English Protestant clergy in slave-owning Virginia in the seventeenth century 'made little effort to convert or instruct the Negroes lest they stir up notions of egalitarianism and rebellion'.[29] The English were less reticent in southern Africa, where at the time they had little at stake. Although many were intensely pious themselves, the Calvinist Dutch settlers and their descendants did not evangelize the Africans. Some of the chaplains of the Dutch East India Company in the Cape made an attempt to teach local natives Dutch (so they could read the Bible) and Christian doctrine, but they had little impact, and when, in 1737, a German Moravian began preaching to Africans, he was very firmly pressed by the Afrikaners to desist. As Templin says: 'For almost a century no concentrated missionary work among the Africans was conducted by any of the Dutch ministers or settlers.'[30] The British administration initially established a colour bar in its territories but was persuaded by John Phillip of the London Missionary Society (supported by evangelicals at home) to renounce it, 'thus placing the Hottentots on an equal footing with white colonists'.[31] The tension between the Christian imperative to save souls and the Afrikaners' desire to maintain their social superiority can be clearly seen in the evolution of the Dutch Reformed Church's (DRC) response to the consequences of its limited missionary work. Segregation was introduced to the Church in 1857 because it was the price demanded by members opposed to 'the propagation of Christianity among the heathen', which at the time meant, not the native Africans, but the Cape Coloureds, a population of people created by the interbreeding of whites and Africans.[32] The DRC's synod of 1881 created the Dutch Reformed Mission Church to bring together the various congregations of Coloureds; the justification betrays the embarrassment many felt at this compromise. The statement asserted the factual unity of the 'church' and hence, implicitly, the equality of humanity, but it defended the segregated organization 'in view of the practical situation'.[33]

The reluctance of the Afrikaners to erode the boundaries between themselves and those they exploited meant that the bulk of missionary work was conducted by English missionaries, which explains why the vast majority of black Christians in southern Africa belong not to the tradition of the first large body of white settlers but to the Episcopalian and Methodist churches.

There is a relevant religious difference here that combines with the location of interests to produce this outcome. The Afrikaners were Presbyterians whose commitment to democracy in the church meant that they were free to reinterpret their religion to suit their circumstances. There was no overarching and external authority that could constrain such adaptions to local interests. The English missionaries either were Anglicans (who accepted a notion of hierarchy) or were employed by London-based missionary societies and hence were answerable to their bishops or funders back home. And, as the British were not yet the major power in South Africa, it was relatively easy for them to put high principle above local interest.

The attitude of Spanish and Portuguese colonists was markedly different from that of Virginians and Afrikaners.

> Slaves in Portuguese Brazil and in the Spanish colonies had roughly the same status as serfs in Eastern Europe. The Spaniards and Portuguese were accustomed to holding Moors and Jews in slavery, and accorded the African a position equivalent to that of their other slaves. They recognized him as a moral person, insisted on his active membership in the Catholic Church, and gave him legal protection against his master's mistreatment.[34]

There were many differences between the American and the Iberian colonies, but the variety of Christianity seems to have been a significant factor. Catholicism is a hierarchical religion that stresses the subordinate status of the laity and that sits easily with the great feudal pyramid. Protestantism is essentially egalitarian. It recognizes no significant differences of status within the community of the godly. Although for much of its history it has accepted the fact of social divisions, it offers them no theological support. On the contrary, it provides a vocabulary of equality that has periodically been used to legitimate rebellion against despotism: the Scottish Covenanters and the English Roundheads, for example. In situations of gross inequalities it was thus paralysed by the hypocrisy inherent in converting slaves to, say, Presbyterianism and then insisting that they remain slaves.

We thus have the irony that the less egalitarian Catholic religion, because it offered no theological objection to profound social inequalities, actually treated the oppressed better than the supposedly more democratic Protestantism. It was unable to square its insistence that we are all the same in the eyes of God with the refusal of many of its members to see other peoples and races in that light. One way to restore consistency to the Protestant position was to reject slavery and that is what the evangelical Protestants of

Britain and North America eventually did. And, to their credit, they not only rejected it but took the leading part in the campaign to have it banned in the British Empire. However, such a radical resolution was much easier for those who had no great investment in slavery and who had not been socialized in that culture. It was much easier for evangelicals in London to denounce slavery than for the clergy of the Carolinas to take the same view. Hence we see the pattern prior to the American Civil War of all the major US Protestant denominations dividing over the issue: northern evangelicals became anti-slavery campaigners and their southern counterparts continued to justify the institution.

Religious identities in India

Compared to the vast Muslim population created in northern India by the Moghul conquest, the direct religious impact of the Raj was slight. Perhaps 4 per cent of population is nominally Christian. If we add in the figures for Pakistan and Bangladesh to get back to the range of British India, the figure would fall to below 3 per cent. Such slight effect is hardly surprising when we remember that the British were a significant presence in most parts of India for less than a century; the Moghuls were there from 1483 to 1858. And, unlike earlier conquerors, the British did not force their subjects to adopt their religion. Even the most enthusiastic critic of paganism proposed only persuasion and the persuaders were thin on the ground. In 1852 there were only 102 European missionaries in the entire principality of Bengal, a country as populous as Britain and considerably larger.

The most far-reaching changes in the religious culture of India did not come directly from mission. They came indirectly from British objections to 'vile customs' or inadvertently from consequences of the ethos of British administration. Even those colonial officers committed to respecting local customs found some of them unacceptable. When faced with institutions that they regarded as barbaric, they outlawed them and justified such intervention by arguing that such abominations were not 'really' religious. Examples are the Hindu institution of *suti* (in which widows were expected to commit suicide on their husband's funeral pyres) and child marriage.[35] Caste was another local institution that offended British sentiment. Class inequalities were as natural to the British as breathing and among themselves they borrowed the language of caste. There was only the slightest irony in the British habit of referring to the Indian Civil Service with the term used for the Brahmin caste: 'the heaven-born'. But even the British were repulsed by the extent to which 'out-castes' were excluded. The Pulayas of central Travancore were regarded by other castes as not just untouchable but unapproachable. Pulayas had to stand at a distance of 90 feet from Brahmins and 64 feet from Nairs. Most were agricultural slaves, held in bondage by their masters and remunerated for their work at a rate that only just prevented starvation. The initial agitation on behalf of the Pulayas came from missionaries, but the decision of the Travancore government to outlaw slave owning came not from any desire to advance missionary work but from the secular consideration that, as the British government had outlawed the better-known African slave trade, it could hardly tolerate an institution every bit as invidious in its Indian territories.[36]

Another inadvertently profound influence on the religious culture of the empire's subject people was the Western notion of a distinction between the public and the private, between religious propriety and public administration. Taking for granted the West European view that religion should properly be a private matter for individuals and their families, the imperialists often and sometimes unthinkingly forced the religions they administered to narrow their reach so that, in the Sudanese example mentioned above, the newly codified shariah was held to apply to 'private' and, to Western eyes, somewhat sacred, matters such as marriage and divorce but not to criminal behaviour.

In many respects the consequences of British rule were paradoxical. On the one side was the obvious Westernization. Many upper-caste Indians were educated in British schools and colleges and brought into the British administration. Many, especially among those who later led the nationalist movement, were educated in Britain and were influenced by liberal humanism and Enlightenment rationalism. Yet, at the same time, the preference for managing India through local elites and in terms of racial and religious blocs encouraged people to think of themselves as, and to seek advantage by becoming more, not less, Sikh or Hindu or Muslim. The establishment of an externally imposed peace meant that the myriad Rajahs and Nawabs (as respectively the Hindu and Muslim princes were known) had less need to rule their territories in a manner that accommodated both minorities within their principalities and each other. With responsibility shifted to the British, they were free to become less concerned with stable administration and more with exemplifying their religio-ethnic groups.

The British criticism of local customs produced local self-awareness that generated both reaction and reform (and mixtures of the two). The Deobandi movement (which was to have a considerable influence on north Indian Islam) started in 1867 as a conscious programme to make Islam impervious to Christian criticism by purifying it of the Hindu accretions it had acquired over the centuries of cohabitation: it was an Islamic Reformation.[37] The Brahmo Samaj, founded by Ram Mohan Roy in Bengal in 1828 (and revived in the 1840s by Debendranath Tagore), was supported mainly by the growing 'middle class'. It aimed to strip Hinduism of those social customs and ritual elements that, in comparison with Christianity, seemed most primitive and to reconstruct it as a monotheistic faith. The Prarthana Samaj formed in Calcutta in 1867 was similar. Most resolutely anti-Christian was the Arya Samaj, founded in 1875 in the Punjab. It was also monotheistic and like the others committed in principle to the abolition of caste, but it based its revivalism on a return to the Vedas as the only authentic Hindu scriptures.[38]

What is interesting about these and the wide range of other 'sanatana dharma' organizations is that they were not just a response to the challenge of Christian ideas and Western values. They also represented the adoption of a particularly British way of conducting business. They had branches with fee-paying members and constitutions and management boards and secretaries. They published regular periodicals and held annual conferences. Through their regular petitions to the government they acted as a rational channel through which Indians could communicate with their rulers.[39] The British were often perfectly happy to work through existing hierarchies, but their administrative culture made them prefer negotiating with organizations such as the samajs, which produced 'officials' whom the British could treat as representative. For India, this bureaucracy was new and hence, as Sen notes, for Indians, such politics required 'social non-conformism'. Hence, contact with the British tended to be disruptive even when the British did not intend it to be. For this reason, 'the ultra-orthodox group within the revivalist camp took a great exception to organized political work'.[40]

Creating a nation from a religion

Although I will discuss nationalism in more detail in the next chapter, this seems a reasonable place to introduce the history of the Sikhs, one of the clearest cases of a nation being created from the interaction of a religious identity and a regional power base. Sikhism was founded in 1469 by Guru Nanak, but its followers remained barely distinguishable from those of many Hindu and

Muslim spiritual orders until the 1699 innovations of the tenth guru, Gobind Singh, who introduced the practice of all male members taking the same name and the five symbols of initiation into the Khalsa (the unshorn hair, the comb, the sword, the steel bracelet and the loin cloth). As Uberoi[41] argues, much of the Khalsa initiation seems to have been designed to invert common elements of Hindu rituals of the time and thus mark the Sikhs off from their surroundings. Guru Gobind also set his followers off from Muslims by prohibiting the eating of meat killed in the Muslim ritual manner. Such differentiation coincided with increased Moghul hostility, which turned into outright warfare in the early eighteenth century. As Moghul power gradually disintegrated over the century, the Sikhs became more powerful, until the guerrilla band led by Ranjit Sikh defeated internal opposition and Ranjit became Maharajah of the Punjab, which he ruled until his death in 1839. This brief period of Sikh power (before the British annexed the Punjab at the end of the 1845–9 war) was accompanied by a weakening of the earlier religious traditions. There was certainly an erosion of the egalitarian spirit in Guru Gobind's promise: 'I shall ever be among five Sikhs. Wherever there are five Sikhs of mine assembled they shall be priests to all priests. Wherever there is a sinner, five Sikhs can give him baptism and absolution.'[42]

It was feared that British annexation of the Punjab would hasten the extinction of the *Panth* or community of Sikhs. Since the start of the nineteenth century, Sikhism as a distinct religious creed had been declining. Until the advent of British rule, the boundaries between Sikhs and Hindus were relatively fluid. Hindus became Sikhs and they relapsed. The Sikhs 'followed many of the practices, customs and traditions of the Hindus and continued to be bound to the Hindus by ties of marriage and kinship'.[43] Although in theory egalitarian, in practice Sikhs accepted the Hindu caste system. Sikhs and Hindus worshipped at the same shrines. 'To the passive influence of the ever-absorbing Hinduism the advent of British rule in the Punjab added the active proselytizing practices of Christian missionaries.'[44]

The effect of British rule was the reverse. Part of the revival came from the conqueror's desire to harness the martial traditions of the Sikhs. After the 1715 and 1745 Jacobite rebellions in Scotland, the British outlawed the cultural symbols of the Scottish Highlanders (including the wearing of tartan) and banned the carrying of arms. Once the Highlanders had been neutralized as a political threat, they were encouraged to enlist in the British army and Highland dress became the uniform of the Scottish regiments. The British did the same with the Sikhs; they enlisted them. Outward signs of Sikh-ness – the uncut hair, the turban, the beard, the ceremonial sword – became the regimental uniform and Sikhs were forbidden to abandon them once enlisted. The Sikhs were so respected for their martial traditions that young Hindu men who wished to enlist would present themselves as Sikhs. As a recruiting officer put it: 'it was almost a daily occurrence for say Ram Chana to enter our office and leave it as Ram Singh – Sikh recruit.'[45]

Rather than weaken Sikhism, Christian missions inadvertently encouraged a reaction. Revival movements such as the Singh Sabha were formed. Reminded of their initially radical rejection of caste by the Christians who did the same, the Sikhs again stressed their egalitarianism and recruited well from the lower castes. In line with the general policy of working with existing identities rather than destroying them, the British actively encouraged the Sikhs to think of themselves as a distinct people by treating them as such. The British administration gave grants of rent-free land to leading Sikh gentry and religious figures. Sir Robert Egerton, the Lieutenant Governor of the Punjab in 1881, became patron of the Lahore Singh Sabha. A new class of educated professionals was encouraged to provide the local administration.

The single most important element of the twentieth-century fixing of Sikh identity was the British acceptance of the claims of one sect of Sikhs to control the religious heritage of all Sikhs. The initiated Khalsa Sikhs, marked by their five k's, were initially only one part of a much wider movement and people. In the early part of the twentieth century there was an increasingly bitter series of battles for control of the Sikh temples or gurdwaras, with militant Khalsa Sikhs seeking to displace the hereditary keepers, whom they accused of religious laxity and profiteering. Although the British administrators were reluctant to become involved, the escalating violence forced them to step in and they vested control of all the gurdwaras in the Shiromani Gurdwara Prabhandak Committee (SGPC), the representatives of a particularly militant and separatist form of Sikhism. This group in turn created the Akali Dal, the political party that came to represent Sikhdom. The 1925 Gurdwaras Act not only gave the Khalsa Sikhs control of a vital ideological resource. It also gave them a great deal of revenue, which allowed them to promote education and charities, to fund an effective political organization and to create jobs staffing the gurdwaras.

Punjab was the home of the Sikhs in the sense that they originated there, had for a time ruled it and were given a privileged position in its administration by the British. But they were far from a majority. In the decade before Britain granted independence to India, at least half the population were Muslims and the Muslim League campaigned for the Punjab to be given to the future Pakistan. India wanted to retain one of the most fertile areas of the country. The Akali Dal wanted independence from both. The first outcome was to divide the country between Pakistan and India. In the Indian Punjab in 1951, Sikhs were 35 per cent of the population and Hindus 61 per cent. The Akali Dal pressed for a further reorganization that would give it power and eventually got its way in 1966 when Indian Punjab was divided into three states: Punjab, Himachal Pradesh and Haryana. Sikhs were a larger proportion of the new unit – about 55 per cent – but the Akali Dal's hope of winning power was dashed by the failure of ordinary Sikhs to play their allotted part in this steady progress to autonomy. They voted for the non-sectarian Congress Party of Nehru. The Akali Dal did form a government but only in coalition with the Communist Party of India and a local Hindu party.

In the late 1970s a separatist element of the Akali Dal emerged under the leadership of Jarnail Singh Bhindranwale. It mounted a number of terrorist attacks in the hope that Hindus throughout India would turn on Sikhs, thus forcing them to return to the Punjab and turn the population balance decisively. Bhindranwale and his supporters blockaded themselves inside the Golden Temple at Amritsar, the most sacred of Sikh gurdwaras. In June 1984 the Indian army, led by Sikh as well as Hindu officers, attacked the Golden Temple and Bhindranwale was killed. Six months later the Sikhs had their revenge when two of her Sikh bodyguards murdered Prime Minister Indira Gandhi. This almost achieved Bhindranwale's goal. It triggered widespread communal violence. Over 2,000 Sikhs were killed across India. In Delhi alone 10,000 were driven from their homes.

After a year of violence, a moderate Akali Dal sought a rapprochement with Rajiv Gandhi, Indira's son, who had been elected in a Congress Party landslide. Some further concessions to autonomy were made. For his attempts to compromise, the Akali Dal leader Sant Marchand Singh Longowal was assassinated by Sikh extremists. In the 1990s, led largely by Sikhs outside India, a movement for an independent 'Khalistan' sustained a campaigning organization but was not widely supported within the Punjab, where the Akali Dal preferred to use its distinctive religio-ethnic identity as a lever to prise greater benefits from the Indian state.

This very brief history of the Sikhs shows the complexity of interaction between religion and other sources of shared identity.

Gradually over five centuries what began as a Hindu sect mutated into an ethnic group and putative nation. Both repression (by the Moghuls and then by the British) and encouragement (by the British after 1849) played their part in strengthening that sense of shared identity.

Conclusion

What conclusions can we draw from these brief sketches of two empires? It would have been convenient if they had been similar in all but religion, but, bearing in mind all the cautions entered in the previous chapter, we can try to draw out some generalizations about the imperial management of religion.

The British Empire was more tolerant of the diverse religions it encountered than was the Ottoman. We may explain some of that by the fact that the Ottoman Empire contained the Muslim home-land of its ruling people while the British Empire was far far away. In that sense the Ottomans legislated for themselves as well as for their 'foreign' subjects, while the British (when they could fend off the evangelical enthusiasts at home) had the luxury of being able to manage others in ways that had no necessary implications for themselves. We should also note that the British had nothing like the same opportunity as the Ottomans to swamp their deviant subjects. The Ottoman Muslims were a large majority in the heart of the empire; the British in India and Africa were a fraction of the total population. We also need to accept that a certain revision of Victorian condemnations of the Ottoman Empire is in order. McCarthy has a point when he says that, 'While surely not perfect governors or always just to their subjects, the Ottoman sultans had a record of governing that can stand against any of the great empires in history. The tolerance of the empire was notable: all the religious groups that were present at the beginning of the Ottoman Islamic empire remained in place when it ended, six centuries later.'[46] But he is too generous. He forgets that Muslim conquest did destroy entirely some non-Muslim communities and drastically reduced others. The Chaldeans of Mesopotamia, the Hebrews of old Pales-tine, the Arameans of Syria and the Lebanon, the Copts and the Assyrians, and the Armenians of Asia Minor either disappeared altogether or were reduced to shades of themselves.

One major difference between the Ottoman and British empires is that in the former the dominant religio-ethnic group was less modern than some of its subject people while in the latter the imperialists were the modernizers. While the consequence of Ottoman rule was often to retard economic and social progress, the consequence of British rule was more mixed. Overall, imperialism may have had a detrimental effect on local economies by requiring them to produce for the British home market and to purchase British goods, but then modern economic development is always to a lesser or greater degree distorted by the fact that some economies are vastly more powerful than others. That is, even if the British had not ruled the countries of its empire, their economies would still have been shaped by their place in global trading networks. Whether we think the following things good or bad is a matter of political preference, but British rule brought to India models of efficient and honest administration, universal systems of justice, well-organized professional armies, elementary schools and universities, literacy, mass media and the rudiments of representative democracy. It also inadvertently created the basis for modern nationalist movements.

This does not necessarily mean that the British had a better attitude to their subjects than did the Ottomans. If the British left India with a better legacy than the Ottomans left to Greece, it is primarily because the Britain that ruled India in the nineteenth century was a liberal parliamentary democracy with an advanced record of human rights at home. It was no keener than the Ottoman Empire to treat its imperial subjects as well as it treated its own citizens, but, because the baseline was higher, so were the standards used to manage the empire.

But this chapter is not a beauty contest for empires. My concerns are more narrowly with the imperial treatment of religious diversity and in that narrow context the greatest difference between the two empires was, to put it rather pompously, the ideological basis of legitimation. The Ottoman Empire was both sultanate and caliphate. It sought the acquiescence of its subjects by claiming that it embodied the will of Allah and that its ruler was the rightful heir to the Prophet's religious mantle. It justified the exactions necessary for government – military service and taxation – as religious obligations and it imposed religiously sanctioned law upon its people. It did so either immediately if they were Muslims or secondarily if they were Christians or Jews, who, in any matter involving Muslims, had their own laws and customs subordinated to those of Islam.

The belief that God had given the British a mission to civilize the world was an important motive for some imperialists, but the way even they carried 'the white man's burden' was not especially shaped by the fact that they were Christians. Although some British imperialists at times justified their empire in religious terms, it was not a theocracy. It only sometimes permitted Christian missionaries to evangelize non-Christians. Where there was no strong local religion to offer robust opposition, it sometimes encouraged such missionary work. As often as not its local officials tried to leave intact local cultures. Of course it is impossible fundamentally to alter an economy, a polity and a society but leave a culture untouched. Irrespective of their intentions, the British in India had a profound effect on the religions they encountered. Unlike the Ottomans, they did not much change the religious composition of the countries they ruled, but their rule considerably changed the nature of those religions.

3

NATION

Introduction

In 1537 Hugh Latimer, the English Protestant reformer, remarked in a letter to Oliver Cromwell that God 'has shewed himself God of England or rather an English God if we consider and ponder well all his proceedings with us from time to time'.[1] The English were not alone in thinking themselves especially favoured by the Creator. That coupling of divine approval and national interest is commonplace and it is the focus of this chapter.

Nationalists like to claim an unbroken and ancient lineage for their nation. They also suppose that the nation has some sort of obdurate objective reality. Its existence may have been hidden by some more powerful neighbour, but, in singing its praise and fighting for its autonomy, nationalists see themselves as doing no more than recognizing facts. In contrast, Ernest Gellner has plausibly argued that the cultural unity of the modern nation state owes a great deal to the ideological and political work of nationalists and that modern nationalism developed when it did because it fitted well with the requirements of industrialization. The nation was the right scale: bigger than the family, the tribe and the city state but smaller than an empire. Nationalism's rejection of the traditional rigid hierarchies of feudal 'estates' and 'stations' in favour of an egalitarian rhetoric of 'brotherhood' allowed a fluidity of social roles and the social and occupational mobility that was necessary for economic modernization. Its insistence on a common culture (a shared language and a common stock of knowledge created by a state-sponsored educational system) facilitated production and exchange within a unit that could attract the emotional attachment of its members.[2]

That nationalism took root in the modernizing economies of eighteenth-century Western Europe does not mean it ended there. On the contrary, the monocultural nation state has become the universal template, spread around the globe by imposition and by imitation. Impressed by their own success, when they came to give up their empires, the great Western powers offered their model of the nation state to groups of peoples whose economic conditions were quite different from those of the Western states. Equally impressed by Western success, many elites imitated the outline of the political model that was assumed to have brought that power and prosperity.

In early statements of his theory, Gellner was perhaps too anxious to establish the contingent or invented nature of the nation. In later versions he made more allowance for the possibility that some characteristics of pre-modern ethnic groups and political units might make it harder or easier for nationalists to succeed in their propaganda work of creating a nation. And it is that more constrained image of social construction that colours this chapter. Nationalism is a creative enterprise, but it must work with the raw materials that are available. In its twin goals of establishing a new basis for political legitimacy (that a regime is acceptable only if it is ruled by our own folk) and identifying the 'us' that should form the unit, nationalism has little choice but to strike an attitude to religion. Religion, after all, has been in the business of identifying 'God's people' and legitimating their rule since time immemorial.

The links between religion and nationalism can be sketched as follows. In the eighteenth and nineteenth centuries, rising nationalist movements, and the states they created, often called on a shared religious identity as the basis for a sense of unity among the chosen people. The new nationalisms of the first half of the twentieth century tended to eschew religion or even to suppress it. By then the dominant model of progress was secular and the new elites thought that discarding their religious heritage was as essential to progress as the replacement of the horse by the tractor. Many of the new nations failed to develop fast enough or failed to spread the benefits of development sufficiently widely and eventually triggered waves of reaction that drew heavily on a religious heritage and identity.

I will begin by describing some common patterns of relationship between nationalism and religion. I will then try to answer two of the compelling questions in this area: why is religion so regularly implicated in nationalist movements and why do unusually pious people often dissent from such linkage? Finally I will consider the contemporary rise of fundamentalism.

Religion and national identity

To give some shape to this grand tour, I will group my illustrations around combinations of two topics: the attitude of nationalists to their religious heritage and the religious composition of the putative nation to be mobilized. As we will see, some nationalists make extensive use of religious symbols while others disdain them. This may be a matter of personal preference: contrast the pious Catholic Polish leader Lech Wałęsa with the avowedly atheistic Joseph Stalin. But separate from what nationalists want is what is possible. It may not be possible to construct a nationalist programme around religion. The racist British National Party in the 1990s quite sensibly avoided religious themes. That Asian immigrants worshipped the wrong God could not feature high on the list of characteristics that made them undesirable, because the native British were no longer very religious. Committed Christians who might object to Muslims and Hindus on religious grounds are principally from the social classes least likely to be attracted to politicized racism. Even if the bulk of a people is godly, that they worship different Gods may oblige nationalists to promote a secular identity. Even if the Albanian communist leader Enver Hoxha had not had an ideological objection to religion, he could not have used it as a source of social solidarity because the Albanians were divided between two forms of Islam and two forms of Christianity.[3]

As will become clear, the division of my illustrations into four groups is largely a presentational convenience: there is considerable overlap. Any particular country would fit under a variety of headings depending on what point in time we begin its story and which particular regions we choose as the main characters in the narrative. Even the division by country cannot be long sustained. It is difficult to talk about the Ukraine, for example, without also talking about Russia. Nonetheless, not everything can be said at once: the written text must be linear.

Nationalists mobilizing strong religious identities
A common religion and an emerging sense of national identity often interact with each other in a circular process of feedback.

Religious changes halt at political, ethnic and linguistic borders; one people converts to a new religion; its neighbours do not. Hence the chequered pattern of the spread of Christianity and Islam in Africa. In Nigeria, the Yoruba may be either Christian or Muslim but the Igbo are predominantly Roman Catholic while the Hausa and Fulani are Muslims.[4] When neighbours go to war, their competing religions provide one source of legitimation for their conflict: we have God on our side; they are infidels. In turn, the fact of conflict can make each people more conscious of its religious identity and more committed to it. When in the 1570s Phillip II of Spain inherited the Dukedom of Burgundy and with it control of the Netherlands, he tried to reverse the spread of Protestantism there and to impose his high Spanish version of Catholicism. The more thoroughly Protestant parts of the Netherlands revolted and seceded: 'the Seven northern provinces became independent and Protestant: the ten southern provinces (half low German and half Walloon) remained loyal to Spain and Catholicism.'[5] That division in turn became the basis for the divergent development of the modern states of Holland and Belgium.

In most settings we can identify an ethnic group and a more or less common religion as two separate entities and explore the connections between them. But before I offer some examples of close links, I want briefly to mention the relatively rare polar extreme of this sort of connection: there are some ethnic groups or putative nations that are defined solely by religion. The Jews are obviously a case in point. Prior to the creation of the State of Israel and the possibility of secular citizenship, what identified Jews was their Judaic religion. We can imagine discrepant cases at the margin. Some Jews might regard themselves as Jewish because earlier generations of their family held to that faith. Some might be defined as Jews by others (such as the officials of the Third Reich) despite not having any active commitment to their religion. But the core of Jewishness is the Judaic faith. A British Jew who abandons utterly his faith is simply British. Another case in point are the Sikhs of the Punjab, who were initially separated from their Hindu neighbours only by their decision to follow the new religion and who gradually came to form a distinct ethnic and then putatively national group because of the decisions of their political leaders and the responses of others to them.

Poland and Ireland   The history of modern Poland offers a classic example of a nation, the identity of which has been shaped and sustained by a religion that united within and divided without.

Poland became Christian in 966 when Prince Mieszko I was baptized into the Catholic Latin stream of Christianity. Although once a great power, for over a century before 1918 Poland had been repeatedly partitioned by its more powerful neighbours, from whom it differed in language and in religion. While the Poles were Catholic, the Germans to the west and the Swedes to the north were Lutheran Protestants and the Russians to the east were Orthodox. Poland enjoyed a brief period of independence between the two world wars, but in 1945 it came under the control of the Soviet Union, which imposed on it a Communist government.

For the next fifty years, the Catholic Church served as a repository for Polish national identity. Although the Church was careful to avoid all-out war with the atheistic government, it did serve as a vehicle for opposition to what was seen as an alien state.[6] The link between Catholicism and national resistance was given an enormous boost by the election of Cardinal Karol Wojtyła of Cracow to the papacy in 1978. It reinforced the widespread notion that God had given Poles a particular mission. As a prominent priest put it:

> The Polish nation is conscious that God is assigning a twofold task to it: one is internal, concerning itself, the members of a nation, and the other is external, concerning other nations, the whole economy of God. In each case Poland has both general and special tasks to accomplish.... Thanks to her identity and her individuality, she serves the other nations, making up what they lack and what the whole Family of Nations lack.[7]

In August 1980 the workers of the Lenin shipyard in Gdańsk staged a strike in opposition to a rise in food prices. What began as local industrial action won unprecedented concessions from the government, including the official recognition of the Solidarity trade union led by electrician Lech Wałęsa. The man who eventually brought down the Communist regime and became its first post-Communist President signed the accord with the government with an outsize souvenir pen featuring a picture of Pope John Paul. He was also wearing a badge of the Black Madonna, the icon of Polish Catholicism. Solidarity was strongly supported by the Church, which over the next decade played a cautious but signal role in negotiating the demise of the dictatorial regime.[8]

Religion played a similar resistance role in the preservation of Irish identity under four centuries of British colonialism. The majority of the Irish remained Roman Catholic despite (or because of)

centuries of Protestant British domination that saw the Episcopalian Protestant Church of Ireland imposed on a reluctant people
and a very large settlement of Scottish Presbyterians in the north-
east of the island. After failing to shift the Irish from their Catholicism, the British government moved to subsidize the Catholic
Church when in 1795 it approved an annual grant to the seminary
at Maynooth and even proposed paying the clergy – an attempt at
incorporation that was firmly rejected. Gradually freed from repressive legislation, the Church built a powerful institutional structure that made it the primary carrier of Irish identity.[9] It is a mark of
the popular power of Catholicism that, when the rebels of the Irish
Republican Army, many of them avowed socialists, launched their
insurrection on Easter Day 1916, their proclamation began 'In the
name of God' and the concluding paragraph started with the
words: 'We place the cause of the Irish Republic under the protection of the Most High God, Whose blessings we invoke upon our
arms....'.[10]

When three-quarters of the island achieved autonomy as the Irish
Free State in 1922, nationalist leaders competed with each other to
assert the Catholic nature of the state. Like the Russian *narodniks*
who supposed that virtue was to be found among the pious peasants of the countryside, Eamonn De Valera was a romantic who
saw liberation from British rule as an opportunity to reject also the
dehumanized utilitarian spirit of modern industrial capitalism. His
imagined Ireland was a country of whitewashed peat-burning cottages inhabited by pious Gaelic-speaking Catholic peasants.[11]
A similar romantic ethos informed the views of Nichifor Crainic
and Nae Ionescu, leading Romanian intellectuals of the 1920s who
argued that the solution to economic difficulties and the lack of
state integration was a return to the authentic spirituality of the
Romanian village and the Orthodox Church. Liberal democracy
was unacceptable because, like communism, it had its ideological
roots in Renaissance rationalism, the Enlightenment and the French
Revolution.[12]

Nationalists mobilizing weak religious identities

Poland and Ireland had an unusually long history of association
between religious and national identities, which was made possible
partly by the coherence and stability of the religious tradition. They
were also unusual in the neatness of the disputes about their
autonomy, which resulted from them being hemmed in by relatively coherent states. More common are situations where religious
diversity, shifting boundaries and changes in regime created a

much less easily deployed religious heritage. The recent histories of Yugoslavia and Russia can provide a number of examples.

Yugoslavia   Tom Gallagher's fine history of the Balkans shows very clearly how specific political actions produced outcomes that could easily have been very different. It is thus a powerful corrective to the view, common in mass-media explanations of the Balkans conflicts, that the recent wars were in some sense inevitable. Nonetheless, it is difficult to escape the conclusion that Yugoslavia, the country of the 'southern Slavs', was inherently much more precarious than most states.[13] Too many of the major fault lines in European history ran right through it: the division of south European Christianity into Latin Catholicism and Slavonic Orthodoxy; the rivalry between the Austro-Hungarian and the Russian empires; and the major divide between West and East.

Once ruled by the Ottoman Empire and then by the dual monarchy of Austria and Hungary, the Yugoslav state was created after the First World War as the home for all the southern Slavs except the Bulgarians. It was a hotchpotch of competing religio-ethnic groups: Catholic Christian Slovenes and Croats, Orthodox Christian Serbs, Macedonians and Montenegrins, and Bosnian and Albanian Muslims. There were also small numbers of Hungarians, Germans, Slovaks, Turks and Jews. Instability was endemic, as was intolerance. The following story is instructive. In 1917 leading Croat and Serbs met to negotiate a settlement they could present to the victors of the war who would determine their future. One stumbling block was the diversity of Bosnia-Herzegovina, which had a majority Muslim population. Stojan Protić, a Serb delegate, announced: 'We have a solution to Bosnia. When our army crosses the Drina we will give the Turks [i.e. Muslim Bosnians] 24 hours, well maybe 48, to return to the Orthodox faith. Those who won't will be killed, as we have done in our time in Serbia.'[14] The Croats were horrified. Protić insisted he was serious.

The Serbs saw the new state as an expanded version of the previous Kingdom of Serbia. As the largest group after the Serbs and the one that had enjoyed some autonomy under Hapsburg rule, the Croats were the main obstacle to the Serb dream and they never fully accepted the new state. The inter-war years were marked by always-unstable government and regular assassinations; King Alexander was murdered by Croat and Macedonian nationalists in 1934. In the Second World War, Yugoslavia was carved up by the Germans, Italians, Hungarians and Bulgarians. The Germans and Italians who occupied it created an independent

Croat state, ruled by the fascist Ustaše, who carried out a vicious campaign of genocide against the Serbs. In May 1941 Ustaše seized the Orthodox Bishop of Banja Luka, shaved his beard, gouged out his eyes, cut off his nose and ears and lit a fire on his chest before dispatching him. In total some 130 Orthodox priests were murdered. The Serb Chetniks replied in kind. After the war, the Communist Party led by Tito (the alias used by Josip Broz) dethroned the exiled king and established a stable government, which allowed considerable autonomy to six republics (Serbia, Croatia, Slovenia, Macedonia, Montenegro, Bosnia and Herzegovina) and to two autonomous provinces within Serbia (Kosovo and Vojvodina).

Tito's enduring problem was that the main parts of his jigsaw had recently enjoyed some political freedom. They had been stimulated by their own nationalists to stress what separated rather than united them. In the 1840s the Serbs had promoted the history of a Greater Serbia: a once-powerful Christian kingdom defeated by the Turks. Although the 1389 battle of Kosovo was probably not vital to the Ottoman conquest of the Balkans, it was assigned a pivotal role by Serbian intellectuals, who conveniently forgot that Christians had fought on both sides. As Gallagher puts it:

> given the nationalist agenda of the Serbian state, a homogenous identity was required which denied such co-existence. New myths emerged. Conversion to Islam was seen as based on cowardice and greed, which justified harsh treatment against Albanian and Bosnian Muslims. The Slavs were seen as Christian by nature and abandonment of Christianity was tantamount to betrayal of the Serbian race.[15]

Religion was also important to the Croats. Indeed, recent history aside, it is pretty well all that distinguished them from the Serbs. They spoke one language but wrote two. Because they were Roman Christians, the Croats rendered the tongue in Latin script; because they were Orthodox Christians, the Serbs rendered it in Cyrillic.[16] One people looked west; the other east.

The country was held together for thirty-five years by the power of the Communist Party, by Tito's personality, and by his policy of federalism. His solution to the rivalry between Serbs and Croats was to create more subdivisions. In 1966 the Bosnian Muslims were raised to the status of an 'ethnic group', even though, as Gallagher notes, 'their lifestyle was mainly secular'.[17] To ensure stability after his death, Tito created a collective and rotating presidency. Yugoslavia would be ruled by a council consisting of one member from each unit of the federation plus the leader of the Communist Party and the federal minister of defence. But, as with all systems that allocate power to ethnic groups (the Lebanese constitution is the perfect example), this structure encouraged the political leaders not to seek common ground but to promote the interests of the people they represented. What was supposed to prevent internal fragmentation simply encouraged it.

After Tito's death in 1980 the Serbs, led by Slobodan Milošević, began to take over the federal republic, first inserting placemen in charge of Vojvodina, Kosovo and Montenegro (and thus ensuring four of the eight votes on the ruling council) and then ensuring command of the Yugoslav army. By encouraging Serb minorities in the other republics to claim to be oppressed, he fuelled Serb nationalism. Despite having been a career communist, Milošević happily encouraged the manipulation of religious symbols. Whereas Tito had very deliberately discouraged the celebration of divisive history, Milošević encouraged the Serb Orthodox Church to make the most of the forthcoming 500th anniversary of the Battle of Kosovo: 'The Serbian Church whipped up a great deal of public interest in the event – and in itself – by transporting the relics of Prince Lazar around Serbia's ancient monasteries.'[18] Many thousands of Serbs gathered on the field outside Pristina where Lazar had fallen five centuries earlier, and, supported by a claque of black-robed Orthodox bishops, Milošević made a speech that effectively ended the federation. Stimulated by such Serbian aggrandisement and made incautious by the collapse of the Soviet Union, Communist leaders in the four remaining republics (especially Franjo Tudjman in Croatia) pressed first for greater autonomy and then for full independence, and Yugoslavia collapsed into war.

In Poland there had been a centuries-long association of a clear national identity and a shared religion, strengthened by periods of national independence. The Yugoslav situation was much more fragmented. Even the most apparently coherent blocs had within their boundaries sizeable minorities of peoples linked by religion and ethnicity to other republics. Although there had been some mobilization of religion in the previous nationalist movements (especially in the 1941–5 rivalry between Croats and Serbs), the long period of Tito's rule had drained some of that spirit. And ethnic identities sometimes competed with religious ones. For example, during the Communist era the Muslims of Kosovo were on poor terms with the leading Muslims in Bosnia, whom they saw as being too close to the federal Communist leadership.[19]

Nonetheless, as each group of nationalists pressed its case, it made what use it could of its religious heritage, and leading clergy of each religion played very public roles in legitimating separatism. Radovan Karadic and Ratko Mladic (respectively the political and military leaders of the Bosnian Serbs) made great play of their Orthodox faith. The Bosnian Serb press agency in Pale distributed a telling photograph of them taking communion together from an Orthodox bishop. The Serbian warlord Arkan, despite his own personal life falling a long way short of any Christian ideal, often wore a cumbersomely large Orthodox crucifix.

The wars that followed the collapse of Yugoslavia gave the leaders of each religio-ethnic bloc cause to 'rediscover' their pre-Communist religious heritage.[20] As well as the romantic function of providing explanations for their fates and justifications for their separatist agendas, there was the rather more practical matter of seeking external support. The term 'Muslim' was applied to one section of the Bosnian people, not so much because they were Muslims (though they were) as because they were not Croats or Serbs, and their conversion to Islam during the days of the Ottoman Empire was the most obvious thing they had in common. In the 1990s they were noted neither for their orthodoxy nor for their piety. However, the West's refusal to arm them forced Bosnian leaders to solicit aid from their fellow Muslims in various Arab countries and from Pakistan. Muslim states provided weapons and money to pay mercenaries and the price asked was a strengthening of Muslim orthodoxy. Many of Osama Bin Laden's Arab fighters, who in the late 1990s were a vital element in the ideological and military apparatus of the Afghani Taliban, first saw service in Bosnia.[21]

Russia and the Ukraine   The collapse of the Soviet Union in 1989 allowed the re-emergence of an array of nationalisms, almost all of them inspired to varying degrees by religious identity and difference.

Russia had long been uniformly Orthodox, with its own autonomous church structure and a fine sense of self-importance. Since Byzantium, the original centre of the Christian Church in the East, had been overrun by Muslims in 1453, the Moscow Patriarchate had seen itself as the heart of Christendom. It was, however, an unusually docile institution. Under Peter the Great the Church was reformed so as to make it entirely a department of state. The Patriarch was subordinated to a committee padded with the Czar's placemen. Peter took the Church's extensive wealth and gave a quarter back in salary payments to the clergy, who became civil servants. Among other indignities they were required to report any whispers of sedition heard in the confession box. Being required to act as government agents 'undoubtedly worked to identify them with the increasingly oppressive state and thus divide them from the people they served'.[22]

In the civil war that followed the Bolshevik Revolution, the Church's leaders were on the conservative side and suffered as a result. Metropolitan Vladimir of Kiev was killed by an armed gang in 1918. Metropolitan Venianin of Petrograd was shot by firing squad in 1922. Many others were sent into Siberian exile. Joseph Stalin, a former Orthodox seminary student before he became a Bolshevik, set out to eradicate religion when he acquired the power so to do. There is no better illustration of that desire than the fate of the Cathedral of Christ the Saviour.[23] This church had its origins in the defeat of Napoleon's invasion in 1812. Czar Alexander I promised to give thanks to God for the providential deliverance from the French army by creating the most magnificent religious edifice imaginable. Building on a site by the Moscva river did not actually begin until 1838 and it took forty-five years to complete, but when finished it was one of the largest and most extravagant churches in Christendom. Its massive bulk dominated Moscow and its interior was finished with marble, gold and jewels. In 1931 Stalin ordered that it be stripped of its riches and flattened to make way for a vast Palace of the Soviets, which, in order to show the superiority of communism over capitalism, had to be bigger than the Empire State Building. This would symbolize the triumph of the Party, not just over the Russian Church, but over all religion. However, there were problems with the site. Foundations were built but kept filling with water. Other interests got in the way and Stalin never found time to finish his building contest with God. In a fitting anticlimax, which humbled the ambitions of the Czars and of Stalin, Khrushchev eventually arranged for the vacant site to become a heated open-air swimming pool for the hardy citizens of Moscow.

The Soviets had two approaches to religion: displace and control. The Party promoted a secular Marxist ideology and created an array of institutions and rituals (such as community wedding ceremonies in the secular Hall of Marriage) that it hoped would serve the social purposes of religion. Such functional substitution and rigorous indoctrination in scientific atheism would kill the demand for religion. If the Church could not be made entirely redundant then it would be co-opted, which was not difficult given its relationship with the Czarist state. The Communist Party merely changed the master.

The speed with which the Soviet regime collapsed in the late 1980s, to leave almost no one who admitted to having actually believed in Marxist-Leninism, suggests that all the secular propagandizing had not been terribly successful. The comparison with the popular oppositional church in Poland is instructive. That Communism left the Orthodox Church in a moribund condition probably had less to do with people becoming convinced atheists than with them losing interest in an institution that was largely controlled by the party.

The situation outside Russia was somewhat different.[24] As in Yugoslavia, the structure of the state inadvertently played a part in turning rather loose amorphous ethnic groups into self-consciously aware political entities. The federal model of the Union of Socialist Soviet Republics required republics. To give the party outside Russia legitimacy, exemplars of the titular 'nationality' had to be promoted to positions of power. A Tajikistan required Tajiks. The result was to encourage Tajiks and Azeris and Uzbeks to see themselves as distinct peoples (albeit united in the great project of building socialism). 'Each of the borderland ethno-republics was provided with a degree of institutional protection that enabled their native languages and cultures to flourish.' In Central Asia, 'by federalizing ethnic homelands into ethnorepublics, the Soviet state created nations whose sense of nation-ness had previously barely existed'.[25] When Soviet control was removed, the republics could compete with each other about peoples who were on the wrong side of the borders. So Armenia and Azerbaijan could argue about which should have Nagorno-Karabakh, and the main difference that could be deployed in such contests was religious identity: the conflict could be construed as Christianity versus Islam.

The restoration of the Russian Orthodox Church to the centre of Russian identity began when Mikhail Gorbachev introduced his reforming programme of *glasnost* (openness) and *perestroika* (efficiency). Gorbachev was the first Party leader openly to acknowledge the utter demoralization of the Soviet state, ruined by decades of repression, corruption and nepotism. He saw Orthodox Christianity as a potential source of shared moral values and, as did Stalin during the Great Patriotic War, hoped that the Party could use the 'church-and-nation' line to encourage loyalty to the unloved Soviet state. In April 1988 he invited Patriarch Pimen to the Kremlin, the first such meeting since Stalin had asked Metropolitan

Sergi for his support during the war. The state sponsored the events to celebrate the Millennium of Russian Christianity with extensive radio and television coverage. It even permitted the printing of 100,000 Bibles and the importing of a further 500,000.

After the collapse of Communist Party rule, the rehabilitation of the Church was accelerated. Many properties were returned to the Church. Khrushchev's swimming pool was drained and very large sums of scarce funds were spent restoring the Cathedral of Christ the Saviour.[26] The Church even got its bodies back. The remains of Saint Serafim, canonized in 1903, had been removed from their tomb in 1922 because it was too popular a place of pilgrimage. He was shuffled around from one museum of atheism to another until he was lost in Leningrad. When communism closed so did the museums of atheism and in a wholesale clear-out Serafim was found. With great solemnity the remains were displayed for veneration in Leningrad and then Moscow before he was finally reburied in his original tomb.

For the first time since 1918 political leaders sought religious legitimation. When Boris Yeltsin was sworn in as Russian president in June 1991, he had himself blessed by Patriarch Aleksi II. Although the Freedom of Conscience and Religious Association law of 1997 announced that Russia was a secular state, it also declared that Orthodoxy had a special place in Russian history and in the development of the spirituality of the Russian nation.[27] History was rewritten so that the godless Marxism of the Soviet era became merely a hiatus in an otherwise indissoluble bond between church and nation.

It must be said that the restoration of the Church to the bosom of the nation was less a result of popular pressure than was the case in many of the neighbouring countries that had been subjugated by Russia in the Soviet era. Unlike the Catholic Church in Poland or Lithuania, the Orthodox Church had not won the respect of the Russian people by acting as a disguised political opposition. On the contrary, it had been thoroughly docile and compromised. After liberation, church attendance briefly picked up but then fell back again. Surveys in the 1990s showed that 75 per cent of Russians described themselves as Orthodox but the proportion of the population regularly attending church rose only from 6 per cent in 1991 to 7 per cent in 1999.[28]

In exile in the United States from 1974 to 1994, the dissident Russian novelist Alexander Solzhenitsyn had argued that the cure for the corruption of the Soviet system was not to be found in the embrace of liberal democracy and capitalism.[29] For all their apparent divergence, communism and capitalism were the twin children of the French Revolution and the rational Enlightenment and both had to be rejected. Only a religious revival could free the modern world from soulless materialism. As he put it:

> the shiny bauble of unlimited material progress has led all of humanity into a depressing cul-de-sac, represented with only slight difference in the East as in the West. I can discover only one healthy course for everyone now living, for nations, societies, human organizations, and above all the churches. We must confess our sins and errors (our own, not those of others), repent, and use self-restraint in our future development.[30]

Some nationalist politicians, missing the point about recognizing their own errors, put a more chauvinistic spin on Solzhenitsyn's slavophile philosophy and promoted Orthodoxy as a tonic, not so much for the ailing soul, as for the political weakness of Russia.

This rediscovery of Mother Russia failed to strike much of a chord with the Russian people. Too many desired precisely the materialism that so offended Solzhenitsyn about the United States and Slavophile nationalism was not helped either by the personal character of politicians such as Vladimir Zhirinovsky or by the cranks it attracted (the restoration of the Romanov royal family was one rather diverting cause they embraced).

Above I made the point that the Russian Church's incorporation in the state prevented it from playing the opposition role that did so much to keep Catholicism popular in Poland, Lithuania, Slovakia and the other Catholic fringes of the Soviet Empire. There may well be another consideration. The Russians were the dominant people of the empire. Though their religious heritage may have had some additional appeal from being the antithesis of the official ideology of an unpopular regime, the Russians did not also have an 'ethnic' grievance that could be framed in religious terms. A religious heritage most effectively supports nationalism when the nation in question is at odds with a more powerful *external* force. Hence, in Yugoslavia, religion was more closely associated with national identity in Croatia than in the more powerful Serbia. The people who enjoy political domination have less need to husband the alternative identities and sources of pride to be found in religious institutions.

The position of the Ukrainians vis-à-vis Russia was in many respects similar to that of the Poles or the Lithuanians and this is reflected in the political role played by the Uniate Church in the

Ukraine. However, there were important differences that stem from the Russians' more effective domination of the Ukraine and from the internal cultural divisions within the region.

The East Slav tribes of the thirteenth century gradually produced three peoples: Ukrainians, Belorussians and Russians. For the next four centuries the first two peoples were under the domination of the Polish–Lithuanian Commonwealth. In the seventeenth century, in return for the promise of autonomy, the Ukrainian Cossacks rebelled against the Poles and allied themselves with the Russian Czar. Predictably that autonomy was steadily reduced until the eastern part of the Ukraine was firmly assimilated to Russia. The western Ukraine, or Galicia, however, remained under Austro–Hungarian control and then passed to Poland at the end of the First World War. When, at the start of the next, Stalin and Hitler carved up the territory between them, along with half of Poland, the Soviet Union took Galicia.

Russian treatment of Ukrainians, under Romanov and Communist czars, generated enormous resentment. Both regimes suppressed the local language and culture and encouraged large numbers of Russians to settle in the Ukraine. Because it had been a prosperous peasant farming economy, the Ukraine suffered particularly badly under Stalin's agricultural collectivization programme. Those peasants who were reluctant to give up their farms to the new collectives had their property confiscated; the Soviets removed all the food they could find. In the subsequent famine of 1932–3 some five million Ukrainians starved to death.

It is no surprise, then, that, when the German army overran the Ukraine in 1941, its soldiers were treated as liberators. Metropolitan Andrij Sheptytsky congratulated 'the victorious German army that has already taken control over the whole of our region with joy and gratitude for liberation from the enemy'.[31] Sheptytsky is reputed also to have supported the raising of the Galician SS division for the German army. When the fortunes of war shifted and the Germans fell back, many Ukrainians chose to retreat with them rather than face the predictable Soviet revenge. After the war the Soviets imposed themselves even more firmly on the Ukraine.

In the Ukraine religion was not as neatly associated with national identity as it was in Poland or Lithuania because there were usually three religions: a version of Catholicism and two competing forms of Orthodoxy. Ukraine had initially been Orthodox, but, during the periods that Galicia had been under Western control, the Church had been assimilated to the Vatican. This hybrid, known variously as Uniate, Greek Catholic or Eastern Rites Catholic, remained

Orthodox in its liturgy and its junior clergy married, but it accepted the authority of the Pope. The Orthodox Church in the Ukraine was divided by ethnicity. Czarist Russia attempted to ensure loyalty by controlling the Ukrainian Church. Of nine diocesan bishops in 1915, eight were Russians. In the war that followed the Bolshevik Revolution, Ukraine sided with the Whites and fought for its independence. It lost. Once they had gained control, the Bolsheviks stripped the Orthodox Church in the Ukraine of its revenue-generating property. Although intended to weaken an opponent, this had the opposite effect. For the first time in its history the Church became completely dependent on its members, who were Ukrainian nationalists. When the Church did not sufficiently distance itself from Moscow, separatists, who had the symbolic advantage of controlling Kiev's beautiful Cathedral of St Sophia, broke away. They created a Ukrainian Autocephalous (meaning 'self-headed'; that is, not under the authority of anyone else) Orthodox Church (UAOC) that by 1924 had over 1,000 parishes and about four million members.[32] Stalin forced the UAOC to return to the control of the Moscow Patriarchate. When Germans replaced Stalinists, the UAOC re-formed. When the Stalinists returned, it was once again disbanded.

Stalin also forced the Uniates to accept Russian Orthodox control, but, despite (or because of) forty years of concerted repression, the 'closet' Uniate Church remained popular in western Ukraine. The fall of the Soviet Union allowed Ukraine to declare its independence, and, once given a choice, almost 2,000 priests and five million members left the Orthodox Church to re-establish themselves as Uniates under the leadership of Rome. The first president of the post-Soviet Ukraine, Leonid Kravchuk, and other former apparatchiks, tried to create a new national church – the 'Kiev Patriarchate' – on the model of the UAOC. Nationalist-minded Christians in the Ukraine were not impressed by this sudden conversion of senior churchmen who had such a short time before been loyal supporters of the Soviet state. Filaret Denysenko, the Metropolitan of Kiev, made an implausible nationalist.[33] When the Soviets were worth placating he banned his clergy from preaching in Ukrainian.

The net result was that Orthodoxy was divided in three: two small organizations very independent of Moscow and one mostly independent. The 1990s saw increasingly bitter conflicts between the Uniates and the various brands of Orthodoxy as they competed over church property and as their relative status came to act as a surrogate for East–West divisions and contests to claim the soul of Ukrainian nationalism. The net result of the divisions was that nationalists were not able to call on a single heritage as the basis for a new sense of identity, and, although each church was able to act as a spokesman for its people, there did not emerge a single strong religio-ethnic bond.

Where two peoples in competition adhere to different religions, the links are simple and strong. As we see with Ukrainian Orthodoxy, it is less easy for nationalists to use their church as a carrier of national identity when those whom they wish to avoid or snub share the same faith. Nonetheless they often try, as we see in the example of Moldova. When the Soviet Union broke up, the Moscow Patriachate happily conceded autonomous status to the Orthodox Church in Moldova, but one leading Moldovan bishop wished to go further in his rejection of the Soviet period. He tried to put history into reverse by subordinating the Moldovan Church to the Romanian Patriarchate: a return to the situation between 1922 and 1944 when 'Bessarabia', as it was then known, was part of Romania. The Moldovan government wanted to be free of Russia but did not want to embrace Romania. Its solution was to place the Moldovan Church under the direct authority of the Patriarch of Constantinople – a convenient two countries distant![34]

Nationalists rejecting strong religious identities

The above examples concern nationalists with more and less success deliberately drawing on religion to mobilize a common national identity. We can also find, especially in more recent cases of nation formation, deliberate attempts to dispense with religion. As we will see in the discussion of African states in the next section, the new 'nation' may be so culturally diverse that appeals to faith are simply not possible. This section is concerned with the different matter of nationalists on principle pursuing a secular path. The main reason for this is the belief that the traditional culture is a hindrance to social and economic progress. Such 'progressivism' can come in Marxist and non-Marxist forms and with varying degrees of abstraction and reach. We have already seen one example of the Marxist form in the Soviet promotion of atheistic communism as the road to utopia. Any number of examples of a less formalized disdain for backwardness can be found in the ways that most metropolitan peoples see their own regional fringes. The Anglophone Presbyterian Scots of the Lowlands despised the Highlanders for their Catholic religion, their barbaric clannish ways and their uncouth language. Progressive educators wanted to create a common culture across the United Kingdom and, along the way, to improve the ignoble savages. As many in the West still do when

thinking about poverty in the Third World, the improvers conveniently overlooked the structural causes of poverty (and in particular the possibility that the rich may have prospered at the
expense of the poor). They supposed the Highland fringes were
poor because the culture retarded progress.[35] So progress required
that Gaelic be replaced by English. Anglophone Protestants in
Ireland took the same view of Catholicism and Irish. And, as late
as the 1920s, we can find the Archbishop of the Episcopalian
Church in Wales describing the Welsh language as 'the last refuge
of the uneducated'.[36]

General Park Chung-Hee, who came to power in South Korea in
1961, firmly believed that Korea's Confucianism and the older
indigenous religion of shamanism were an impediment to social
and economic development. He ordered religious officials to be
harried: 'in a campaign accompanying the New Village Movement,
designed in the early 1970s by the government to foster rural
development, local reformers imprisoned shamans and destroyed
their shrines to eradicate allegedly superstitious practices; traditional Confucian and yangban leadership was equally targeted
by this campaign.'[37] With political stability and increasing prosperity came greater confidence and a more positive assessment of
Korea's past. Religious traditions were restored: this time rather
tamely framed as 'heritage'. In the 1980s a new paired contrast was
devised. Instead of 'old' and 'new', politicians started to talk of
'Western ways' and 'our ways'. Heavily criticized for the authoritarianism of the South Korean state, the Korean political elite found
a defence in separating 'modernization' (which was good) from
Westernization (which was bad). As the new metaphor put it, the
ideal Korea would be built on 'Western hardware but Confucian
software'.[38] Attempts to justify an illiberal regime on the grounds
that it was indigenous may have been self-serving but there has
been a genuine revival of interest in traditional culture. In 1998 a
Ministry of Culture and Tourism was created with the remit to
promote national culture. Folk religious festivals were encouraged
and Buddhist temples and Confucian shrines were restored.

Turkey, Egypt, Syria and Iran   Even before the Ottoman Empire
chose the wrong side in the First World War and was dismembered
in the peace negotiations, its loss of power was obvious and groups
least incorporated in the old order were pushing for radical change.
In 1908 a cadre of army officers, bureaucrats and intellectuals under
the banner of the Young Turk movement tried to reform the empire
on the lines of secular nationalism. They promoted Turkish lan-

guage and culture through educational and administrative reforms. This naturally offended the Arabs and traditional Muslims, who accepted the primacy of Arabic as the language of the Qur'ān and of the Prophet. The changes necessitated by the defeat in 1918 were hastened by the 1919 Greek invasion. Inspired by Bishop Germanos's vision of re-establishing the Orthodox Christian Byzantine Empire, the Greek army tried to regain control over the Greek-speaking parts of Asia Minor. The army of the new Turkish state defeated both the Greeks and the conservative Muslim forces led by the Sultan. The net result was the consolidation of the new Turkey, as many thousands of Turks and Greeks shifted to be on the right side of the new boundaries.

Kemal Atatürk, the founder of the new state, was a militant secularist. His populism contrasted the old corrupt (and Muslim) ruling elites and the potentially vibrant spirit of the Turkish nation. In 1925 he banned the wearing of the fez. The following year he instituted civil marriages and outlawed polygamy. In 1929 the use of Arabic in publications was banned and the Latin alphabet was imposed. Most significantly for a Muslim culture, Atatürk encouraged women to become active in the public sphere. Fourteen members of his Republican Party executive were women.[39] Initially Atatürk expected the private sector to fund economic development, but when it failed to do so he used state bureaucracy to promote growth. In 1931 the party declared that Turkey was nationalist, republican, secular, statist, revolutionary and populist. These 'six arrows' became the guiding principles of the nation and were six years later written into the Constitution.[40]

Similar principles inspired Nasserism in Egypt.[41] In 1922 Egypt became an independent constitutional monarchy but Britain retained a military presence and control over a large part of its affairs. Severe hardship after 1945 and Egypt's failure in the Palestine War of 1948–9 led to violent popular protests against the British presence and against corrupt and incompetent monarchy. In 1952 junior army officers led by Gamal Abdul Nasser took power, abolished the monarchy and negotiated Britain's withdrawal from the Suez canal. Some 90 per cent of Egyptians are Muslims and the Christian minority was much resented for the privileged position it had enjoyed under British rule.[42] It would have been possible for reaction to take the form of an Islamic revival and there were organizations that wished for just that; the Muslim Brotherhood, founded in 1929, for example.[43] But, like Atatürk, Nasser was convinced that his country could advance economically only if the social and cultural heritage that Islam had legitimated was set aside. The initial programme of his one-party state was secular in its social mores (in particular it encouraged the advance of women, who were granted the vote and the right to stand for public office in 1952). Nasser's domestic programme, called 'Arab socialism', consisted of state-controlled capitalist development. In 1956 foreign enterprises were seized and put under local management. Land reforms were slight but they were an important symbol of a break with the past.

There is no doubt that the Nasser regime was popular: 'due in no small measure to Nasser's political style and personal charisma. He spoke to the people in colloquial Egyptian rather than the standard Arabic that was imperfectly understood by the majority of Egyptians.'[44] His stand against Western imperialism and his ability to symbolize hope for the future made him a hero throughout the Arab world and further afield.

Egypt's defeat in the 1948–9 Palestine war caused its leaders to want to buy modern weapons systems. The United States refused to supply Egypt because Nasser refused to support the West against the Soviet Union and instead became a leading exponent of non-alignment, so Nasser turned to Czechoslovakia. Britain and the United States withdrew their funding for the vital electricity-generating Aswan Dam project. Nasser then decided to nationalize the Suez Canal and use the income from transit fees for the dam. Britain and France (because Egypt supported the Algerian War of Independence) and Israel (for the usual reasons) invaded. Egypt was again humiliated by Israel but this time a political success was forged out of military defeat when the United States and the Soviet Union combined to force Israel to withdraw. The Canal was returned to Egypt and Nasser's standing as the leading figure of Arab nationalism was restored.

In 1958 Egypt formed a short-lived union with Syria in the United Arab Republic but this collapsed under the strain of differing interests and the active hostility of the United States, which feared the formation of any bloc powerful enough to threaten its interests in the Middle East.

Nasserism failed as an economic programme. Whether one blames this on Egypt's own weaknesses or on the Western powers (particularly the United States) that could have done far more to assist it, the point is still failure to produce economic growth fast enough to satisfy the growing aspirations of the people.[45] To this was added the repeated failure to defeat Israel. When Nasser died in 1970, Israel was still occupying the Egyptian territory of Sinai and the Egyptian economy was in a deepening crisis. His successor,

Anwar Sadat, reversed many of Nasser's policies. In particular, he removed the ban on the Muslim Brotherhood and encouraged it as a balance to growing left-wing forces. But his willingness to make peace with Israel in return for Sinai deeply offended more militant Islamic groups and in 1981 Sadat was shot dead with a gun that had 'In the name of Allah the Avenger' engraved on its barrel.

As an aside and because it reminds us that different religious traditions can generate identical political actions, it is worth adding that the same willingness to put political pragmatism before principle also caused the death of the Israeli Prime Minister Yitzhak Rabin fourteen years later. In November 1995 Rabin was shot dead by Yigal Amir, an ultra-Orthodox Jewish theological student, for the treachery of negotiating a 'land-for-peace' deal with the Palestinians.

Syria, another state created from the ruins of the Ottoman Empire, has a similar history.[46] It was under French colonial rule until 1946, when it became an independent constitutional monarchy. Since 1963 the country has been ruled by the notionally socialist and pan-Arab Baʿathist party. The central premiss of Baʿathism is that the Arabs form a single nation that was artificially divided, first by the Ottomans and then by Britain and France. Such a view had particular appeal in Syria. Although most post-Ottoman states were created with more concern for British and French interest than for any intrinsic sense of identity, Syria was unusually artificial, especially after the French had decided to create the State of Lebanon in part of what was regarded by many Syrian politicians as their land.

The Baʿath party in Syria followed a Nasserist programme of secular reform, state-led investment and military expansion and similarly failed to promote indigenous economic growth.[47] After the coup of 1970 had brought Hafez-al-Asad to power, it became essentially an authoritarian military dictatorship. It was further distanced from its own people by a discrepancy of religious affiliation. The majority of Syrians are Sunni Muslims, but the Baʿathist leadership is predominantly drawn from the small Alawi sect (the Muslim identity of which is rejected by most Shias and Sunnis) and the Druze (a small offshoot of the Ismaili branch of Shia Islam strongest in the mountains of Lebanon). When Asad died in 2001, the Baʿathist party demonstrated how completely it had abandoned democracy by anointing his son to succeed him. It retains power only by maintaining an enormous military apparatus (that consumes about half the domestic budget). The one respect in which it differs from the Shah's Iran (of which more below) is that its foreign policy does not offend directly against Arab Middle Eastern interests. Syria has not courted the West and has remained more robustly anti-Israel than has Egypt. Nonetheless economic deprivation has combined with resentment at the political power of the Alawi and Druze communities to create strong popular support for Islamic fundamentalist movements. What distinguishes Syria from many of its neighbours is the force with which it has repressed such opposition. In 1982 the army destroyed the city of Hama and killed some 20,000 of its own people in order to put down an uprising by the Muslim Brotherhood.

A fourth example of secular nationalism was the White Revolution of the Shahs of Iran. Iran differed from its neighbours in a number of ways that have implications for any generalizations made from its circumstances.[48] It had a long history of autonomy. Although it was overwhelmingly Muslim, it was Persian rather than Arab in language and its Muslims belonged to the minority Shia strand of Islam. It also had one characteristic that is crucial for understanding why fundamentalists succeeded in gaining power there when, as of 2002, they have failed to do so in Turkey or Egypt. In other Islamic states (such as twentieth-century Tunisia) religious taxes and endowments were controlled by the secular authorities, but in Iran the Shia clerics were able to maintain their political freedom because they first retained their financial independence. That practical advantage was underpinned by an element of Shi'ite thinking that accidentally created an unusually effective sort of social organization. Although in theory all Muslims are equal in the eyes of God, in practice those who were well trained in the interpretation of the Qur'ān and the Hadith enjoyed considerable social influence. Towards the middle of the nineteenth century, the idea became widespread among Shi'ites that every Muslim should adopt a 'source of imitation', a Muslim scholar with the right to interpret the canon, and follow his judgements. Those leaders came to be ranked in an informal hierarchy of judicial insight. There thus evolved an all-encompassing but highly flexible hierarchy of authoritative religious leadership that was able to provide an important counter to the power of the Shahs of Iran. For example, in 1891 the Shah sold the tobacco concession to a British subject. The most influential 'source of imitation', Ayatollah Shirazi, declared that it was now unlawful for any Muslim to use or deal in tobacco. His lead was so widely followed that the monopoly had to be abandoned.

So Iran, unlike Turkey or Egypt, had a powerful religious institution. Iran was also different in the extent to which it had remained underdeveloped. Both Britain and Russia claimed influence over Iran and both were content to have it remain agrarian. Hence when in the 1930s its rulers began a programme of deliberate modernization, the speed of change was much greater than in many other Islamic countries.

Reza Khan, the army leader who became Prime Minister in 1921 and five years later made himself Shah, initially played secular nationalists against religious traditionalists, but his preference to free himself from his country's Islamic past was made clear when he chose the name 'Pahlavi' for his dynasty, a name that claimed links to the purported rulers of pre-Islamic Iran and thus tried to suggest long lineage and heritage while bypassing the more recent tradition that gave legitimacy and power to his rivals: the mullahs.

The Shah was quickly successful in building a coherent nation state. He expelled foreign troops from Iran's soil and established government control over what was, for its population, a vast country. The nomadic tribes were forced to settle permanently; when they protested, he turned the army on them. Resources were devoted to development projects such as the building of a trans-Iranian railway that both enhanced national prestige and consolidated a sense of national identity.

The Shah believed that economic development required social and cultural reform. Like Atatürk, he saw traditional dress as a sign of backwardness, so he banned it. The chador was a mark of poverty, so he banned veiling. He established a network of secular courts and required that their judges hold a degree from his newly established Teheran University. He thus disbarred the graduates of the Islamic colleges. He further deprived them of income and social prestige by removing the power to notarize and register legal documents. When the religious leaders protested, he turned the army on them. In 1928, when Ayatollah Mohammad-Taqi Bafqi protested at the inappropriate dress of some female members of the royal household visiting the shrine at Qom, Reza Khan dragged the Ayatollah out of the shrine and beat him up. In 1935 Reza Khan sent the troops into a shrine at Masad to break up prayer meetings at which preachers were complaining about his modernizing schemes. Dozens were killed and thousands were injured.

The Shah thus thoroughly alienated the traditionalists. Unfortunately, and here we see another difference with Turkey, he also alienated the secular nationalists who could have formed a popular support base. He took power from the religious institution but, rather than vest it in secular democratic institutions, he turned it into royal prerogatives, which gradually became ever more regal.

As the Ottoman Empire had done in 1914, and for the same reasons, the Shah backed the wrong side in the Second World War. The Shah resented the power of Britain, the United States and Russia and saw a German victory as his liberation. Britain was worried that it might lose the Iranian oil that fuelled its ships; Russia was worried that the Germans might use Iran as the base for an attack on its southern flank. When the Shah refused the Allies the use of the Trans-Iranian railway to supply the Red Army from the West, British and Russian troops invaded and deposed the Shah, putting in his place his 22-year-old son, the second and the last member of the Pahlavi dynasty.

The new Shah continued his father's programme of modernization and continued to be challenged by radicals. To keep them happy he made Dr Mossadeqh his Prime Minister and, in 1951, Mossadeqh nationalized the country's oil and removed it from the control of the Anglo-Iranian Oil Company. The logic of the Cold War did not permit small countries to remain neutral. If the West did not control the oil, perhaps the Soviet Union might. Caught between the radical nationalists (many of whom were pro-USSR) and the West, the Shah fled in 1953 and was restored to power by an army coup inspired and paid for by Britain and the United States. He pressed on with his White Revolution that was ever more dependent on Western capital and political leadership. As the Bolsheviks did in the Soviet Union and military leaders did in Egypt, Libya and Iraq, the Shah tried to create a series of all-embracing state-wide institutions of party, youth movement and women's movement. He tried to replace Islam as the country's binding ideology with a secular nationalism that had its own heroes, public holidays, slogans and songs. In 1975, the 2,500th anniversary of the Achaemmenids' pre-Islamic glory, he presided over an extravagant imperial spectacle at the palace of Darius and Xerxes in Persepolis.[49] And when these confections failed to win popular support, he became ever more dictatorial and repressive.

The impact of oil on the Middle East was paradoxical. It provided unprecedented wealth and that wealth could fund economic development, but it was always dependent progress: dependent on the goodwill and the skilled workers of the West. Instead of promoting indigenous and sustainable development, it further distorted the economy. Oil delivered great prosperity to some but it did so in ways that undermined socially significant parts of the traditional economy: in particular the small traders and craftsman of the bazaar. The failure of centrally directed development in Iran was more spectacular than in Egypt but it amounted to the same thing:

statism had failed. Oil could restore Muslim pride, but it also showed Muslims just how backward they had become because it could be turned into wealth only through the cooperation of the Great Satan. And the Shah's response to increasing criticism was to strengthen the repressive state.

The religious opposition to Reza Khan and his son was slow to evolve and it was at first narrowly self-interested. Though they sympathized with the desire for national autonomy, the mullahs were not naturally on the side of the secular reformers. They were not democrats and were comfortable with authoritarian monarchs, so long as they did not challenge the religious institution. The gradual expansion of the targets for religious opposition can be seen in the positions taken by Ayatollah Khomeini, a cleric of growing influence in the symbolically important spiritual centre at Qom. Khomeini's first public criticisms were made in 1941, shortly after the first Shah had been forced to abdicate. In *The Unveiling of Secrets*, he blamed the Shah's failures on his 'deliberate policy of ignoring Islamic principles and undermining the religious community'.[50] Khomeini was no more impressed by the second Pahlavi Shah. The *ulama* (the 'community of the faithful') of Qom mounted a campaign of opposition to the Local Council laws of 1962, which permitted women and non-Muslims to vote, and forced the laws to be abandoned. What is noticeable about that campaign is Khomeini's elision of a number of traditional enemies. The new laws, he suggested, 'were perhaps drawn up by the spies of the Jews and the Zionists ... The Koran and Islam are in danger. The independence of the state and the economy are threatened by a take-over of the Zionists, who in Iran have appeared in the guise of Baha'is.'[51] Understanding why the Baha'is should figure in such a list tells us a lot about the limits to Islamic tolerance. The product of an 1860s schism from the Iranian Shi'ite tradition, the Baha'is were the least troublesome minority in Iran, but they were particularly persecuted because they had once known the truth and abandoned it. They also gave a much higher position to women than most Islamic sects and discouraged polygamy.

An important encouragement to militancy in Iran was the worldwide wave of movements for independence from colonial rule that shook Africa and Asia. Although adopting the language of freedom fighting and anti-colonialism had its dangers for them, the ayatollahs saw its advantage in allowing them to claim leadership of a spectrum of anti-Shah movements. Khomeini, for example, said: 'Islam is the religion of militant individuals who are committed to truth and justice. It is the religion of those who desire

independence. It is the school of those who struggle against imperialism.'[52] For the ayatollahs, Western imperialism had triumphed,
not because its technology and social organization had given it
superior military and economic might but because Islamic leaders
had betrayed the faith. As one put it:

> Islam was defeated by its own rulers, who ignored Divine Law, in
> the name of Western-style secularism. The West captured the im-
> agination of large sections of our people. And that conquest was far
> more disastrous for Islam than any loss of territory. It is not for the
> loss of Andalusia [a reference to the Moors being driven out of
> Spain] that we ought to weep every evening – although that remains
> a bleeding wound. Far greater is the loss of sections of our own
> youth to Western ideology, dress, music and food.[53]

The details of growing opposition to the Shah are complex but the
causes of unrest are simple. His White Revolution raised expectations and threatened traditional occupational groups and networks, but failed ultimately to provide sufficient rewards to win
popular support. The fundamentalists responded to the Shah's
attempts to create a modern bureaucratically rational state by creating a national network of small groups, often meeting in private
homes. That network became the frame around which the disaf-
fected and uprooted could create a sense of self-worth. From that
base, the fundamentalists moved into the public sphere by taking
over mosques and using youthful vigilantes to 'encourage' mosque
attendance and adherence to Islamic requirements. They also
created alternative institutions: Islamic banks, sex-segregated student buses and self-help groups. They persuaded people to bypass
the state's secular courts and settle their disputes by the traditional
appeal to the judgements of trusted Islamic jurists.

In retrospect what is striking about the Iranian revolution is the
brittle nature of the Shah's repressive regime. Through the 1970s,
his secret police had been feared as being as brutal and as effective
as anything created in Communist Eastern Europe, but, when the
secular and religious opposition movement finally combined under
the leadership of Ayatollah Khomeini, then in exile in France, the
state collapsed and in 1979 the Shah of Shahs fled Iran.

As soon as the revolution succeeded the secular–religious coalition unravelled. Once in power the fundamentalists turned against
the secular radicals and against other Islamic groups that did
not share Khomeini's commitment to the creation of a rigorously
Islamic state. Their opposition movement had been built on a

network of popular social ties that, in contrast to the bureaucratic state, could be described as 'civil society', but once in power they preserved the state structures created by the Shah and turned them into a vehicle for the imposition of the shariah.[54]

It is worth returning briefly to the country with which I began this section in order to make a point about the simplicity of divisions. Korea was a poor backward country that was helped to prosperity by the sort of US interference that proved so unpopular with Muslims in the Middle East. Yet most Koreans remain very positive towards the West. There are, of course, many differences and this selection may be contentious but I would note the following. First, Christian missionaries were very active in the country in the nineteenth century and their work in establishing schools and hospitals was popular. Although some Buddhists and Confucians resented their presence, this encounter between East and West was not coloured by centuries of conflict between natives and Christians. Christian missionaries came without much stigmatizing historical baggage and had some considerable success. Large numbers of Korean became Christians; the first president of the Republic of Korea, Syngman Rhee, was a Methodist.

The second important difference is that, although Korea suffered from colonial oppression, it did not come from the same source as Christianity but from Japan. During the period of Japanese imperial rule, Korean Christians distinguished themselves in nationalist movements and thus established their loyalty. A quarter of those charged with unrest by the Japanese were Christian.[55] Whatever reservations Koreans may have had about Christians and about the Western powers, its most recent oppressors were not Christians.

India   The final example of a state that deliberately pursued a secular road to modernization is India. The India that the British ruled for less than a century, from the Government of India Act of 1858 to independence in 1948, was in language, ethnicity and religion an extraordinarily diverse country: an empire in its own right. Only too aware of this, many of the leaders of Indian nationalism were wary of playing the religion card, but it was always hard to suppress the religious identity of the majority Hindu population. Mahatma Gandhi spoke the language of religious ecumenism and tried to create a common Hindu–Muslim front to campaign for independence, but his movement drew sufficiently heavily on Hindu symbolism to alienate many Muslims. He often used the phrase 'Ram Raja' (rule by Rama) to describe the righteous society he desired to succeed the British Raj. While some Muslims joined his Indian Congress, others founded the Muslim League that eventually argued for a separate Muslim state of Pakistan. As independence came closer to a reality, more secular Hindu leaders such as Rabindranath Tagore and S. C. Bose were pushed aside and in reaction even thoroughly Westernized secular Muslims such as Muhammad Ali Jinnah found it necessary to deploy religious rhetoric. Gandhi's commitment to non-violence did not save him from militant Hindus. The independent India he had laboured to create for thirty-three years was only a month old when he was murdered by Hindu nationalist Nathuram Godse. Looking back fifty years later, his brother and fellow conspirator Gopal Godse said:

> if you ask me, did I feel any repentance, my reply is no, not in the least.... We knew that if we allowed this person to live any longer, he would do more and more harm to Hindus, and that we could not allow.... We had done away with someone who was not only satisfied with the creation of Pakistan; he wanted to see Pakistan progress; he was in fact the father of Pakistan.... We killed with a motive, to serve the higher interests of our people.[56]

With Gandhi's death the leadership of India fell to Jawaharlal Nehru, a Western-educated modernizer who shared the Atatürk and Pahlavi dislike for traditional religion and who had the additional problem of managing a multicultural society. Although the creation of Pakistan and the subsequent migrations had removed the majority of Muslims, India was still only some 80 per cent Hindu, with Muslims and Sikhs as powerful blocs. Nehru's conclusion was that 'the government of a country like India, with many religions that have secured great and devoted followings for generations, can never function satisfactorily in the modern age except on a secular basis'.[57] India's three neighbours, Pakistan, Nepal and Burma, adopted constitutions that gave pride of place respectively to Islam, Hinduism and Buddhism, but India was established as a formally secular society.

With only two very short breaks the Congress Party led the country and the Nehru family (Nehru was followed by his daughter Indira Gandhi and his grandson Rajiv Gandhi) led Congress from independence to 1991. They were all Western-educated technocrats who saw their primary goal as promoting economic growth and who saw India's religious traditions as impediments. Unfortunately for the modernizers, the project of planned state-led growth faltered. By 1975 there was such unrest that Indira Gandhi introduced a state of emergency. When she returned to power in

1980 she produced a complete U-turn and abandoned central state-led development for economic liberalization. Far from solving what was taken to be a crisis of low productivity, the reforms (rather like those that followed the end of the Soviet Union) delivered great benefits to a small section of the rich, who were able to buy public assets at knock-down prices. By 1990 India's debt was a massive 63 per cent of GDP and the International Monetary Fund was called on to prop up the Indian economy.

In explaining the rise of the campaign to build a Hindu temple to Ram on the site of a Muslim mosque at Ayodhya, Rajagopal offers a succinct summary of the forces that lay behind the rise of the Hindu nationalist Bharatiya Janata Party (BJP). That the majority of Muslims in British India had opted for their own country (which had since fought with India over contested territory) had left a residual suspicion that Muslims could never be properly loyal Indians.

> There was in addition: the anger of aspiring lower middle classes at a sense of exclusion from the political process and from the social mainstream; peasants and farmers responding to the call of the faithful; upper castes perceiving a conservative means of political assertion that did not challenge the caste hierarchy; sections of the intelligentsia finding in the movement an echo of their own frus-trated ambitions for national greatness; non-resident Indians abroad, thinking that a strong national party would bolster the country's reputation abroad, and hence their own expatriate situation; and businesses seeking a strong nationalist party to replace the Congress, and to become...what the Congress had never been, namely an ideologically based party articulating a distinct and explicit consen-sus.[58]

Although the BJP did succeed in winning power in the federal elections of 1999 and in a number of states, it has not achieved much of the assertive *Hindutva* (or 'Make India Hindu') programme it supported in opposition. In the northern Hindi states where it is strongest, it has done a few things to advance its cause. In Gujarat and Uttar Pradesh it removed laws that prevented civil servants being members of the Rashtriya Swayamsevak Sangh – ostensibly a cultural organization but closer to a paramilitary force and the major mover behind most Hindutva campaigns. The BJP has pro-moted Hindu prayers in state schools. It has also encouraged na-tionalist historians to produce a new school of historical writings, which, its critics claim, demonizes Christians and Muslims and creates a false (and falsely long, glorious and consistent) history for Hinduism. But there has also been unexpected moderation. The BJP has opposed plans to build a Hindu temple on the site of the Ayodhya mosque. In the light of the Hindu nationalist view of Gandhi presented by Godse above, it is significant that the BJP Prime Minister, A. B. Vajpayee, has very explicitly condemned Gandhi's assassination.

There are two possible explanations of BJP moderation in power and it would be invidious to apportion weight to them. It may well be that being responsible for managing India, rather than merely trying to win elections, has brought BJP leaders to appreciate, as Nehru did, the costs of disunity. Or it may be that the necessity to form coalitions (in the Punjab, for example, the BJP formed an alliance with the Sikh Akali Dal) has moderated it.[59] Either way, what we can forget when we concentrate on the gradual decline of the secular Congress Party and the corresponding rise of the BJP is that India remains a formally secular democracy. For all the periodic outbreaks of communal violence, it has not become a Hindu state in the sense that Pakistan is a Muslim state.

I will return to these themes in the final chapter, but it is worth briefly saying something here about the constraints that Hinduism as a religious culture places on Hindu nationalism. Although Hindus share some sense of common identity (which is reinforced when confronted with Islam, the creed of India's main political rival in the region), the religion is hindered in its ability to act as the basis for either a theocratic regime or a sustained religio-ethnic movement by both its internal variegations and its permeable boundaries. It is often said with some accuracy that Hinduism is not one religion but many; nineteenth-century Hindu nationalists were aware of the problem, and the sanatana dharma associations briefly mentioned in chapter 2 were intended to increase cohesion. The difficulty was that each wanted every other to conform to its view of what was essential Hinduism! That there is less in terms of belief or ritual that is common and essential to all Hindus than there is to Jews, Christians or Muslims makes a radical division between the godly and the ungodly more difficult to sustain. It is significant in this context that Hindu nationalism is associated with a particularly monotheistic strand of Hindu religion. Those people who have been trying to create a sense of national identity based on a shared religion have also been active in promoting a vision of Rama as a creator God that mirrors the Christian and Muslim views of a single being with a special relationship with his chosen people.

A further problem for the Hindu nationalist is the deep division based on caste that is central to the religious tradition. All religions, even those such as Sikhism that rhetorically reject it, can live with social stratification. In a verse of 'All Things Bright and Beautiful' now tactfully omitted, Victorian Christians in Britain lustily sang: 'The rich man in his castle | The poor man at his gate | God made them high and lowly | And ordered their estate.' But Hinduism is unique in making stratification a central part of its religious culture. It is worth returning here to Gellner's account of the origins of nationalism. At the heart of nationalism is the view of the nation as a horizontal community of equals. At the heart of Hinduism are caste divisions that allocate groups (based on inherited membership) different degrees of religious virtue and purity and different ritual obligations.

Caste presents the BJP with an obvious problem for the consistency of its ideology and for its search for power in a parliamentary democracy. The one element of religious particularism in India's federal politics is carried over from British models of representation. In order to advance the interests of those variously called outcastes, harijans (children of God) or Dalits (the oppressed), special constituencies were created that could be contested only by members of those populations (though voting for the reserved seats is open to all): about 15 per cent of the seats in the Lok Sabha, the Indian Parliament.[60] Partly because it needs to win the seats, and in order to show that it is inclusive, the BJP has always made a point of fielding Dalit candidates (as it has with Muslims). In the 1990s, the BJP won between 30 and 39 per cent of those seats, but it did so largely because its Dalit candidates were elected on upper-caste votes. Survey data show that, despite the BJP's attempts to widen its electoral base, the support it received from the scheduled castes fell from 15 per cent of those voters in 1996 to 12 per cent in 1999.[61]

As we would expect from the fact that its nationalism is built on a religion that accords an honourable position to the 'twice-born' upper castes and excludes as 'untouchable' a large part of the Hindu population, the BJP, despite its attempts at inclusion, remains a caste party.

Hinduism is also prevented by its internal variations from asserting that a particular way of life is divinely ordained. Although some Hindus regard particular practices such as *suti* and arranged child marriages as being essentially Hindu, many of these are rejected by others who have equally good claims to be Hindus. There is certainly nothing like the social code of the shariah that could be the basis for a theocratic state. In brief, though we can expect that the patterns of uneven social and economic development that have encouraged Islamic fundamentalism will drive certain groups to turn to their traditional religion as a source of reassurance and shared identity, Hinduism is unlikely to generate movements of the same potency.

Nationalists rejecting fragmented religious identities

My fourth group of examples consists of cases of nationalists deliberately downplaying religion, not because they see it as an impediment to modernization but because for a variety of reasons (diversity being a common one) it is unsuitable for use as a source of national cohesion.

Albania offers a case in point. According to a 1942 census, 70 per cent of Albanians were Muslims, 20 per cent were Orthodox Christians and 10 per cent were Roman Catholics. In addition, the Muslims were themselves divided. Most were Sunni Muslims but perhaps 25 per cent were Shi'ite Sufis: members of the Bektashi Order. Albania gained its independence from the Ottoman Empire in 1912. Ahmet Zogu became president in 1925 and three years later declared himself king. King Zog fled when the Italians invaded at the start of the Second World War. He was unable to return after the war because his country was liberated by Communist partisans led by Enver Hoxha, who imposed a 'dictatorship of the proletariat' that remained effectively dictatorial (if hardly proletarian) until his death in 1985 and then collapsed completely in five years. In pursuit of national unity, Hoxha responded to his country's religious divisions by banning them all. As he put it:

> All the religious sects existing in our country were brought to Albania by foreign invaders, and served them and the ruling classes of the country. Under the cloak of religion, god, and the prophets, there operated the brutal laws of the invaders and their domestic lackeys. The history of our people demonstrates...how [religion] engendered discord and fratricide in order to oppress us more cruelly, enslave us more easily and suck our blood.[62]

Sub-Saharan Africa   None of the new nations of sub-Saharan Africa immediately followed Hoxha's dictatorial lead (though many got there depressingly quickly). Their first governments were all modelled on the West European parliamentary democracy and all formally guaranteed religious freedom. But the same problem that confronted Hoxha was one of the reasons all chose to construct a sense of shared identity that made little or no reference to religion. It is difficult to summarize the role that religion has played in the post-independence histories of all the countries beyond the reach of Islam, but some general points can be made.

Although the new nations were secular, and emerged from former European colonies that had supported extensive missionary work, there was not the same animosity towards Christianity that was seen in the Middle East or India. One obvious difference concerns the solidity of the indigenous religion that was either displaced or symbolically threatened. The missionaries were competing with small fragmented tribal religions rather than with large well-established and articulated religions deeply embedded in long-standing social structures. They might sometimes provoke hostility but they did not create a common religious reaction. The violent Kenyan Mau-Mau rising of 1952–6 is one of the few examples of a liberation movement that was overtly anti-Christian, and even it was not informed by a positive religious alternative.

The other difference is that, in most African contexts, nationalist leaders could clearly distinguish colonial oppression (a bad thing) from the effects of the missionary work that had accompanied it (a mixed blessing but probably a blessing). There were three reasons for this. In the first place, the missionaries converted a sufficiently large number of Africans (in some of the new states almost the entire population) for Christianity to become indigenous. Secondly, the Christian churches quickly 'Africanized' their clergy. Indeed, they were often ahead of the secular institutions of colonialism in promoting an indigenous leadership. Thirdly, many African leaders were committed Christians. Julius Nyerere, the founding father of Tanzania, was the product of a Catholic mission school. John Chilembwe, who led a rebellion against British rule in Nyasaland in 1915, was an American-educated Protestant clergyman. Hastings Banda, who took Malawi to independence, was a Scottish Presbyterian. Abel Muzorewa, who was briefly Prime Minister of Zimbabwe in 1979, was also the first black bishop of the United Methodist Church. Jomo Kenyatta, the father of modern Kenya, was mission educated, his brother-in-law was a Catholic priest and the first African Archbishop of Kenya was a close relative. Kenneth Kaunda, who led Zambia to independence in 1964, was a former Methodist lay preacher.

So, although some churches in some places (the Dutch Reformed Church in South Africa, for example) might continue to be regarded as alien and oppressive, there was little chance of African nationalism being aggressively anti-Christian. Equally well, Christianity could not play a positive part in the self-image of any new African state. The associations with colonialism were too obvious and recent and the religion was too new to most countries. It had displaced the tribal religions only in the previous century (and, in some cases, within living memory). There was thus no possibility of creating Christian foundation myths for the new nations. In the Balkan examples discussed above, the peoples who drew on their shared religion to give sense and shape to their national liberation movements in the 1850s had adhered to those faiths for many centuries. It is comforting to believe that God has chosen and shaped your nation, but the icons of that relationship have to be ancient: a fourteenth-century Prince Lazar, for example. There is little heroic or inspiring about God having discovered your people twenty centuries after he chose the Jews or ten centuries after he chose the Arabs. Equally well the pre-Christian and Islam religions of the region could not much help build a sense of shared identity because there were too many of them and their reach was too short.

Cultural diversity was a general problem. For Tanganyika's leaders to make much of Christianity would have endangered the sought-after union with predominantly Muslim Zanzibar: 'From independence until the late 1980s, ethnicity, race and religion were explicitly excluded from national political life because the ruling political party believed that they had no role to play in a secular social agenda of *kujenga taita* (nation-building).'[63] Nigeria had a similar potential for conflict between Christians and Muslims.

Although not involved in national consciousness, organized religion has played two important roles in the politics of a number of sub-Saharan African countries. In some countries specific churches have become associated with the identity and interests of one ethnic group within the new state. In others, churches have become the main vehicle for criticism of the government.

It was partly a consequence of which European country was the imperial power and it owed a lot to the accident of which missionary society fetched up where, but the competing Christian churches converted Africa into a patchwork quilt of churches, sects and denominations. This in turn meant that, because most of the new 'nations' were ethnically fragmented and those ethnic identities were carried into parliamentary democracy as ethnic parties, there was always the potential for ethnicity, party affiliation and denominational identity to become merged. For example, Protestant–Catholic tension was a feature of Uganda's early history as an independent state. Because the Uganda National Congress (UNC) came to be dominated by Protestants, Catholics formed the Democratic Party to represent their interests. The traditionalists in

Buganda formed the Kabaka Yekka (the King alone) party, which, in alliance with the successor to the UNC, formed the first government and gave power to Milton Obote. When Obote's desire to consolidate his power led him to undermine the autonomy of the Bugandans and in 1966 to abolish the old kingdoms, the departing Bugandan king visited the Anglican bishop Nsubuga and told him: 'We are going. You should look after Buganda.'[64] However, such religion–ethnicity links were never as strong in any African country as they were, for example, in Poland or Ireland, largely because, as I have noted, all the Christian churches were too new a presence to have acquired the deep roots that allow Poles commonly to use the expression 'Polak-Katolik': 'to be a Pole is to be a Catholic'.[65]

One positive parallel with Eastern Europe is the way in which, as the new nations have become more authoritarian and corrupt, and as the ruling parties have systematically destroyed social institutions and networks that threatened their power, the churches have sometimes come to act as unofficial oppositions. Under the rule of Daniel arap Moi, the leaders of the Anglican, Catholic and Presbyterian churches in Kenya collaborated to criticize Moi's government because there was no effective political opposition.[66] On the first anniversary of the military coup that brought Sergeant Doe to power in Liberia, Methodist bishop Arthur Kulah publicly criticized his rule. Doe replied by telling the clergy 'to preach about Christ and lead their flocks to the throne of grace rather than engage in politics'.[67] That the churches have not been more active in opposition to dictatorial rule and tribal preference politics is probably explained by many of them being pervaded (to a lesser degree) by the same corruption.

This final point allows me to take up a theme of the previous section: the failure of secular nationalism. With very few exceptions the modern African states have failed in the two primary purposes of government: to ensure the safety and security of their people and to produce economic growth. As with Ba'athism in Syria, the inclusive secular enlightened philosophies articulated at independence turned into their antithesis. Kwame Nkrumah's pan-Africanism made him a hero to millions, but his Ghana became a repressive one-party state and then a military dictatorship. Kenneth Kaunda of Zambia called his secular philosophy 'Humanism', but it used the language of commitment to the national good as justification for a one-party state. Obote's response to the fragmented nature of Uganda was to promote a pan-African nationalism coloured by state-directed socialism. He followed the 'Common Man's Charter' with the 'Move to the Left'. In Kenya Moi promoted *Myoyo*-ism or

'Footsteps'.[68] Behind all the high-sounding rhetoric was nepotism, corruption, tribalism, oppression, authoritarianism, communal violence and an economic performance that was truly dreadful. At the end of the 1980s, the typical African was 40 per cent worse off than at the start of the decade. In Nigeria in 1993 the real income per head of population was one-tenth what it had been eight years earlier.[69] In Paul Gifford's dismal analysis: 'The continent is slipping out of the Third World and into its own bleak category of the nth world.'[70]

It would be wrong to tie these things too closely, but it is noticeable that the economic decline of Africa has been accompanied by the defection of many African Christians from the older missionary churches such as the Methodists or the Presbyterians to Pentecostalism.[71]

> In any African city, from Harare to Freetown, from Nairobi to Kinshasa, these new churches were to be found every Sunday in schoolrooms, cinemas, theatres, halls and hotel conference rooms. Some, in the space of a few years have become mega-churches with a very high profile. Idahose's Church of God Mission International in Nigeria, Otabil's International Central Gospel Church in Accra, Wutawanashe's Family of God in Zimbabwe, Leslie's Abundant Life in Kampala, Gitonga's Redeemed Gospel Church in Kenya, are now huge churches that simply did not exist twenty . . . years ago.[72]

Much could be said about the spread of Pentecostalism in Africa and I will confine myself to the political repercussions. Initially what was striking about the pentecostal churches was their stress on the believing faithful individual. While they may well in the long term encourage the sort of personal character well suited to economic and democratic development (that will be considered in the final section of the last chapter), the first effect seems to have been to release people from ascribed and inherited identities and social obligations. Members stress the immediate family and the congregation and then the next level up is the world.

The political passivity of the Pentecostal churches may be temporary. As the new congregations and organizations become more confident of their place in the world (and their growth relative to the old mainline Christian churches), they may become more assertive and politically involved. Certainly in Zambia in 1991 a number of prominent Pentecostal leaders campaigned openly for one presidential candidate and in Ghana in 1993 Pentecostal churches willingly blessed President Rawlings (the former military dictator, now returned to office through an election) when the mainstream churches refused to give thanks for his victory. Gifford suspects that such Pentecostal dabbling in politics is not part of some US-inspired global conservative movement. It 'does not stem from ideology, but probably from something far more pragmatic, the desire for the respectability conferred by government recognition, and for the material rewards a well-disposed president can dispense'.[73]

Imposing toleration

The new African nations tried to integrate their peoples with secular conceptions of the nation – an obvious response to the lack of a religious heritage shared by those whom accidents of colonial map making had deemed a nation. Indonesia's solution was not to avoid religion but to invent a new religion.

It is not difficult to see the problems of cohesion and identity facing General Sukarno when his 1945 revolution created an independent state out of a series of islands that spread over 3,000 miles east to west (about the distance from the west coast of Ireland to Azerbaijan). Indonesia encompassed over 150 different languages and, although Islam was the majority faith, it included viable communities of every major world religion.[74] The battles between 1945 and 1949 to prevent the Dutch regaining their former colonial possessions gave the Indonesians some cohesion, as did the decision to promote Bahasa Indonesia as a distinct national language. This had the advantage over Hindi in India in that it was a new composite language rather than the tongue of one previously dominant ethnic group. Some Muslim activists argued that their preponderance should be recognized in the new state's constitution and social policy. Sukarno and his military rulers came to the quite different conclusion that social harmony would best be advanced by creating an official state philosophy that embraced key elements of all the monotheisms and that was justified by the claim that this represented the original spirit of indigenous Javanese religion. *Pancasila* ('the five principles') required that Indonesians believed in one God, in humanitarian ideals, in national unity, in democracy guided by the wisdom of representative deliberation and in justice. Although Indonesians might express their belief in God in the manner of their particular confession, agnosticism and atheism were declared illegal.[75] The Social Organizations Law of 1985 requires all major social institutions and associations (including religious organizations) to acknowledge that *pancasila* is their foundation. This puts Indonesia in the remarkable (and, I suspect, unique) position of insisting that its citizens believe in God but not minding which one. When asked what sort of man he would select as his vice-presidential running mate, Dwight Eisenhower (possibly apocryphally) replied that he wanted a man who had religious convictions but did not mind what they were. That tale is usually told to illustrate the shallowness of both Eisenhower and the 1950s suburban USA he represented. Indonesia made it a keystone of national policy.

The economic success of Sukarno and his successor Suharto restricted opposition to their authoritarian *pancasila* democracy, but, as the regime became more patently corrupt in the 1980s and 1990s, so the legitimacy of the state philosophy was undermined. As opposition grew, particularly from radical Muslims, Suharto responded by demanding ever greater commitment to *pancasila* and by increasing the resources that were given to indoctrination. The policy failed. As *pancasila* had no history, no rituals, no specific God and no very detailed content, it is not a surprise that it did not win hearts and minds. It was less a religion in its own right than a set of limits on what religions could teach. So it did nothing to weaken the attachment of particular peoples to their own religions. When things were going well, people were more tolerant. When they were going badly, they became more mindful of their own rights and prerogatives. Public opposition forced Suharto's successor President Habibie to relax the *pancasila* policy. The legal powers to enforce it were revoked. Habibie built alliances with Islamic groups, as a counter to Suharto's previous reliance on Christians.

Across Indonesia there has been a steady increase in communal and inter-racial violence. Although the demands for independence in East Timor were not confined to Catholic Christians, they were an important stimulant. In Acheh province, Islamic militants demand an Islamic state. In the Moluccan islands there have been outbursts of savage Muslim–Christian violence. *Pancasila* has not proved the panacea.

Why religion?

It is not difficult to show that religion is intimately associated with nationalism. Put positively: a shared faith was a vital part of most nineteenth-century new nation states and national liberation movements. Put negatively: most states that have sought legitimacy from secular nationalism have not prospered. Where a shared popular faith has been rejected by nationalist leaders, the secular state has been taken over by fundamentalists (Iran), or sustained by a military dictatorship (Turkey) or some combination of the two (Egypt, Syria). It is very hard to write about nationalism and national identity outside Western Europe post-1945 without writing about religion. But, beyond demonstrating that faith remains central to communal identity, I want to consider the reasons for that connection. Why is a common religious heritage and identity so often at the heart of nationalism? The answer involves history and function. Much of this may seem obvious but it is worth spelling out.

The history point is simple but important: religion was there first. Gellner is right that nationalism is a modern phenomenon. In the Middle Ages no one who mattered cared what the peasants thought about anything, let alone expected them to feel an emotional attachment to the political unit they inhabited. If anyone had asked the ordinary people what they looked for in a ruler, race would rarely have figured in the answer. That he was less corrupt, less vicious and less greedy than his predecessor is a more likely response. Whether we assign the rise of nationalism to 1792 (the French Revolution), 1815 (the Congress of Vienna), 1919 (the break-up of the Ottoman and Austro-Hungarian empires) or 1947 (the end of the Raj), the date will be centuries after the peoples who formed the putative 'nations' acquired their religion. The Serbs were Orthodox Christians long before they were Serbs. At the risk of stating the obvious, I will add that the historical primacy of religion over nationalism and the effective nation state feeds into the functional explanations. If people wanted certain things done, then the fact that organized religion was there already doing that sort of thing explains why the needs were addressed through that medium. For those who find the biologist's language of functions and needs unhelpful when talking about societies, the same point can be made in a slightly different way: what characteristics of organized religion could readily be adapted to nationalism or used by the nation state?

One such characteristic is the dual feature of dividing without and uniting within. Most religions create a clear divide between those who adhere to the true faith and the heathen, the infidel and the pagan. More often than not they also create suspicion, animosity and resentment. There is no God but Allah. My God is a jealous God. Confessional loyalty is almost always turned into a rule for close association. Adults marry only those of the same religion or insist that spouses convert. People may teach their children two languages but they do not teach them two religions.

As well as dividing one community from another, religion unites within its reach. All religions periodically throw up radical sects that allow membership only to those who meet exacting standards, the religious virtuosi, but generally religions seek to encompass an entire people. They will not tolerate rebellion but they will accept considerable laxity in ritual performance and moral life.[76] Almost all religions confer membership at birth: hence baptism and the analogous rituals that incorporate babies and children into the community of the faith. Furthermore, most major religions at least pay lip service to the notion of equality. Hinduism, with its complex system of castes and the ritual requirement that the upper castes avoid contamination from contact with the lower castes, is exceptional. More usual is the assertion of equality in the eyes of God combined with easy acceptance of the social divisions that humankind has created.

Put together, those characteristics fit very well the structure of the world according to nationalism: a theoretical comradeship within the community and abrupt divisions between this community and the aliens, us and them. That religion often unites a group of people and divides them from their neighbours, and has done so for some long time, means that, when nationalists are seeking for the spirit of the entity whose interests they are trying to promote, their shared faith will always be a strong candidate. In the case of the Sikhs in the Punjab and Croats and Bosnian Muslims in Yugoslavia, religion was the only candidate: it was all that distinguished these people. As noted above, after the collapse of the Soviet Union, republics that had never previously shown any great desire for autonomy now found themselves required by the assumption of modern politics to acquire a 'nation' to go with their 'state'. Their elites felt the need 'to *essentialize*, to identity one trait or characteristic in codifying a national or ethnic grouping... through searching for... a pre-colonial cultural purity'.[77] In many such regions, that cultural purity was most easily provided by religion. That the former Soviet republics of Turkmenistan, Uzbekistan, Kazakhstan and Kyrgyzstan are all concerned about the threat of Islamic fundamentalism has caused them to be careful of laying too much stress on Islam as a basis for legitimation, but the first presidents of each signalled very clearly their Muslim identities. Two made a very public show of making a pilgrimage to Mecca; the other two swore their oaths of office on the Qur'ān.

The primacy of religion also owes much to more mundane functions than identity creation. Before the rise of the modern bureaucratic nation state, a religion's network of officials often formed what little there was by way of social organization beyond the local feudal estate. Monasteries and cathedrals provided the embryonic framework for national administration and the religious institution provided the main source of trained literate officials. The church educated the nobility and could provide secretarial services. When the Scottish nobles wanted to assert their independence from English rule, they turned to Scotland's leading churchman: the Scottish Declaration of Arbroath was written by Cardinal Beaton.[78] Most European countries had senior clergymen holding high office. Cardinal Wolsey ruled England from 1515 to 1529 as Henry VIII's Lord Chancellor. Cardinal Richelieu, who ruled France from 1621 to 1642, perfectly illustrated his own conviction that the church's training provided a cadre of honest, loyal and disinterested officials who could serve the modern state far more effectively than those whose only qualification was a blood relationship with the king.[79] As his successor he recruited the Italian cleric Mazarin. Richelieu also compiled his *Political Testament*, a series of maxims for the government of the new state that was one of the first and most widely read textbooks of modern government.

The stability and continuity of the religious institution mean that churches were often keepers of records and artefacts. When the English King Edward wanted historical justification for his claims to the Scottish throne, he turned to the only place likely to possess historical documents: the monasteries. For centuries annalists had added notes to the margins of the calendars that were used to keep track of the round of religious offices. Although the gradual extension of secular education eventually produced cadres of secular intellectuals, well into the nineteenth century in most European countries clergy played important roles in producing histories of their people that could be turned to nationalist purposes.[80]

Their distribution and organization meant that the network of clergy could perform thoroughly secular state roles. The Protestant reformation in Sweden had initially been as cynical as Henry's in England, but under Gustavus Adolphus (1611–32) Lutheran doctrines began to take popular hold. Adolphus 'bolstered his doughty Lutheran clergy and they in turn mixed patriotism with religion, performing such thankless civil jobs as collecting the local taxes'.[81]

One virtue of religion is its durability. It generally outlasts regimes. It might have been possible for the fifth generation of a ruling family to talk of the divine right of kings, but such continuity is extremely rare. The mundane origin of kingship was all too obvious in the German states in the seventeenth century or the Balkans in the early nineteenth century. In Greece, Serbia and

Bulgaria, local notables argued about whom they might invite to be the first occupant of the thrones of their new formed kingdoms. Their choices had to be approved by Britain, France and Russia (the guaranteeing powers), and those considered for the job haggled about terms and conditions.

Even language may change abruptly. The Polish journalist Ryszard Kapuściński reports a sad conversation with the writer Yusif Samedoglu, the leader of the Azerbaijan National Front.[82] He had stopped writing. He could no longer write, because his language was being abolished. As an act of cultural self-assertion, the new state was abandoning the Cyrillic script, the language of the former Russian oppressor. Now Azerbaijanis would use only the Latin alphabet or perhaps even go back to Arabic. He could, of course, be translated, but, as he told Kapuściński, who would bother? An act of state had made him illegible.

Of course, the earthly representatives of God also change. Anyone who lived in England between 1534 and 1558 and paid much attention to church affairs changed allegiance three times: from Catholic to Protestant to Catholic and back to Protestant. In the Balkans church authorities manoeuvred for autonomy from the Greek Orthodox leadership in Constantinople as much as the local notables tried to free themselves of Ottoman rule. But many of the rituals remained stable, as did many of the beliefs. Both as a world-view and as a structure, religion generally enjoyed far greater permanence than the more obviously human affairs of politics and hence could serve as the basis for a sense of shared identity better than mundane creations. The Orthodox Church leaders who celebrated a thousand years of Russian Christianity in 1988 might have hoped but they could not know that Soviet Communism was shortly to collapse. The commissars lasted a mere seventy years.

In addition to such practical considerations, religion also provides ideological justification for arrangements in this world. Rulers have always sought divine justification and support. For many centuries European monarchs sought the blessing of the Pope. In their disputes over the independence of the Scottish throne from England, both English and Scottish monarchs petitioned the Pope for his approval. The Catholic Church in France was so firmly associated with the aristocracy that its influence was radically diminished by the French Revolution and the subsequent development of a strong national consciousness was secular led. But in other countries the church found it relatively easy to shift from supporting and legitimating monarchs to the new democratic task of sponsoring national identity.

There is one particular way in which a church enjoys an unusual advantage over other social institutions in a society threatened by an external alien force: if the aliens are of a different religion, they cannot infiltrate the church. In Yugoslavia the more powerful and numerous Serbs increasingly settled in Croatia and they enjoyed privileged access to positions of power and influence. Although they made up only some 15 per cent of the population of Croatia in the 1980s, they were 40 per cent of the police force (more in the senior positions) and a disproportionate part of the ruling Communist Party. But, being Orthodox Christians, they could not take over the Catholic Church – which was left in the hands of Croats. The Soviet policy of exporting Russians to neighbouring republics meant that the churches of Orthodox countries could be officered by aliens, but the Catholic and Lutheran churches of the Baltic states could not be so manipulated. Likewise the English and Scots settlers in Ireland: they might take the best land and dominate the magistracy and the polity, but they could not displace the natives from the Catholic Church.

Anthony Smith has drawn attention to one particular way of promoting national identity that is uniquely in the gift of religious institutions.[83] Religion also provides a powerful repertoire of myths of election. We are glorious because God chose us. We do not need to be too cynical to appreciate the value of exalting base interests and the advantages in the high rhetoric of divine approval. On 16 December 1838 white Afrikaners circled their sixty eight wagons beside the Ncome river and awaited the onslaught of thousands of Zulu warriors. The Afrikaners prayed and made a pact with God that if they were spared they would keep the day holy and build a monument on the site. In the event some 3,000 Zulus and only three Afrikaners died. The Battle of Blood River (as it was aptly renamed) became a central theme of Afrikaner ideology: proof that God would preserve his people. One of the political virtues of religious myths of election that Smith notes is that they allow assertions of moral superiority: in the minds of the Afrikaners they triumphed not because they had rifles but because they had divine approval.[84]

Pious dissent from religio-ethnic linkage

In all the above examples, I have viewed the mobilization of religion for nationalist and nation-building purposes from the point of view of the nation and nationalism. I would now like to add an important qualification that comes from viewing the relationship the other way round.

The first corrective is to note that God is not always willing to be co-opted for political purposes. The seriously pious, especially among the clergy, may often resist incorporation. As I noted in the first chapter, what makes most religions a potential threat to any political order is that the believers set their God above all temporal authorities. The two exceptions are Shinto in Japan and Confucianism in China, where the spiritual and the temporal are pretty much the same thing.[85] Put most generally, while religion may often legitimate and encourage particular political arrangements, this-worldly ties may well offend the religious zealot. In most religious traditions there is a tension between the roles of priest and prophet. The institutionalized religion becomes comfortable with the regime, with the social order and with the mundane world. Periodically radical sects challenge that close association between the divine and the commonplace. The Old Believers rejected the Russian Orthodox Church's close association with the Russian state. The Quakers rejected the Church of England. Particularly pious individuals may regret compromising their faith for worldly ends. Thomas Becket was made Chancellor in 1155, the first Englishman to hold such high state office since the invasion of the Normans a century earlier. He was a highly effective statesman and diplomat until he was made Archbishop of Canterbury in 1162. In that office, he became a religious zealot and fell out of favour with Henry II because he objected to his king's attempts to make the clergy subordinate to the state. He was murdered in his own cathedral by four knights doing what they took to be Henry's wishes.

The point can be made from a survey of religious and political attitudes in Northern Ireland in the mid-1970s. Ian McAllister discovered that, against his expectations (and they would not have been mine), for the Protestant respondents in the survey, there was no strong connection between being 'ultra' in religion and in politics.[86] The most conservative and observant Protestants were not also the most conservative and committed Unionists. We might conclude that, while religion obviously defined the major political division – Protestants were unionists and Catholics were nationalists – it had no separate effect on the strength of individual attachment to those political agendas.

The correct explanation is quite different: it is that the zealots can be found at either end of the scale and thus cancel out. It is clear that some highly committed evangelical Protestants (such as the Reverend Ian Paisley and the activists of his Democratic Unionist Party) associate the will of God with the political ambition to promote Ulster Unionism and to preserve Northern Ireland from absorption in a Catholic Ireland. But a large number of equally sincere and committed evangelicals have serious doubts about the propriety of so linking faith and politics. Even senior members of Paisley's own Free Presbyterian Church, though they would vote for Paisley in elections, privately express reservations about many aspects of the connection. The political struggle distracts Paisley from his primary task of preaching the gospel. The close association of church and party means that those who do not share Paisley's politics will be blind to the more important spiritual message. Some will go so far as to admit, as one minister put it to me, 'politics is a dirty business. Politicians have to do things that a Christian will find disturbing.'

A similar divide has occurred in Sinhalese Buddhism, where religious reformers have found themselves increasingly at odds with Sinhalese nationalists: 'The purists have had to sit by, dismayed, as the popularity of Hindu elements and especially of things magical and demonic have grown enormously...since World War II. They have also seen people turn increasingly to violence, which the purists regard as contrary to Buddhist principles.'[87]

In the USA in the mid-1850s, the anti-Catholic American Party (also known as the 'Know-Nothings' because of its secretive nature) enjoyed a short burst of success. It briefly controlled Massachusetts and in 1856 its presidential candidate Millard Filmore won 21 per cent of the vote cast. Yet that support melted away. One reason was that pious evangelical Protestants came to dislike the secrecy, the cabals and the intrigues. Nineteenth-century US politics were just too sordid.[88]

Leaving aside any specific dirty work that politics may require, there is always the more general problem that the actual people fall short of the people of the myth. And even if they do not, what Burns called 'the unco-guid' will suppose they do. John Newton, the anti-slavery campaigner and writer of *Amazing Grace*, described his countrymen as 'perhaps the most sinful in Europe'.[89] The nationalist religion will impute virtues to Afrikaners or Ulster Protestants or Polish Catholics as a whole, but many of those so valorized patently fail to live up to the ideal (or even make the effort). The close linking of church and people means that believers and the political constituency can be spoken of in the same terms.

So when Paisley talks of 'the Protestant people of Northern Ireland', he may have in mind born-again Christians, unionist voters or all those who are not Catholics. But he is periodically aware that the first group is only a small subset of the other two. Other evangelicals less involved in politics will be even more sensitive to the accusation that by eliding the religious and the political they are guilty of hypocrisy. In order to think of a divine destiny for the people as a whole, they must overlook defects in the majority of those people, and there are usually sufficient outsiders to remind them of this tension. Scotland's Orange Order perfectly illustrates the problem. Almost all of its members are secular and drink alcohol. But they march under the banners of evangelical and temperance lodges. In the late nineteenth century, when a much larger proportion of Orangemen were churchgoers, it was common for Presbyterian clergymen to be members and to fill the office of Lodge chaplain. Now no Church of Scotland clergy belong to the Order. The Serbian warlord Arkan wore a large crucifix and defended the actions of his paramilitary Tigers in Croatia in the early 1990s with references to divine approval of the Serb cause, but he was a former bank robber whose men funded their campaigns by smuggling and looting.[90] Afrikaners divided. Clergymen and other middle-class Christians were willing to join the *Broederbond*, a secretive Masonic-like organization that paved the way for the triumph of the National Party in 1948, but they did not join the paramilitary *Ossewa Brandwag*. When Afrikanerdom started to fall apart in the 1980s, the 'rough' element joined the thuggish paramilitary AWB. Its actions alienated the evangelicals, who began to shift the Dutch Reformed Church away from its traditional position of legitimating Afrikaner nationalism.[91]

The disjuncture between rhetoric and reality may be a particular problem if the political mobilization of religion is tinged with the millennialist expectation that some divine climax is due and can be brought on by the behaviour of the godly. Agrippa d'Augibué, a French Protestant of the late sixteenth century, said: 'All things will be granted to you when your sins no longer repel Him who has all victories in his hand.'[92]

We cannot treat religious commitment and national consciousness as two simple variables that are so neatly correlated that the extremes on each axis match. To think of religion as a single property and imagine that what matters is whether someone is more or less committed to the traditional faith is already a gross simplification. But if we accept that for the moment, we must recognize that at the high end there will be a divide: while some committed believers will promote the political cause (the Croat Catholic priests who fought for the Ustaše, for example), others will have reservations. Some will reject the nationalist project altogether as ungodly – as did one strand of Orthodox Jewry before the successful establishment of the State of Israel changed the terms of the debate.

This is a small but important point. Religion (and again we must exempt Shinto and Confucianism) never loses its prophetic potential. Because it supposes a final authority beyond the powers and principalities of this world, it may always inspire a challenge to the mundane order. Hence those people who are most deeply committed to the religion will rarely be dependable spokesmen for the close association of God and people, the traditional religion and the nation. Nor is the association safe at the other extreme. Those members of the ethnic group or nation who are not at all religious will not be much moved by assertions that God is on their side. It is actually those of middling faith, whose religion is largely conventional and taken for granted, who are best mobilized by God the nationalist recruiting sergeant. The deeply religious will be suspicious and the largely irreligious will be indifferent.

Global fundamentalism

Finally in this chapter, I would like to return to the theme introduced in the brief histories of some recent secular nationalisms: the fundamentalist backlash.[93] We should appreciate the modern nature of fundamentalism. Although its promoters routinely disclaim innovation and insist that they offer a return to the golden age that obtained before the dreadful illnesses of 'Westoxification' and 'Occidentosis', most fundamentalism is neither conservative nor traditional. The Iranian ayatollahs were not turning the clock back in some revenge of the countryside on the city. They used the past as a source of rhetoric and symbolism, but their religion was not the magical saint cults of the villages. Just as the Protestant Reformation advertised a radical programme as a return to the spirit of primitive Christianity, so the ayatollahs invoked the past while preaching a radical reform of Islam and promoting the society-wide imposition of puritanical high Islam (only made possible by the modern state) as the way forward. Iranian fundamentalism is the social equivalent of Oliver Cromwell's radical Protestantism.[94] The same is true of fundamentalist movements in the Islamic states of the former Soviet Union, where small groups of radicals, heavily influenced by the Wahhabi Islam of Saudi Arabia, are trying to displace the Islam of the Sufi orders.

A number of social trends – urbanization, political centralization, incorporation in wider markets, labour migration – were moving people away from their old world and weakening the local paternalistic social ties that sustained the old religion. Had the Shah of Iran's White Revolution succeeded in meeting the aspirations it raised, then Westernization might have succeeded (as it did to a much greater extent in Turkey, for example). It failed and the Shah's only response was increased repression. People were in the market for a new analysis of, and solution to, their problems. Their traditional leaders, the ayatollahs, provided it and they did so by reconstructing the past.

Of course it is a simplification to talk about a 'natural' course of economic development, but we can clearly identify one particularly 'unnatural' feature of the recent history of many states that have experienced powerful fundamentalist movements. It is not an accident that radical Islamist movements are supported not in the main by the poorest sections of any population but by young male graduates. In the 1960s and 1970s Egypt, Afghanistan, Iran and many other Muslim countries succeeded in producing a cadre of educated young men (and women, which is a separate problem) without also creating the wealth to sustain a bureaucracy large enough, or a level of manufacturing high enough, to provide them with well-paid jobs.[95] In the 1980s a new source of frustration appeared with the popularity of qualifications in business studies. Young men from countries such as Bangladesh acquired MBAs in the misguided hope that they would bring affluence.[96] There was thus a very specific source of relative deprivation.

The point about gender is also vital. Although there are marked differences between Islamic cultures in the status they accord women, fundamentalist movements have in common a desire to curtail the autonomy that women acquired during the Westernizing period of secular nationalism. This is defended as a return to the shariah. No doubt the increasing independence of women is seen by orthodox Muslims as a specifically religious problem: it is a threat to their ability to reproduce their religion. But there is a more mundane tension: educating women for work outside the home creates competition for scarce high-status jobs in economies that are generating ambition faster than they are generating the means to satisfy it.

This may seem like stating the obvious, but any regime can call on two sources of legitimation: efficiency and cultural acceptability. A regime that effectively safeguards its citizens and allows them to prosper will be accepted, as will any that can persuade its people that its rule is legitimated by a widely shared value system. The difficulty for most post-1918 states (especially those of the Middle East, Africa and Asia: that is, the poor parts of the world) is that they sought legitimacy on the grounds of effectiveness and believed that to be effective they would have to jettison their traditional cultures. And they failed to be effective. Without the popularity that would have resulted from material success, the new states were forced to seek value legitimation. Hence the popularity of a movement such as the Muslim Brotherhood in Egypt was always the inverse of the success and popularity of the secular modernizing innovation: in this case Nasserism.[97] Fundamentalism is fuelled by the failure of various forms of the secular nationalist project to improve greatly life for the mass of the peoples of traditionally religious countries. A liberal version of Islam might have triumphed had it not been for 'the unfortunate coincidence and association between imperialistic Western domination and Islamic liberal theory'[98] and the failure of the modernizers to deliver. If the West is seen as both the inspiration for change and the cause of its failure, then circumstances will be ripe for religious fundamentalism.

Class divisions are common to all societies, but those of Third World economies are particularly acute, because the ruling classes use their position as conduits for the wealth generated by contact with the West to advance themselves and their children well ahead of the rest of their people. And in many kleptocracies they compound the problem by exporting that wealth to some safe haven such as Switzerland, to which they retreat when the inevitable coup arrives. In a context of increasing class divisions, where the differences in life chances are so clearly related to contact with the West, there will be considerable scope for Islamic fundamentalist parties to act as an enduring opposition, representing the interests of the deprived and dispossessed and framing their problems as the work of the Great Satan. In that sense, we can expect that modernization will always create a market for fundamentalism. This is not just a story about globalization. Although fundamentalists usually present their cause in the widest most universal terms, there are persistent local problems. The incompetence and corruption of the first generation of nationalist leaders have created a powerful demand for change and parties that can present themselves as religious and virtuous will find a ready audience.[99]

The limits to fundamentalism

However, to suggest that there is something normal about fundamentalism is not the same as suggesting that it will triumph.[100] In explaining why not, I will first consider a possible internal weakness of fundamentalism and then return to the main theme of this chapter: the power of the nation state.

This is highly speculative, but I do not believe that Islamic fundamentalism has yet developed a social order (as distinct from a religious culture) that will in the long run provide a viable alternative to Western liberal democracy. This should not be mistaken for some optimistic assessment that the benefits of Western civilization are so obvious that it will win over the entire world. Rather I mean that if, as they hope, Islamic states prosper, they will continue to be faced with demands for greater personal freedom, greater egalitarianism and greater equality in gender roles. They may not be able comfortably to accommodate those demands but nor do they seem to have designed a viable alternative. Despite their programme having initially been extremely popular and despite commanding considerable repressive powers, Iranian fundamentalists are losing ground to liberal reformers.

Furthermore, just as Communist regimes collapsed because their citizens could not be shielded from the fact that those of capitalist countries enjoyed vastly more of the good things that communism promised than they did, so greater contact with the West (while it may generate all manner of resentment and hostility) will also serve to remind Afghans or Iraqis or Egyptians that there are alternatives. Although it is possible for specific local circumstances to isolate a society from the rest of the world (war being the classic case), any increase in prosperity will bring greater international integration. Despite the enormous pressure to do otherwise, middle-class Iranians and Saudis watch American and European television programmes and they travel widely. While they may disdain some of what they see, many will desire the degree of personal freedom that is common in the West. The rich are able to resolve the tension between the liberty they claim for themselves and the constraints their ideology demands by cheating: they conform in public and deviate while abroad or behind the closed gates of their compounds. But such hypocrisy cannot be sustained in a regime that claims an ideological basis of legitimation. It is precisely the same cancer that rotted the Soviet Union from the top down: those whose apparent loyalty to the party brought them positions of power used it privately to betray the principles of the revolution. The end result was that no one believed in communism.

Religious fundamentalism requires belief. Stability and prosperity will increase the demand for personal liberty, especially from women, and a more liberal version of the faith. If the religious culture is not relaxed but instead the powerful cheat, they will do even greater damage to the faith.

A sensitively documented illustration of the tensions between old and new worlds can be found in an anthropological study of Jordanians who had studied and worked abroad and then returned to their village.[101] Its shows that, in weighing up the benefits and costs of life in Europe or the United States and life in Jordan, the returnees were thoughtfully selective. They talked with insight about differences in relations between men and women, and parents and children, and about the relative merits of individualism and communalism. One respondent who had trained as a doctor and worked in Germany had come home because he preferred the Jordanian model of family life to what he saw in the West. He also objected to the secular culture of the West. Nonetheless, in talking about how the Jordanian economy could develop, he explicitly admired the Western stress on the primacy of science, and commended a system of differentiated roles, with differential training and a hierarchy of knowledge, and a system of credentials. He wanted secular science and technology and the rational bureaucracy that went with it and thought those more important than the tribal and ethnic identities that played such a large part in Jordanian village life.

There are also constraints on fundamentalism that stem from religion being in competition with other sources of social identity. That the circumstances that generate fundamentalist reactions to modernization are distributed very widely does not mean the fundamentalist rhetoric of a universal movement will be able to transcend more mundane divisions, and, to the extent that it cannot, the legitimacy of fundamentalism will itself be called into question.

One constraint is internal division. What is sometimes forgotten is that the country that has given fundamentalism its greatest success – Iran – is unusually homogeneous. Fundamentalist movements elsewhere have often been internally weakened by ethnic divisions. The history of Afghanistan provides many examples.

Although the Pashtun tribes of southern Afghanistan provided a reasonably stable foundation, its integrity has always been threatened by the large Turcoman, Uzbek and Tajik minorities in the north and west of the country, who share a common language and sense of ethnic identity with their fellows in the former Soviet Republics of Turkmenistan, Uzbekistan and Tajikistan. These divisions became particularly apparent when the loose alliance of Mujahaddin fighters succeeded in driving out the Soviet troops who had supported the fragile Communist government from 1979 to 1991. As soon as they were in power, they fell apart. Ethnic divisions also played a large part in the downfall of the Taliban in 2001. US 'daisy-cutter' bombs destroyed the Taliban as a physical force, but the regime had never managed to win the hearts and minds of the non-Pashtun peoples of Afghanistan.[102]

Divisions within Afghanistan were exacerbated by Pakistan, Iran and Saudi Arabia, each of which promoted its interests through proxies. This reminds us of another constraint on the political success of religious fundamentalism as an international movement: the nation state. Most Middle Eastern states are recent creations, the boundaries of which made little sense in terms of shared characteristics of their peoples, geographical features or trade routes; indeed, anything except the convenience of Western powers. Many have failed to improve much the lives of their people and many have experienced enormous internal instability. Nonetheless, their boundaries have remained fixed and they have slowly won a degree of popular acceptance. Certainly their elites have come to associate their interests with those states. The result is that competition between states can moderate the development of fundamentalism's potential. A good example is the failure of Iran to export its brand of revolutionary Islamic fundamentalism to its immediate neighbours. The only place its Party of Allah has been welcomed is in southern Lebanon – two countries away. One obvious reason is that its attempts to provoke a similar revolution in its immediate neighbour, Iraq, produced a war and a consolidation of Iraqi identity.

Conclusion

To summarize, there are good reasons why religious fundamentalism has become an important part of the political culture of many countries, especially but not exclusively of the Islamic world, since the 1960s. But there are also good reasons why it will not become the international force that communism was at its height. While a universalizing religion can appeal across national boundaries, it does so most effectively when, as in the case of Pentecostalism, it combines a highly abstract imagined international community with a local voluntary association of self-selecting like-minded believers. Universalizing religion does not seem able effectively to undermine the nation state, even though, as we have seen, fundamentalism is most popular in the least effective nation states. Although Islamic fundamentalism may seem in its own terms to be the very antithesis of nationalism, asserting the primacy of the universal God over any local loyalty, it has been most effective as a political force when it has served the rather old-fashioned role of uniting the diverse class and regional fragments of a nation against an oppressive neighbour. When the success of the Khomeini regime in Iran threatened the Saudi Arabian claims to the leadership of the Muslim world, the Wahhabi Saudis attempted to belittle the Islamic Republic of Iran by describing its ethos as 'Persian nationalism'. It was a cheap shot, but it accidentally expressed an important truth. Like Catholicism in Poland, Islam in Iran became powerful because it provided the spiritual justification for nationalism. And the Polish example is useful because it reminds us that the yoking of religion to nationalism means that, when the latter becomes less arresting and salient, so does the former. We come back to the internal tensions. If peace and stability and prosperity weaken the appeal of the fundamentalist insistence that all other differences be set aside in defence of the City of God, then class and gender and the demand for greater personal freedom will return.

4

PARTY

Introduction

Chapter 2 considered the politics of empires and the various methods for managing peoples of diverse religions. In chapter 3 the magnification was increased to consider the role of religion in the formation and behaviour of nation states. This chapter again increases the magnification. It is concerned mainly with the role of religion in party politics within modern states. My primary interest is the effect that religious institutions, identities and values have on more or less democratic politics; that is, I am concerned with the political preferences and choices of individuals. For that reason the examples are drawn primarily from European countries and their colonial offshoots in the twentieth century – states in which, however much we suppose our choices shaped by social forces, we are still free to choose.

As most European countries are Catholic, I will begin by considering two very different sorts of Catholic politics: where the interests of Catholics as a bloc are expressed rather directly and where the links between Catholicism and political preferences are mediated by social class. I will then consider the effect of religious affiliation on political preferences and voting since the Second World War. I will also consider whether religion influences political attitudes more widely. Finally, evidence for the influence of religion on a variety of contentious socio-moral issues will be examined.

Closed Catholic politics

Given that most countries of continental Europe are historically
Catholic, it seems sensible to begin with a description of Catholic
politics. In his magisterial study, John Whyte made a useful distinction between 'closed' and 'open' Catholic politics.[1] For fairly
obvious reasons, the political behaviour of Catholics differed quite
markedly depending on the size and power of the Catholic community relative to the rest of the population. It is never quite this
neat, but in settings such as Belgium or Austria, where Catholics
were a majority or a very substantial part of the population, they
acted in concert and in tune with official Catholic Church social
thought: Whyte's closed Catholic politics. In settings such as the
United States or Australia, where Catholics were only a small part
of the population, their politics were much less obviously Catholic
in any institutional sense and were marked more by class interests.

In the nineteenth century the Catholic Church was generally
hostile to liberal democracy. This is not surprising. The Church
was deeply rooted in the old order of feudal monarchies that had
served its interests well. Any change was unwelcome and it was
particularly so in Italy where nationalist attempts to create a united
country meant depriving the Pope of the papal states. Second, the
Catholic vision of human nature, sinful since the expulsion from
the Garden of Eden, created a general affinity with the pessimistic
views of the right and made alien the progressive ideology of left-
wing movements. Third, the Church's self-image was built on the
general assumption that the truth was best preserved by a divinely
inspired elite. There was certainly no reason in Catholic thinking to
imagine that the common people could be relied upon to prefer
truth over error.

Various nineteenth-century Popes offered no encouragement
to participatory democracy. In his encyclical *Mirari vos* of 1832,
Gregory XVI, who had to endure rebellion in the papal states, set
himself firmly against elected assemblies, freedom of the press,
freedom of conscience and the separation of church and state. With
more than a little self-interest, he invoked the divine origin of the
papacy as justification for his continued rule over large parts of Italy.
Pius IX, in *Quanta cura* (1864), repeated the attack on freedom of
conscience and described representative democracy as a 'pernicious
opinion'. The *Syllabus of Errors* ended with a wonderfully sniffy
condemnation of the very idea 'that the Holy Roman Pontiff can

and ought to reconcile himself to what is called progress, liberty and modern civilization'.[2] Four years later, the first Vatican Council proclaimed the dogma of papal infallibility. Protestants saw this as a direct challenge to the legitimacy of Christians outside the Catholic Church, but the claim that, under certain circumstances, the Pope was protected by the Holy Spirit from making a mistake was actually directed at a much wider target. It was intended as a rejection of the whole ethos of liberal thought and politics. The Catholic position was logical. *The Catholic Encyclopaedia* of 1908 said of the radical French priest de Lamennais: 'He was wrong . . . in believing that liberty was the positive foundation of everything; hence the justice of the reproach cast upon his formula, "God and Liberty": either *Liberty* was superfluous, since it is already implied in *God*, or the phrase was illogical, since there can be no question of liberty unless it harmonizes with social order.'[3] 'Social order' here means 'what the Catholic Church says God says the social order should be'. If there is a God and if the Catholic Church knows his wishes, then it follows that its teachings should trump mere human philosophies and values.

From the revolutions of the 1840s, organized bodies of Catholics were usually to be found opposing liberals in their attempts to broaden the franchise, to create secular social institutions such as national school systems and to solidify national identity. However, the Catholic Church had not maintained its institutional integrity for centuries by remaining completely indifferent to popular currents and, in 1891, Leo XIII's *Rerum novarum* marked a signal change. Although this statement enthusiastically denounced socialism, it did accept that the state had a significant role to play in human affairs. As states were stabilized and made increasingly democratic, the old system of small elites haggling over competing interests was replaced by the competition of mass political parties and there were electorates to be mobilized.

The distinctive political vision promoted by the Church offered an alternative to both the individualism of the liberal right and the class solidarity of the left. Its key theme was *corporatism*. The Catholic ideal of an orderly society was one in which people bonded together in functionally specific guilds. Instead of the anarchy offered by liberal economic theory, there would be a disciplined (a frequent motif in Catholic thought) structure of corporations of workers, managers and employers which negotiate rational and just outcomes that respected the interests of all. Not surprisingly, much of the appeal of the idea of corporatism came from its flexibility: it was understood very differently by different interests. In practice, it favoured the already powerful, who saw it as a new vehicle for managing the lower orders.

Consistent with the Church's vision, Catholic countries spawned a large number of associations. And the clergy came to the fore. When politics was a matter for small ruling elites, Catholic interests were usually represented by Catholic aristocrats. In the era of mass mobilization, the clergy became highly active both in social movements and in electoral politics. Priests led political parties in France, Belgium, Holland and Germany. We should note, however, that the Church leadership was not entirely in favour of such involvement: 'The danger was that Catholic political parties and social organizations threw up strong leaders who might show a disconcerting independence.'[4]

As Whyte notes, Catholic politics became less salient after the First World War, largely because the issues that had provoked so much conflict in the 1880s had been settled one way or another. With the integrity of the Italian state firmly established, there was no point in campaigning to have the papal states returned to the Church. State aid for the Catholic Church no longer aroused strong feelings either in France, where it had been withdrawn, or in Italy and Belgium, where it remained. And the issue of schooling had mostly been settled. But the main reason for the sidelining of Catholic parties was the rise of a new claimant to the political right. Catholicism's role as the bulwark against communism was usurped by fascism, which divided the Catholic camp. Fascism's worship of the mighty state was contrary to Catholic teaching and offended many Catholics, and fascist social organizations were intended to displace Catholic ones. On the other hand, the corporatist approach of fascism resonated with Catholic teaching and many of the sentiments to which fascism appealed – 'nationalism, solidarity, a longing for order, a desire for scapegoats'[5] – appealed as much to ordinary Catholics as to other people.

Catholicism and the right

One of the main goals of this study is to establish if, and to what extent, we can generalize about the political effects of different religions. One of the most frequently advanced propositions is that Catholicism offers a fertile soil for authoritarian regimes or, to recast it in the form familiar in Protestant countries: Protestantism encourages democracy. At first sight there is much in the politics of the twentieth century to make such an association intuitively plausible. Below I will discuss a large number of extremist right-wing movements[6] in Europe. To those we could add the military dictatorships of Latin (that is, Hispanic and overwhelmingly Catholic) America. And we can connect the two sets of examples: there is good evidence that the Vatican helped a large number of Nazis and fascists to escape to Latin America from Europe in 1945.[7]

It is no surprise that many European states succumbed to some form of authoritarian government in the years between the end of one world war and the start of the next. The states of central Europe were novel and awkward creations, devised with less attention to the political identities of their peoples than to the interests of the victors in the war. The economies of Europe had been severely damaged by the war and little more than a decade later were hit by worldwide depression and financial collapse. Old social orders were being disrupted: in the long term by industrialization and in the short term by defeat in the war. Like the babies of alcoholic mothers, being born out of failure meant that many new states began life with a major handicap. In states denied the legitimacy that follows from venerable age or material success, the rise of extremes is understandable. Countries were torn between communism on the left and authoritarianism on the right; generally, conservative Catholics supported the right. In Martin's summary: 'It was the first world war which deepened to the point of near-disaster the struggle between passionate political dogmatisms and so reinforced Catholic proclivities to side with the organicist right wherever the Church was part of the established order.'[8]

Italy gave the world both the word 'fascist' (after the Latin *fasces*: the bundle of sticks and projecting axe that was a symbol of the authority of the Roman consul) and the first fascist movement. Although Italian Fascism was initially anticlerical, Mussolini quickly appreciated the need to find an accommodation with the Church and the Church was happy to reciprocate. In the Lateran Pacts of 1929, the Church accepted the Kingdom of Italy in return for the state accepting the autonomy of the Vatican City, the right of the Church to teach Catholic doctrine in the state schools, and the Church's moral authority. Many senior clergy actively supported Mussolini and played a prominent part in devising elaborate civic liturgies for the Fascists. The Church also approved Mussolini's conquest of Abyssinia (now Ethiopia) and his assistance for Franco in the Spanish Civil War. And the views of ordinary Italian Catholics are clear from the popular support Mussolini enjoyed until the Axis powers began to lose the war.

The attitude of German Catholics to Nazism is less easy to discern. The longer history of representative politics meant that

German Catholics were already well organized into parties and organizations with which the Nazi party competed. Catholics were initially more reluctant than Lutherans to support the Nazis, but that probably has more to do with loyalty to existing right-wing Catholic organizations than to ideological distaste.[9] In many predominantly Protestant states, Catholics initially opposed Hitler, but in overwhelmingly Catholic Bavaria the Catholic BVP advocated cooperating with the Nazis. Franz von Papen, who became Hitler's vice-chancellor in January 1933, was a conservative Catholic and leader of the Catholic Centre Party. He not only provided an acceptable civilian front for Hitler; he was also active in negotiating the 1933 concordat between Hitler and the Vatican that saw the Church drop its opposition to the Nazis and dissolve its Centre Party in return for the protection of Church interests. Parts of the Catholic press encouraged their readers to support the Nazi revitalization of Germany. The Church officially supported Hitler's first international challenge (the occupation of the Saarland in 1935) and his 1938 hostile takeover of Austria. Many German lay Catholics and clergy bravely opposed Nazism and suffered the consequences. In 1941 the Bishop of Munster preached three sermons criticizing the police state and the forced euthanasia programme. He was too prominent to punish, but a number of Catholics were executed for circulating copies of the sermons. In 1943 a group of Catholic students in Munich tried to provoke a revolt and were executed for their troubles. But, as Roger Griffin concludes: 'In general, however, overt anti-socialism and illiberalism combined with the covert nationalism and anti-Semitism of established Catholicism to preclude the possibility that German Catholics would turn against Hitler *en masse*.'[10] Konrad Adeneur, a pious Catholic who went on to become Chancellor of West Germany, certainly believed the Church could have done more to resist Hitler.[11]

A persistent obstacle to making confident inferences about the influence of religion is that religion can rarely be separated from other considerations. The case that Catholicism in some sense 'made straight the way' for Nazism would be more compelling if there was clear evidence of Lutheran opposition to Hitler. But how Lutherans behaved has to be interpreted in the context of their very strong support for the previous incarnation of German imperialism in the Second Reich of Bismarck and Kaiser Wilhelm.[12] As Griffin puts it, German Protestants instinctively rejected the weak social democracy of the Weimar Republic and aligned themselves with the ultra-conservative and anti-socialist German National People's Party and the figure of the veteran soldier and war hero von

Hindenburg. Hence we might expect them to be more favourable to Hitler than their Catholic counterparts. However, and to their credit, when Hitler tried to co-opt the Lutheran Church by having his candidate elected as the first 'Reich Bishop', a third of the Protestant clergy rebelled and followed Martin Niemöller and Dietrich Bonhoeffer into the 'Confessing Church'.[13] Niemöller was sent to a concentration camp in 1937 and in 1944 Bonhoeffer was executed for his part in the plot to murder Hitler.

The two Catholic states of the Iberian peninsula both fell to dictators. On 17 July 1936 the Spanish army in Morocco rebelled against the government of the Spanish republic, which it accused of dismembering the fatherland (that is, negotiating with Basque and Catalan separatists) and of Bolshevism. With considerable assistance from Germany and Italy, Francisco Franco won the three-year war and began a dictatorship that survived until his death in 1975. The Catholic Church did not hesitate to support the rebels. As a leading Spanish Jesuit said: 'This nation has Catholicism inscribed in its heart with letters of fire. Even more, Catholicism is so incorporated and conaturalized within its very being, that it cannot cease to be Catholic without ceasing first of all, to be a nation.'[14]

Portugal avoided a civil war but it also abandoned democracy for clerical authoritarianism. For most of the nineteenth century Portugal had enjoyed a liberal constitutional monarchy. In 1910 it was displaced by a more left-wing republican government, but it never managed to consolidate its position and it was overthrown by a military coup in 1926. In 1932 António de Oliveira Salazar became Prime Minister. In 1933 he introduced an authoritarian corporatist regime that stayed in place until 1974. Salazar's childhood friend became Cardinal Cerejeira, the head of the Church in Portugal. He was initially delighted by the 'Estado Novo', but was later alienated by Salazar's suppression of the para-church movement Catholic Action. Salazar was unwilling to permit networks and movements he could not control.[15]

Like Salazar, Franco gave the Church far less than it hoped for. Hitler and Mussolini were enemies of the Christian churches who pretended otherwise so long as they gained from the deception. Rather different are the cases of fascism and authoritarianism in the states that were formed from the ruins of the Austro-Hungarian Empire: Austria, Hungary, Poland, Romania, Yugoslavia and Czechoslovakia.

In many rural areas of Austria the Catholic Christian Social Party worked closely with the right-wing *Heimwehr* (or 'home guard') militia and this support brought Dollfuss to power in 1932. In

February 1934 he crushed the social democratic militias in Vienna and four months later he promulgated his authoritarian constitution: 'We shall establish a state on the basis of a Christian Weltanschauung.'[16] By Christian he meant Catholic. Pope Pius XI was impressed. In 1993 he told Austrian pilgrims to Rome that Dollfuss was a 'Christian, giant-hearted man...who rules Austria so well, so resolutely and in such a Christian manner. His actions are witness to Catholic visions and convictions. The Austrian people, Our beloved Austria, now has the government it deserves.'[17]

Poland's war did not end in 1918. On its eastern borders it had to battle with Ukrainians and Bolshevik Russians, who signed an armistice in Riga in late 1920. The constitution of 1921 granted very wide powers to the parliament and reduced the position of president to being largely ceremonial. The war hero General Piłsudski, who had been made head of state in 1919, refused to contest the election and withdrew from public life in a sulk. The first elected president was murdered. Frequent parliamentary conflicts led to a succession of short-lived cabinets. The economy declined. In 1926 Piłsudski came out of retirement to lead a military coup. Parliament was effectively sidelined by increasingly presidential government. Opposition politicians were arrested, imprisoned and then exiled. Although Piłsudski died in 1935, the authoritarian one-party government he had established remained in power until it was destroyed in September 1939 by the German Blitzkrieg.[18]

After 1918 Hungary had a brief spell as a liberal democracy before an even briefer 'dictatorship of the proletariat' led by the left-wing Béla Kun. Finally it became a fully independent kingdom effectively ruled by Admiral Miklós Horthy. With very strong support from the Catholic hierarchy, he sustained a mildly authoritarian democracy until 1944. Hungary had joined the Axis powers at the start of the war so that it could annex territory from Czechoslovakia and Romania. That achieved, it was a reluctant partner in the Axis war effort and in 1944 the Germans invaded their supposed ally and imposed a dictatorship of the fascist Arrow Cross Party.[19]

In 1941 German and Italian forces occupying Yugoslavia allowed the Croats to fulfil their ambitions of an independent state and put in power the fascist Ustaše (or 'Upright' or 'Resurrection') movement under its Poglavnic (or 'dictator') Ante Pavelić. As Conway notes: 'The new state was eager to make much of its Catholic character, nominating members of the clergy to prominent posts and passing laws against freemasonry, contraception and even blasphemy.'[20] In the Ustaše state and in the parts of Bosnia and Herzegovina that it controlled, Orthodox Serbs and Muslims were forcibly converted to Catholicism or expelled. Orthodox priests were particularly targeted and hundreds of Orthodox churches were destroyed. Archbishop Stepinac of Zagreb initially reacted enthusiastically to Croatian independence and in April 1941 issued a pastoral letter urging clergy to follow the Poglavnic in which he wrote: 'It is easy here to discern the hand of God.'[21] The Pope granted Pavelić a private audience, which he must have known would be interpreted by the Croatian faithful as a mark of approval. As the record of atrocities built, Stepanic became more cautious and by the end of the war was snubbing the regime, but he did not discipline his own clergy, 'some of whom fought alongside the militias and took part in forcible conversions and atrocities'.[22]

Czechoslovakia, another state formed from the ruins of the Austro-Hungarian Empire in 1918, was dismembered at the start of the Second World War. Having annexed the German-speaking Sudetenlands in late 1938 under the terms of the Munich agreement, Germany seized Bohemia and Moravia in March 1939, and established a fascist regime in Slovakia under Catholic priest Josef Tiso, who had led the Slovak People's Party during the brief period of liberal democracy. As well as being head of state and head of the security forces, Tiso was the leader of the paramilitary Hlinka Guard, which wore the Catholic Episcopal cross on its armbands. 'The new state took on . . . the air of a modern theocracy. The Catholic clergy and laity were prominent at all levels of the regime, which in its corporatist and educational policies explicitly based itself on the principles of papal encyclicals.'[23]

Romania was originally formed in the second half of the nineteenth century from the Danube principalities. A constitutional monarchy, it was significantly expanded after the First World War with the addition of Transylvania, Bessarabia and Bukowina. The inclusion of larger numbers of Hungarians (about 10 per cent of the population) added to the complexity of what was already an ethnically diverse state. It had a failing economy, and, in common with many other successors to the Austro-Hungarian Empire, a rapidly growing university sector that was producing more graduates than the already bloated state bureaucracy could accommodate. It also had a thoroughly corrupt monarch whose personal life was such an open cause for scandal that he had for a time been exiled to England by his father. King Carol 'steadily undermined an already fragile democracy by playing all the major politicians off against one another'.[24] The main focus of opposition was the Legion of the Archangel Michael, better known by the name of its paramilitary wing: the Iron Guard. Led by Corneliu Codreanu, the Legion was anti-Western and anti-democracy. It was deeply anti-Semitic, and, like the Slavophile movements in nineteenth-century Russia, its proposed solution to economic crisis and obvious corruption was a return to the Orthodox Church. The Church reciprocated. It is estimated that a fifth of the Orthodox clergy joined the Iron Guard.[25] In the elections of 1937 Codreanu's All for the Nation Party took enough of the vote to prevent King Carol forming a government from any of the tame royalist parties, so he seized power and arranged for a rigged referendum to confirm a new constitution that allowed the closure of the universities, the suppression of the judiciary and the dissolving of all political parties.

> A last-ditch effort to domesticate Codreanu had failed weeks before when Carol offered him the Premiership on condition that the Iron Guard recognize Carol as its Captain.... The xenophobic and anti-Semitic Codreanu was unlikely to jeopardize his credibility by bending the knee to a corrupt monarch who obstinately clung to his influential Jewish mistress, a woman widely seen as a combination of Messalina and Rasputin.[26]

Carol took on the Iron Guard. He had Codreanu imprisoned and then shot 'while trying to escape'. The Iron Guard responded by killing the premier. Carol ordered the prefects of every county to execute between three and five prominent members of the Guard and to expose their bodies in public squares. Not being sure of the outcome of the struggle between Carol and the Guard, some prefects took the precaution of complying only superficially: they executed and exhibited common criminals rather than the intended targets.

It is worth noting that it was not just the fascist opposition to Carol that tried to mobilize religion as a source of inspiration and legitimation. Despite his personal character, Carol also tried to use his country's religious heritage, and he managed to persuade the leader of the Orthodox Church in Romania, Patriarch Miron Cristea, to serve as Prime Minister during the first period of his dictatorship. It was, as Gallagher dryly puts it, 'a sign of the willingness of the Church to align itself with secular power irrespective of its character'.[27]

Given that Romania was Orthodox rather than Roman Catholic in its religion, it may seem to deviate from the theme to put it in this list. However, I will shortly draw out the connection after introducing a few more examples of European authoritarianism.

Although it took the German invasion and the creation of the puppet Vichy state in the southern half of France to bring them to the fore, there were powerful authoritarian Catholic tendencies in France during the inter-war years. One instance was Action Française (AF), founded by Charles Maurras, a poet, journalist and editor of a newspaper of the same name. The movement campaigned for the return of the monarchy and for aggressive action against Jews. Although its relationships with the Catholic Church were not always easy, it was supported by eleven out of seventeen cardinals and bishops and a great many priests. One Abbé sent AF a donation of five francs 'for a rug made out of the kike's skin that I can put beside my bed and step on every morning and evening'.[28] Pope Pius X told Maurras's mother: 'I bless his work.' The next Pope, Pius XI, ruled that the faithful should not support AF. His unhappiness stemmed from the fact that the movement was not under Church control and it encouraged violence.[29]

Whatever the official Vatican position, AF enjoyed its strongest support from conservative Catholics and it enjoyed considerable influence on the Vichy regime. Although Maurras had been fiercely nationalistic and anti-German, he firmly opposed the Resistance and allied war effort. He proposed that, if the Gaullists would not cease their fight, their families should be taken hostage and executed. The AF line was that the Germans had not really wanted to conquer France. It was the German Jews who made them do it and it was the French Jews who had so sapped the spirit of France that the Germans won. By this reasoning one strand of French nationalism reconciled itself to the German occupation. Xavier Vallat, a Catholic member of AF, was the first Vichy Commissioner for Jewish Affairs and an enthusiastic implementer of Vichy's anti-Jewish legislation. He willingly deported Jews to a certain death at Auschwitz.[30]

To this list we could add the Christus Rex (or Christ the King) movement in Belgium, led by Léon Degrelle, which took 12 per cent of the vote elections in 1936 on a platform that consisted largely of denouncing democratic politics and demanding the reassertion of the primacy of Catholicism.[31] The Irish Free State, an overwhelmingly Catholic country, had its Blueshirt movement, led by General Eoin O'Duffy, who had been sacked from his post as chief of police by Eamonn De Valera. Blueshirt units fought in Spain with their fellow Catholics in the Falange. It is worth noting that, when De Valera wrote a new constitution in 1937, the preamble assigned a special place to the Catholic Church, and, although he retained democratic elections for the lower house of the parliament, he created a corporatist upper chamber that was filled with people nominated by professional associations and interest groups.

The Protestant side of the equation is harder to construct, largely because there were so few Protestant states in Europe. Britain had Oswald Mosley and his Blackshirts, but, beyond orchestrating anti-Semitic violence in London, they had no political success and absolutely no religious legitimation. The only predominantly Protestant country to acquire a fascist regime was Norway and that owed almost nothing to local popularity. Vidkun Quisling had a brilliant army career and was made a general staff officer at the age of 24. In 1931 he entered politics and two years later he founded the fascist Nasjonal Samling party. It was never popular and Quisling came to power entirely through the agency of the German army. Quisling helped Hitler prepare for the invasion of Norway and was rewarded by being appointed Prime Minister – an office from which he was forcibly removed in 1945.

The history of the Baltic states usefully complicates the issue.[32] Lithuania, Latvia and Estonia achieved their independence in the aftermath of the First World War, when the major powers on either side were weakened: Germany by its defeat and Russia by the civil war that followed the 1917 Bolshevik Revolution. After two years of small-scale battles, the three countries rid themselves of German, White Russian and Soviet troops, established liberal democracies and in 1922 were admitted to the League of Nations. All three more or less willingly abandoned democracy for authoritarian dictatorship. First was Lithuania. Antanas Smetona and Augustinas Voldemaras took power in a military coup in 1926 and became respectively President and Prime Minister. Voldemaras's rule was opposed in conservative Catholic circles: most clergy supported the Christian Democrat Party rather than the Nationalists. A failed assassination attempt in the spring of 1929 seems to have forced him over some personal hurdle, from authoritarian to fascist. He devoted the summer to building up the paramilitary Iron Wolf organization, to the neglect of his official duties. Smetona asked him to resign. He refused and was dismissed. He was arrested and sent into provincial exile. The Iron Wolf association was suppressed. Smetona ruled Lithuania as a one-party state until the Soviet invasion in 1940 put an end to the nation's brief life.

The world economic crisis of the early 1930s devastated the Baltic states and increased pressure for reforms to constitutions that, by encouraging the formation of very large numbers of small parties, were preventing effective government. In Estonia, a number of alternatives were put to the people in a series of referenda. The one that was finally approved was promoted by the 'Vaps', members of the Vabadussõjalaste Liit (Association of Liberators or Freedom Fighters). This was initially an organization for veterans of the 1918–20 wars of independence, but in 1929, inspired by the German example, it had become a fascist political movement. The new constitution would vest dictatorial power in the new office of president; its supporters talked approvingly of the 'führer principle'. Rather than wait for the new dispensation to come into force, Prime Minister Konstantin Päts, one of the heroes of the struggle for national autonomy, took advantage of his position as acting President to declare a state of emergency, proclaim martial law and imprison some 500 Vaps. Like Smetona, Päts remained in power until the Soviet invasion.

The story of Latvia is similar. Karlis Ulmanis, a popular political leader who had been instrumental in the creation of the new state, used economic crises and the threats from extreme right-wing groups as justification for increasing his powers. The local fascist movement, the Fire Cross, was banned in 1933 but immediately reappeared as the Thunder Cross (Pērkonņkrutieši). In 1934 Ulmanis became Prime Minister and, immediately declaring a state of emergency, suppressed both the Thunder Cross (which was chauvinistic and anti-German) and the Baltisher Bruderbund, a pro-German paramilitary organization.

It would be an exaggeration to class Päts, Smetona or Ulmanis with Hitler and Mussolini: benign despotism would be an accurate description of their regimes. None persecuted his enemies, and, although none allowed free elections or tolerated organized opposition, all were able to persuade leading politicians from other parties to serve in their administrations.

It is the nature of those administrations that suggests the strongest links with Catholic social teaching. In Latvia, Ulmanis sought legitimation and popular input by creating a series of corporations modelled on the medieval guild. Chambers of commerce, industry, agriculture, artisans and labour elected members to a National Economic Council. There was also a State Cultural Council drawn from a chamber of the professions and a chamber of 'Literature and the Arts'. Päts followed a similar model in Estonia, seeking to replace the fractious bickering of a fragmented parliament with a more manageable (and malleable) State Economic Council of 25 members. Ten he appointed himself; the other fifteen each represented one of fifteen corporations.

Like Romania, the Baltic states complicate the association of Catholicism with authoritarian politics because, of the three coun-

tries, only Lithuania was predominantly Catholic; Latvia and Estonia were majority Lutheran countries! One might want to argue
either that the Thunder Cross and the Vaps recruited primarily
from the Catholic minorities in Latvia and Estonia respectively or
that the more benign forms of despotism that prevented them
seizing power were similarly more popular with Catholics than
Lutherans, but there is little evidence for either claim and some
evidence that suggests otherwise. In Latvia, Ulmanis's first attempt
at constitutional reform was opposed by delegates from the Latgale
region, where Catholics were concentrated. And even the influence
of Catholic social theory on the corporatist strategies pursued by
the dictators may be more apparent than real. Jackson suggests that
the fondness for guilds and corporations as a model for civil society
is probably explained by the influence, not of Catholicism, but of
the Baltic Germans who had ruled the region for centuries and
who, since the time of the Teutonic knights, had a fondness for
hierarchical aristocratic guildlike societies: 'A visitor to one of the
Tartu Corporations would imagine himself in a German
Burschenschaft: the same initiation ceremonies, the same insignia,
the same drinking bouts, the same endurance tests.'[33] But it is
worth noting where Catholics stood in relation to the benign des-
potisms of the Baltic. They were not liberal critics. If they were
hostile it was because, especially in the case of Smetona in Lithuania (and this is true also of Piłsudski in Poland), the dictator did
not pay sufficient respect to Catholic associations and leaders.

What then are we to make of the political record of Europe in
the inter-war years? Against the proposition that Catholicism has
a special affinity with authoritarianism, we can note the following.
First, authoritarianism was so widespread that much of the appeal
either of outright fascist movements – or of the slightly more
benign regimes that prevented fascists taking power – clearly derived from the political and economic problems of the time and
the place and the limited repertoire of solutions that were popularized by the initial success of Italian and German dictatorships.
With those models leading the debates, much of the behaviour of
leading Catholics could be defended (and this was their justification) on the grounds that they were holding the line against a
greater evil. Thus Owen Chadwick could assert that Pope Pius XI
was 'one of the world's leaders in the fight against Nazism and
fascism'.[34]

Second, we should be wary of exaggerating the popularity of
fascism. Many fascist movements achieved power only with the aid
of German and Italian military might.

Third, in many settings, religious identities, even when channelled through political parties, were clearly subordinated to ethnic and national ones. The Baltic port of Memel (or, to the Lithuanians, Klaipeda), part of East Prussia and 80 per cent German and Lutheran, was given to Lithuania in 1919 as compensation for losing its capital Vilnius to Poland, but its population never accepted their new status. A branch of the Nazi Party was established and in 1938 won twenty-six of twenty-nine seats in the local council. The party was founded by a Lutheran Pastor and its membership was overwhelmingly Lutheran. That the alien Lithuanian rulers were Catholic doubtless gave the Memel Protestants an additional reason to be attracted to a potent vehicle for opposition, but Nazism appealed primarily because it was German and successful. The point can be made in reverse. Lithuania and Poland were both Catholic but that did nothing to blunt their animosity over disputed territory. Smetona was willing to put Lithuanian interests before those of the Vatican. He was impotent to force the Poles to give up Vilnius, but in the second-best world of church boundaries he was determined to win back some pride and insisted that Vilnius be included in the Church's Lithuanian province.

Fourth, as we have seen with the Baltic examples and with the Legion of the Archangel Michael in Romania, it was possible to build extreme right-wing nationalism on the foundations of a shared Orthodox or Lutheran faith. It was not solely a Catholic disease. Hence, if we are to sustain the claim for an affinity between Catholicism and authoritarianism, the causal links have to be extendable to these other branches of Christianity.

Even with these reservations, some causal connections can be traced and, in defence of the thesis, I would note the following. First, while the manifest problems facing much of Europe in the 1930s obviously explain the market for extremist politics, that the right triumphed over the left (even before German and Italian military success tipped the balance) suggests the power of the institutions of the old order and primary among them was the church.

Second, in most cases there is clear evidence of Catholic Church leaders taking advantage of instability to promote, not just their religiously inspired corporatist vision of the good society, but also the more mundane interests of the Church. For example, Church leaders in Portugal were fiercely opposed to the 'First Republic' that was overthrown in 1926 because its formally secular constitution diminished the role of the Church.

Third, we have the abundant record of the Church's lack of enthusiasm for democracy. By its own account, it was illiberal, authoritarian and, of particular relevance to the fascist right in most countries, anti-Semitic.[35] Although it reluctantly accepted the need to work within the institutions of liberal democracies, it remained opposed to the fundamental principle that people should be free to choose. The leading English Catholic Father Ronald Knox in 1927 wrote that: 'a body of Catholic patriots, entrusted with the government of a Catholic state, will not shrink even from repressive measures, in order to perpetuate the secure domination of Catholic principles among their fellow-countrymen.' More telling, he made it clear that the Church's involvement in liberal democracy was opportunistic: 'For when we demand liberty in the modern state, we are appealing to its own principles, not to ours.'[36] Pope Pius XII, who thought Soviet Bolshevism a much greater threat than Nazism, spent much of the first post-war decade defending the Church's record and it took considerable pressure from the German bishops to push the Vatican to change its tone.[37]

In the case of Germany, Italy, Spain and Portugal it seems appropriate to conclude that Catholicism played a largely passive but nonetheless important role. Despite such obvious anti-Christian features as the cult of the leader, hyper-nationalism, veneration of the state and willingness to use violence against scapegoats, fascists managed to 'appropriate the normative energies of Christianity as a moral authority [and] to convince many thousands (and where they seized power, millions) of ostensibly devout Christians, including some high-ranking clergy, to become enthusiastic recruits to their cause, and hence prepared to connive with, or even participate personally in, acts of repression, violence, racial persecution, and war'.[38] That authoritarian movements shared some common values with Catholic social teaching and were mostly willing to protect (and in some places promote) Catholic church interests was enough to persuade the Church to acquiesce. In the case of the Central European states created from the Austro-Hungarian Empire, I think we can go further. As Sugar notes: 'Obligatory religious instruction in the Successor States survived World War I, just as the close connection between church and state did, and continued to inculcate in the young the belief in a divinely sanctioned . . . and highly structured sense of values.'[39] While only two movements, the Slovak and the Romanian, went so far as to choose religious symbols, all of them recognized the importance of the shared religious heritage. 'Thus emerged the corporate–Christian plank of their program in which Christian stood for nothing that any traditional, conscious, or thinking Christian would have recognized. Here we have a truly "native" feature of Eastern fascism.[40]

The most important connection between Catholicism and authoritarianism concerns not so much religious values as their structural consequences. Remember that any causal connection has to be capable of being extended, in a minor key, to include Orthodox and Lutheran cultures. And, although I have not dealt with the rise and spread of communism here, the fact that communism became successfully embedded in Orthodox countries suggests that whatever we cite as predisposing Catholic cultures to authoritarianism should also be found in Orthodoxy.[41] The key variable is organicism. The Reformed branch of the Protestant tradition (as opposed to the Lutheran strand found in Germany, Scandinavia and the Baltic) is schismatic. It readily divides into competing sects. It also inadvertently encourages individualism and weakens obedience to authority. Catholicism, Orthodoxy and, to a lesser extent, Lutheranism, with their insistence on the primacy of the institution of the church, are much more likely to see the state as the political embodiment of 'the people' as a community rather than as the expression of the preferences of individuals. In that sense the general ethos of these brands of Christianity provides a more suitable structure for the corporatist visions of totalitarianism than Reformed Protestantism with its stress on the believing individual.

That Catholicism is an organic or communal religion forms a second roundabout connection with right-wing authoritarianism: it quite inadvertently encouraged the leftist opposition that helped destabilize the nascent democracies. This may seem counterintuitive but it is an important point and I will say more about it in the final chapter. A form of religion that asserts that it is the only true faith leaves little space for religious dissent. The Catholic Church's insistence that it and it alone had the ear of God and its close association with conservative forces meant that those who opposed particular aspects of the religious establishment were driven out of religion altogether and become thoroughly anticlerical. Hence the common pattern of the states of Western Europe with the strongest and most conservative Catholic traditions – France, Spain, Portugal and Italy – producing the most popular left-wing parties. The reformed strand of Protestantism created a variety of sects that could absorb some of the energies that could have fuelled militant political dissent: the Quakers, the Baptists, the Methodists, the Salvation Army. So religion itself did not become a key principle of division. People who otherwise might have been drawn to revolutionary and destabilizing Marxist positions could express their opposition in more moderate forms. Hence England and Holland and the United States did not experience the same polarization as many Catholic states.

In summary, the association between Catholicism and right-wing extremism is probably best explained, not so much by specific features of Catholic teaching (though those are certainly implicated – anti-Semitism, for example), but by a more abstract structural feature of Catholicism, which it shares in great measure with Orthodoxy and to a lesser extent with Lutheranism. Two principle conditions for the rise of authoritarianism are a communalist attitude to society and political extremism. The 'church' form of religion deliberately encourages the former and, by ensuring that radicalism cannot be accommodated within the religious culture, inadvertently permits the latter.

Open Catholic politics

In most ethnically and nationally diverse political units, the fault lines are not just vertical but also horizontal. For example, the Catholic Irish who migrated to Britain in the nineteenth century were ethnically and culturally different; they were also poor.[42] They entered the labour market at the bottom. They possessed no capital; those who could afford to do so migrated to North America. They had none of the skills necessary to secure well-paid jobs in an increasingly industrial economy. Many of the natives among whom the Irish settled seemed determined to add to their natural disadvantages.[43]

However, the Irish formed only a small part of the unskilled working class of England or Scotland. A combination of push and pull encouraged them to form tight, self-contained communities. The native Scots and English were generally a little unwelcoming and the Catholic Church (fearful of losing its people) did its best to keep them under its wing. When the Irish Home Rule crisis was at its height, the Irish immigrants and their children did have a distinct politics: an overriding concern with the status of Ireland and a set of internal divisions that mirrored the party divisions in Ireland. But, when the Irish question was shelved with the creation of the Irish Free State in 1921, the Irish in Britain turned to the domestic politics of their new land. With the immigrants too few to sustain a Catholic party, their class position naturally drew them to the labour movement. Church leaders were at first hostile; for many, secular trade unions were anathema. But the moderation of the British trade union movement and the Parliamentary Labour Party won them over. Catholics became involved in the Labour Party in Britain to an extent well out of proportion to their numbers. The link became so firm that it survives even though British Catholics no longer have an unusually low class profile.[44] Describing data from surveys in 1991 and 1992, Kotler-Berkowitz says:

> If the Catholic middle class were unaffected by its religion, it should vote for Labour against the Tories as the same rate as the Anglican middle class. That the Catholic middle class continues to give more support to Labour...is solid evidence that the traditional linkage between Catholics and the Labour party continues in the contemporary period, especially among Catholics whose class interests should have moved them to greater rates of Conservative voting.[45]

The same pattern can be found in bolder form in Scotland.[46] There the greater concentration of migrant Irish Catholics interacted with the more radically Protestant religion of the natives (who were Presbyterians rather than Anglicans and Methodists) to deepen social divisions. In addition to Catholics overwhelmingly supporting the Labour Party, working-class Protestants tended disproportionately to support the 'Conservative and Unionist' Party (as the main right-wing party was known). The idea that the urban Protestant working class of the industrial Lowlands formed a Conservative-voting Orange Order bloc is an exaggeration, but there was a significant number of skilled Protestant workers who voted for the Unionists because they were opposed to Irish independence.[47]

A similar association between religion and political affiliation can be seen in US politics. The founding fathers were white Anglo-Saxon Protestants. To be precise, fifty-five of the fifty-six men who signed the Declaration of Independence on 4 July 1776 were Protestants; Charles Carroll from Maryland (a colony set up to take Catholics from England) was the exception. A century later, when Catholics settled in large numbers in the north-eastern states, the WASPs formed an elite. The typical northern Episcopalian, Presbyterian or Congregationalist was richer and better educated than the Irish and later Italian and Polish immigrants who filled the cities. The inherited divisions of the Civil War period make a simple left–right analysis of US party politics difficult. Irrespective of social class, whites in the Confederate states tended (until the Reagan presidency in the 1980s) to support the Democratic Party, but within the northern states, because they were mainly second-wave immigrants and their descendants, Catholics tended to be Democrats. One only has to list the leading Democrats of the 1970s – Daniel Moynihan, the Kennedy brothers, Tip O'Neill – to see the strength of that connection. Particularly in the cities of the north-east, Catholics were able to exercise considerable local power through the Democratic Party.

We can see a similar pattern in Australia and New Zealand, where it was reinforced in the early part of the twentieth century by the close ties with the struggle for Irish independence. Although the class differences between Irish and British settlers was not great, it was sufficient to lay a foundation on which animosities over the British Empire and the Irish question could build. Catholics (who, until the 1970s, when substantial numbers of Central and Southern Europeans migrated to Australia, were descendants of the Irish) were much more likely than non-Catholics to be active in trade unions and to support the Labor Party. Once the British connection had been weakened by the decline of imperialism and the salience of the Irish question had been reduced by the creation of the Irish Free State, the authoritarian right-wing tendency came more to the fore and in the 1930s a section of the Australian labour movement became heavily influenced by the right-wing ideology of Catholic Action – so much so that the party split with the Catholic faction forming the conservative Democratic Labor Party.

In none of these examples is religion *as such* a principal consideration. As I argued above, in so far as Catholicism does encourage a particular political vision, it is one of the right not the left. That in Britain and in its former white colonies Catholics are generally found on the left owes nothing to Catholic ideas and everything to the patterns of social evolution and migration (and specific disputes about Ireland) that saw Catholic migrants enter labour markets at the bottom, where they became involved in labour unions and left-wing party politics. We can see the resulting tension between culture and social location in the nature of the labourist parties in which Catholics formed a major part; they were conservative in values and authoritarian in ethos.

Religious dissent and class formation

In the above examples the connection between religion and social class resulted from a secondary link: a migrant people of one religion entered an economy at the bottom and hence naturally tended to support the party with the closest links to the labour movement. There is a very different way in which religious identity can become associated with a certain class and that is when the dominant religious tradition fragments. Religious innovations are not often concerned only with competing claims about the will of God, or the correct path to salvation. Arguments within churches often draw on competing social visions so that a schismatic movement appeals particularly strongly to one particular social class.

The point can be easily illustrated from the history of the state Church of England. The Episcopalian Church of England, like its Roman Catholic elder sister, was a pyramid of religious authority. With some small variations from time to time, it was supposed that at the summit, and closest to God, was the Archbishop, who ordained his bishops, who in turn ordained the lesser clergy. The Church hierarchy determined the institution's beliefs and liturgy and decided what was and what was not pleasing to God. It was supposed that the Church collectively pleased God through its performance of a calendar of rituals. The laity were expected to accept the Church's authority, use its offices to seek salvation, support it financially and attend the major services, but they were not expected to be enthusiastic committed individual believers of the type we now associate with Protestantism. The pyramid and the passive laity perfectly fitted the social structure of feudalism: the notion of an organic community arranged in a firmly delineated hierarchy, with everyone knowing his or her place and never getting ideas 'above his or her station'. In the case of the English Church, the structure of religion was not only a replica of the social structure of feudalism but it was actually linked at every level. Even before Henry expropriated large parts of the lands and wealth of the Church and passed them over to the lords and the gentry, the ties were in place. After the expropriation, they were even stronger. The leaders of the Church were members of the most powerful feudal families, and, at parish level, the right to nominate a clergyman to a 'living' lay with the major landowners.

Some of the Protestant sects that defied the Church were self-consciously also movements of political dissent, but even those that stressed their loyalty to the established order were nonetheless radical in that the religious changes they promoted had powerful political resonances. First, the rejection of the claim that the ordination of priests gave them peculiar sacramental power reinforced an essentially egalitarian spirit: we are all in the same boat in the eyes of God. Second, most innovations were puritanical. They denounced wealth and indulgence and corruption and argued for a return to the simplicity of the early Christian Church. Not surprisingly, this none-too-subtle way of criticizing the rich had its greatest appeal to those rising social classes that were relatively free of feudal domination: independent small farmers, skilled craftsmen in towns. In part this was a practical matter. Only those who were independent could afford to defy their masters. But there was also a more subtle connection. Those people whose own financial circumstances allowed them to think of themselves as being as good as anybody were attracted to revisions of the dominant religious tradition in directions that suited their view of the mundane world. Those who had no liberty to think for themselves in any other part of their lives were not so attracted to the idea of thinking well of themselves in religion.

That those who left the state church in England tended to occupy particular social class locations (at its simplest neither the poorest, who had no choice, nor the richest, who chose the state church) meant that the various organizations into which the Church of England fractured tended to have a particular class profile, which, as the franchise was extended in the nineteenth century, led to an association between type of Christianity and political preference. The upper classes and those whom they controlled, the Church people, voted Conservative or Tory. The Liberal Party became the vehicle for English nonconformists. As well as representing their class interests, it also promoted their cultural and social interests by campaigning against the privileges of the established church. As a Bristol Anglican cleric put it: 'A Tory dissenter is one of the most anomalous creatures in existence, and is as rare as he is strange and unnatural.'[48]

The denomination underpinning of the English two-party system would eventually be undermined by the extension of the franchise to all working men and the rise of the Labour Party as their preferred vehicle, but it was also weakened by one issue that reminds us of the difficulty of separating ethnicity, religion and class: Ireland. Many nonconformists (especially Scottish Presbyterians) abandoned the Liberal Party at the end of the nineteenth century because of Gladstone's support for Irish Home Rule. Their religious (promoting Popery) and nationalist (the threat of the Irish to British stock) objections to Gladstone led to many Liberals describing themselves first as Liberal Unionists (that is, they favoured the maintenance of the Union of Ireland and Great Britain) and then moving over to what became the Conservative and Unionist Party. However, although the political allegiances of nonconformists shifted, the other side of the equation endured longer. Until as late as the Second World War, most Church of England bishops were members of the old landowning ruling class. A study of forty-seven diocesan bishops between 1920 and 1939 showed thirty-two separate links to the aristocracy.[49]

As I have already argued, the important difference between the UK (and it was repeated in the USA) and European mutations is that Protestantism readily permits schism. It allows political dissent to remain within the Christian ambit and thus softens the divisions. Catholicism, because it insists on a central organization, forces dissent out into anticlericalism.

Religion and West European politics post-1945

One major consequence of the Second World War was to reconcile the Catholic Church to participatory democracy. The Church hierarchy lagged some way behind its laity. In the 1970s the Catholic Church in Ireland had to accept that it had lost the battle to force the government to continue its ban on contraceptives. A 1973 press statement drew a distinction between morality and law: 'what is wrong in itself remains wrong, regardless of what state law says. It does not follow, of course, that the state is bound to prohibit the importation or sale of contraceptives. There are many things that the Catholic Church holds to be morally wrong and no-one has ever suggested, least of all the church herself, that they should be prohibited by the state.'[50] Whoever wrote that was either being disingenuous or had a very short memory for it was not so long before that the Church had maintained precisely that the state had an obligation to prohibit what the Church believed to be wrong. In 1948 John Courtney Murray, a US Jesuit theologian, presented a conference paper on 'Governmental Repression of Heresy'; he politely suggested that a good Catholic need not be in favour of it. Murray was condemned by his superiors and had his writings banned by the Holy Office, the section of the Vatican that decides what is true. It was not until 1960 that a papal commission decided that toleration was a virtue and that a Catholic state should not enforce religious orthodoxy.[51] It was a further nine years before the Catholic hierarchy in West Germany decided it should no longer use its pulpits to instruct the faithful how to vote. Lay Catholics had less trouble learning the lessons of the previous two decades. The failure of fascism brought a remarkable turnaround in Catholic politics. With the exception of Spain and Portugal, which had remained neutral and relatively untouched by the war, all European countries outside the control of the Soviet Union produced Catholic Christian Democrat parties that were genuinely committed to the principles of liberal democracy.[52]

Religion and party

In this section I want to look at the impact of religion on party choices in the last quarter of the twentieth century. Asking if religion is associated with political preferences may disguise two rather different questions. We might want to know if people of different faiths are drawn to different sorts of politics (as in the above discussion of fascism). Or we might want to know if, within a single religious tradition, the devout differ in their politics from the indifferent.

Certain answers to that question were discussed in the previous chapter, where I looked at the role of religion in ethnic or national identity. Clearly religion matters politically a great deal if it creates or reinforces deep social divisions, justifies conflict and encourages movements that question the boundaries or basis of the state. For example, in addition to a large number of class- or occupation-related political parties, Latvia in the 1920s had parties for Russian Old Believers, Russian and Greek Orthodox and Polish Catholics, as well as three Jewish parties. In addition, each of the class parties had a religious shadow: the Latgallian region (where Catholics were concentrated) supported separate local organizations. The collapse of the Soviet Union has unleashed many separatist religio-ethnic quarrels, but there have been relatively few such divisions in Western Europe post-1945. This is partly a feature of greater toleration. It also reflects the large-scale population movements during the war and the wiser decisions about boundaries made after it. The division of the Northern Ireland electorate into Catholics who overwhelmingly vote for nationalist parties (that is, those who wish to join the Irish Republic) and Protestants who almost entirely vote for unionist parties (that is, those who wish to stay united with Great Britain) is one of the few exceptions. I want to leave aside what we can think of as unresolved national disputes and concentrate on a variety of ways in which people's religion might influence their political preferences within the range that are routinely offered to the citizens of, say, France, Italy or Scotland.

As Whyte noted, the big issues of church–state relations were largely solved by the start of the twentieth century and they did not reappear in the post-1945 reconstruction. Even in Spain, which in the 1930s was torn apart by a civil war in which the power of the Catholic Church was a major consideration, the status of religion has not been terribly contentious since the 1960s. José Ramón Montero and Kerman Calvo demonstrate that religion had little effect on Spanish voting between 1982 and 1996 and explain that by the quite deliberate decision of elites of both the right and the left not to make the Catholic Church an issue.[53]

But even when the political privileges of particular churches are not contentious, relationships between blocs of believers can be. Some of Whyte's 'closed' Catholicism was carried through to the second half of the twentieth century. Holland, for example, was what political scientists call 'pillarized'. Catholics, Protestants and Liberals were all content to remain Dutch, but they lived somewhat separately; hence the image of three distinct columns. Each pillar had its own mass media, schools, trade unions, social agencies and political parties. And the Catholic clergy in particular was keen to maintain the divisions. As late as 1954, the Dutch bishops issued a pastoral letter threatening to excommunicate any Catholic who joined a trade union affiliated to the socialist federation. It was also forbidden to read socialist newspapers or to listen to socialist radio stations.[54] But the wishes of the Catholic Church to preserve its people from integration could not prevent the gradual collapse of the pillars. In 1946 just over half the electors voted for denominational parties. In 1967 the corresponding figure was 47 per cent and, in 1994, only 27 per cent voted for denominational parties.[55] One way of conveying the extent of that change is to note that the government formed after the 1994 election was the first in the seventy-six years since the introduction of universal suffrage not to include the Christian Democrats.

The cracks first appeared in the foundations of pillars in the 1960s with a clear decline in church involvement. In 1958 three-quarters of Dutch people had some church connection. By 1975 that had declined to 58 per cent and, in a 1992 survey, it was 43 per cent. Lessening church involvement in turn led to greater intermarriage, which reinforced the growing indifference to historic identities. In the early 1970s the separate confessional trade unions merged and the three main religious parties responded to the declining vote by forming an electoral front as the Christian Democratic Appeal; seven years later the coalition became a single party.

In Holland we see two separate processes of change intertwined. First the number of Protestants and Catholics who wished to differ enough to sustain separate parties declined to the point where the parties merged. Enough still separated them from the non-churchgoers to sustain one party. A clear majority of those who regularly attended church voted for the Christian Democrat Alliance (CDA) (55 and 62 per cent of churchgoing Protestants and Catholics respectively). But there was also a second change, which explains the CDA's loss of power: by 1994 regular churchgoers were only 27 per cent of the population.[56]

Most European countries, because they are almost religious monocultures, begin where Holland has ended: with a basic left–right divide. Those people for whom religion remains personally important tend to be more conservative than people with no religion. But that pattern is getting fainter. A 1952 survey of French voting showed a very strong association between mass attendance and political preference. None of those who supported the Communist Party described him or herself as 'devout', but 50 per cent of Gaullists and 73 per cent of Christian Democrats did. Seventy-seven per cent of Communist supporters never attended church, but only 12 per cent of Gaullists and 2 per cent of Christian Democrats were similarly divorced from France's major religion. Using voting patterns in presidential elections from 1965 to 1997, Bréchon shows a very clear and fairly steady decline in the influence of religious identity on political choice, but this has quite complex origins.[57] It is not the case that devout Catholics are markedly less likely in 1997 than in 1965 to be right-wing. The two main changes are, first, that, as the number of voters who are 'not devout' Catholics has grown, so they have become less distinct and in particularly less likely to be committed socialists or communists. That is, the link between atheism and the left has weakened as France has become more secular. Second, there are simply fewer devout Catholics, so that their effect on political outcomes is reduced.

Italian politics used to be strongly influenced by religion. In 1959 the Vatican confirmed its historic view that socialists and communists should be excommunicated and 67 per cent of Italians thought that a good Catholic could not be a communist or vote for communists.[58] Again the connection has weakened, and it has done so in the same ways we have seen elsewhere. There has been some softening of views among orthodox Catholics. By 1974 only 41 per cent thought that a good Catholic could not vote communist and twenty years later the figure was 15 per cent. Regular churchgoers still tended to vote to the right. In 1990 65 per cent of regular mass attenders voted for right-wing parties, while those who attended only irregularly or not at all voted for the left. But the overall impact of this connection was far less than it had been in the 1950s or even the 1970s, because the proportion of regular mass attenders in the electorate had declined. In 1956 it was 69 per cent of the population. At the end of the century it was less than 30 per cent. In West Germany in 1990 there was a huge difference in support for the Christian Democrats between devout and nominal Catholics: a full 30 per cent. But again regular mass-attenders formed only a quarter of the electorate.

The general secularization of Europe naturally reduces the market for Christian parties, but the experience of Scandinavia suggests that a niche market may endure.[59] The Scandinavian Christian parties were founded much later than their counterparts in Catholic Europe and enjoyed far less success. The Christian People's Party in Norway was formed provincially in 1933 and became a national party after the war. It came to power in 1965 as a tiny part of a four-party coalition. It polled 12 per cent of the vote in the 1970s, dipped in the 1980s and then reached its to-date highest peak in 1997 with 14 per cent. Finland's Christian League, formed in 1958, has since 1975 fluctuated between 3 and 5 per cent of the poll. Christian parties have been more successful in Sweden. The Christian Democratic Union, formed only in 1964, initially took less than 2 per cent of the vote, but in the 1990s the Christians passed 10 per cent. The last formed, Denmark's Christian People's Party, has been the least successful. Its best performance, 5 per cent of the poll, was achieved in 1973 and since 1977 it has not polled more then 3 per cent.

The Nordic Christian parties have a narrow base. They are supported mainly by evangelical Protestants: either Lutherans who supplement their church connection with membership of a mission or dissidents who are outside the church. They are conservative on social issues such as homosexuality, abortion and recreational drug use, but, unlike the English Tories, they are not aggressively anti-state. For example, they tend to be in favour of foreign aid, environmental protection and social welfare. Madeley suggests that the secularity of Scandinavia and Finland has a paradoxical effect. We can imagine a point at which so few Swedes or Norwegians are Christian that a Christian party will be pointless. We can also think back to a time when the culture was so permeated by Christian values that all politicians (other than Marxists) would have thought of themselves as Christian. It is as a society moves from the thoroughly religious to the secular end of that spectrum that the conditions for a specifically Christian party are created. As the rest of the population has become secular and liberal, the remaining evangelical Christians become more aware both of their shared identity and of their minority status. Hence the niche market.

As I noted above, Scotland offers a good example of what Whyte called 'open' Catholic politics. In so far as religion influenced party politics, it did so because Catholics (especially Irish immigrants and their descendants) and Protestants differed in their support for essentially secular parties. From the 1930s to the 1960s Scottish politics had a strong sectarian flavour. Largely because of their position in the labour market, Catholics voted disproportionately for the Labour Party. Protestants generally supported the Scottish Conservative and Unionist Party. For each bloc there was a cultural component that transcended social class. Many middle-class Catholics voted Labour and many working-class Protestants (especially in the industrial Lowlands where sectarian conflict was strongest) voted Conservative and Unionist. That second relationship was threatened by a steady decline in Protestant church involvement (especially among the working class) over the twentieth century, but it was further weakened by a deliberate change of policy on the part of the Conservative Party. For Scottish conservatives, the term 'Unionist' in their party's title was important. It signified their commitment to the United Kingdom (seen as virtuous because it was Protestant) and to the empire. With the loss of the empire, English conservatives shifted to a more secular right-wing ethos. Because it was so much larger, the view of the English party prevailed and in 1965 the Scottish party dropped the word 'Unionist'. The Conservative response to the Northern Ireland crisis (and it has been the attitude of all British governments since 1971) was to buy peace by conceding Irish nationalist demands. Because Scots conservatives were closer (geographically, genetically and spiritually) to the Protestants of Northern Ireland than were the English, this alienated many Scottish unionists. Prime Minister Margaret Thatcher may have said that Northern Ireland was as British as Finchley, but she did not mean it. Nor was she any fonder of Scotland or Wales, which she quite rightly regarded as corporatist backwaters, reluctant to embrace her neo-liberal attacks on state management of the economy. The net result of making the Conservative Party in Scotland conform to the wishes of English Conservative voters was a collapse of the Conservative vote in Scotland. In 1955 the party took 50 per cent of the vote – a figure not matched before or since by any party. By 1997 the Conservative vote in Scotland had fallen to 18 per cent. The final outcome was to hasten the political integration of Catholics and Protestants. In the 1950s Catholics, the religio-ethnic minority, were deviant and their deviation was to support Labour. By the end of the century Labour was the party of choice for Scots of every religion and none.

Some convergence was a result of change on the Catholic side. In our analysis of the 2001 Scottish Social Attitudes survey data Tony Glendinning and I produced a rough-and-ready substitute for a longitudinal study by dividing our respondents into three age cohorts. In the 1999 elections for the first Scottish Parliament, over 90 per cent of Catholics aged 55 and over who voted, but just under half the Protestants, voted Labour. For the middle group, aged 35–54, Catholic support for Labour was reduced to 75 per cent and, for those under 35, it was 62 per cent – not much different from the figure for the rest of the sample.

One issue that traditionally divided Catholics and Protestants was Scottish autonomy. Catholics had long been unenthusiastic about the possibility of either outright independence or even devolved government for Scotland because they feared that an autonomous Scotland would be more overtly Protestant than a Scotland that was just a small region in a more secular and religiously diverse United Kingdom. When the Scottish National Party made its electoral breakthrough in 1974, it was supported by a third of non-Catholics but only one in eight Catholics. However, by 1997, when a Labour Party committed to Scottish devolution was returned to power at Westminster, the Catholic hierarchy was sufficiently convinced that the overall climate of Scotland had changed for Cardinal Thomas Winning to announce that he was confident Catholics had nothing to fear from a Scottish Parliament. In the devolution referendum a larger number of Catholics than non-Catholics did not vote, but, of those Scots who did vote, Catholics were as likely as other Scots to have voted for a Scottish Parliament.[60]

In brief, as has been the case in other European countries, religion in Scotland has lost much of its political associations. Yet it remains the case that Conservative voters are overwhelmingly Church of Scotland and Scots who attend the Church of Scotland are disproportionately likely to be Conservatives.[61] The resolution of the apparent paradox lies in noting that both populations in that second sentence – Conservatives and churchgoers – are now very small when once they were large. Less than 10 per cent of Scots vote Conservative or regularly attend the Church of Scotland. As with the cases of France, Germany and Italy discussed above, much of the secularization of politics in Scotland has come, not from churchgoers changing their politics, but from secularization in a more usual sense: there are fewer churchgoers.

The contexts are very different and he is concerned more with general value positions than with party preferences, but James

D. Hunter argues that for Americans a more general left–right or traditional–progressive division is overriding denominational or confessional identities. In *Culture Wars* he makes a strong case for the importance of a new divide *within* most faith communities between the traditionalists who stress the importance of authority, family, self-discipline and control and the progressives who stress freedom of expression, individual autonomy and personal preference.[62] In an attempt to test this claim with large-scale survey data, Kellstedt and his associates found some support for Hunter's view. As well as dividing respondents into the traditional categories of Catholic, mainline Protestant and evangelical Protestant, they also used a battery of theological questions to divide each into traditionalist, moderate and modernist. When they explored links between these groupings and political preferences, they found that the denominational associations were, to some extent, moderated by the conservative–liberal dimension. For example, while all three subdivisions of evangelicals 'feel closer to conservative than to liberal groups ... there are internal divisions among Mainline Protestants and Catholics'.[63] Traditionalist Catholics joined traditionalist and moderate evangelicals in supporting the Republican Party, but moderate and modernist Catholics leaned to the Democrats. Religion remained important in determining political preferences; indeed, it explained alignments better than class, education and other demographic variables, but the traditional ethno-cultural patterns were moderated by a general conservative–liberal division.

In our Scottish survey, voting for anything other than Labour is so rare that it is difficult to pursue political differences between mass-going and nominal Catholics, but, for Britain as a whole, Kotler-Berkowitz finds that, for all confessions and denominations, church attendance 'consistently reduces Labour support'.[64] If we attach this observation to the above point about US traditionalist Catholics leaning towards the Republicans and similar findings from Australia and New Zealand, we can speculatively construct a general pattern. The first section of this chapter suggested that there was a basic affinity between Catholicism and authoritarianism. The specific history of Catholics migrants to Britain, the USA, Australia and New Zealand gave them a good class reason (compounded by anti-British imperialism) to lean to the left. My guess is that in all these countries, with a decline in churchgoing, the erosion of differences in socio-economic status and increased intermarriage, religion is changing from being an organic community identity, acquired at birth along with a considerable weight of social and cultural baggage, to being a matter of individual

theological and spiritual preference. And, once religious preferences become detached from communities, with their histories of
competition and conflict, so their political associations become
simpler. The sectarian animosities that pushed Catholics and Protestants apart are now largely forgotten. As the ethnic association
fades, what is left is what we see in societies that are religious
monocultures: the committed Christians tend to be slightly (and it
is only slightly) more right-wing than the unchurched.[65]

A final thought: it may seem obvious but it should be said that
the party political consequences of religion will depend on what
party choices are available. As we saw in the Scottish case, one
cause of the convergence of Catholics and Protestants was the
Conservative Party becoming so unpopular that very few people
of any stripe vote for it. Political choice may also be removed by
the major parties becoming so similar that there is little to choose
between them. We do not have to be so flamboyant as Francis
Fukuyama when he spoke of 'the end of history' to acknowledge
that there is no longer a significant Marxist presence in European
politics.[66] Even so-called socialist parties accept the economic primacy of capitalism and conservative parties now accept the social
liberalism of what thirty years ago would have been denounced as
'the permissive society'. When there is very little to separate the
agendas of a Jacques Chirac and a François Mitterrand, it is hardly
surprising that religious identity no longer greatly influences the
choice between them.

Socio-moral values

Although the mechanics differ according to specific features of
every state, the above brief review of recent studies points very
clearly to the secularization of European politics. What of socio-
moral attitudes? Gallup's evidence on US attitudes to abortion over
twenty-five years is clear and consistent. Two-thirds of the very
religious respondents think abortion should be legal in few circumstances or not at all – 'exactly the same as the percentage of non-
religious Americans who think abortion should be legal in all or
most cases'.[67] Europeans are less divided. Bernadette Hayes looked
at predictors of attitudes towards homosexuals in public life, Aids
victims, artificial insemination and pornography. At first sight, the
study suggests a strong religious influence: on all issues people
who disclaimed any religious identity were markedly more likely
than the religious to profess liberal views.[68] However, the relationship disappeared when she controlled for other characteristics.
Much more of the difference in attitudes was explained by the

age, the political partisanship and the levels of education than by the religion of the respondents.

Our analysis of the Scottish Social Attitudes data suggests the same conclusion. Most Scots are liberal on most issues. Religion does remain an influence: members of conservative Protestant sects are anti-homosexual, most churchgoers believe adultery is wrong under every circumstance and older Catholics are firmly opposed to abortion. But for most people and most issues, age, class and education are a stronger influence than religion.

Conclusion

Religion might inform political preferences in three areas: the privileges of churches, left–right divisions and moral issues. In retrospect we can see that, read in that order, the three fairly well describe a common pattern of mutation and secularization. In the nineteenth and early twentieth centuries, in the early days of mass voting, religion was itself a political issue. The expansive modern state and the weakening church had to come to terms with each other and societies had to decide just what privileges they would accord the common religion (as in France and Spain) or how they would balance the claims of competing religions (as in Britain and Holland). Those arguments were mostly settled before the First World War. The inter-war years were dominated by the ideological clash of left and right, and that continued to be the dominant association with religion in the world post-1945: the devout, the pious and the religiously observant voted to the right while the nominal church members and the irreligious voted to the left. That too faded away, partly because the convergence of parties on a common centre ground removed the extremes from politics. In some countries we can still identify a denominational difference on left–right issues such as the role of the state in managing the economy, but it is small. The major difference now is not between the adherents of competing religions but between the religious and the non-religious and it rests on socio-moral issues. Hayes uses survey data from the early 1990s to compare the political attitudes of respondents from the USA, the UK, Norway, Holland, Italy, and East and West Germany. She found that, even after controlling for gender, age, marital status and education, there was still a clear independent effect on attitudes of religion.[69] Those respondents who declared they had 'no religion' were more liberal than either

Protestants or Catholics. But, the USA aside, these are small differences and they tend to be concentrated on one or two particularly contentious items of personal morality such as abortion and euthanasia.[70]

A useful point on which to conclude this chapter is with some consideration of why socio-moral issues do not have a major impact on European politics. In the final section of the next chapter I will consider the unique vulnerability of US politics to well-organized pressure groups. Here I will just note that the electoral systems of most liberal democracies do not encourage the politicization of moral issues. Polities that use some version of proportional representation in their voting systems allow small parties to survive and hence permit a degree of particularism, but even in such systems there is a strong tendency for parties to seek the widest possible support. Hence they concentrate on what are irreducibly the main concerns of the state: defence, foreign policy, management of the economy, and law and order. They try to avoid becoming associated with specific issues that may alienate as many voters as they attract. The major parties that have the greatest role in setting agendas generally have little interest in striking a clear position on abortion, homosexuality, euthanasia and the like.

Second there is the position of religion itself. Most liberal democracies regard religion as a private matter. The way to reconcile individual liberty and religious diversity (even in the form of a divide between those who adhere to the traditional religion and those who do not) is to create a religiously neutral public sphere while protecting the rights of individuals to pursue their religions in private. From that follows a distinct reluctance for political parties to strike postures on what may be seen as private matters. In the British legislature, where parties normally exert almost complete control over the voting of their members, on the rare occasions that 'matters of conscience' such as the death penalty or abortion are forced on to the agenda, the parties permit a free vote – a recognition that matters religious or spiritual should not be treated as the stuff of party politics.

5

PROTEST

Introduction

It is a mark of our secular age that we tend to be cynical about those who claim religious motives. Especially when they are engaged in political campaigns, we readily suppose that what really motivate people are the material benefits that political power can deliver. In this chapter I want to consider four very different examples of groups of people engaging in protest politics, not because they stand to gain, but because they believe that wrongs should be righted. We can, if we wish, maintain our cynicism by insisting that what really drives our pious protestors is the boost to their self-esteem of seeing others accept their values. It is thus not the status of certain values that is at issue: it is the status of those who promote them.[1] There is always an element of truth in such claims. Even the most saintly and self-effacing campaigner will derive some personal satisfaction from the success of the crusade. Shaftesbury, of whom more shortly, wrote in his diary in 1842: 'I am beginning to be a little anxious. I wonder now whether I am so for myself, or on behalf of the cause. I know full well that there is in all these things a leaven of personality.'[2] However, it seems clear that those whose actions we consider in this chapter were primarily driven by a cause. Most could have enjoyed greater social approval and worldly success had they not committed themselves to protests and reform campaigns that risked them being ostracized for fanaticism. And, even if their sense of self-worth became entwined with the campaigns they promoted, such campaigns were still importantly different from much politics. Trade unions, for example, exist to create or acquire power that will improve the working conditions and rewards of their members. Religiously inspired moral pressure groups exist to promote the status of a particular set of values, and the campaigns they pursue are generally for the benefit of some other group of people.

I intend to consider four religiously inspired movements. All are similar in being led by Christian clergy and religious virtuosi. The first three have in common that, while their inspiration was religious, their goals were primarily secular. I will briefly describe the English campaign for social reform led by evangelicals in the late eighteenth and early nineteenth centuries, the US civil-rights movement of the late 1950s and early 1960s and Catholic clergy opposition to military dictatorships in Latin America in the 1970s. I will then draw from these a number of general observations about the value of religion for the pursuit of secular goals. In the second half of the chapter I will consider the New Christian Right in the USA. Although it draws on the same religious heritage as the first three, it is in some senses their opposite. Although it often uses secular language to promote its goals (a profound sign of the extent of secularization in the West), it is narrowly religious in intention. After describing the movement, I make some general observations about the limits that modern democracies place on religious particularism.

Taming industry

In 1780, when the 21-year-old William Wilberforce was elected to Parliament for the city of Hull, Britain was the world's first industrial economy and first urban nation. That, a century later, it was also a relatively civilized country owes more than somewhat to the reforming efforts of evangelical Christians such as Wilberforce and his colleagues in what was known (to friends and enemies alike) as the 'Clapham Sect', after the London suburb where they clustered.

The Clapham Sect and their country friends were evangelicals first and reformers second. Their main interest was in winning souls for Christ. What made them reformers was the appreciation that Britain had a submerged and unchurched population whose social conditions prevented them attending to their souls.[3] Their preferred weapon in the war against evil was personal philanthropy, which they held to benefit the giver as much as the receiver.

Especially for gentlewomen, who were excluded from manufacture, trade, government and politics, good works provided an excellent and improving occupation. Evangelicals gave large amounts of money and time to voluntary activity. Dr Barnado founded a network of children's homes. The Quaker Elizabeth Fry led in penal reform and prison visiting. Octavia Hill and George Peasbody promoted improvements in working-class housing. Hannah More pioneered free schools for the poor in the rural Mendips. Anthony Ashley (Earl of Shaftesbury from 1851) campaigned on behalf of the climbing boys who were used to sweep out the vast chimneys of London's Georgian houses, shoe blacks, crossing sweepers, factory children and those in the mines. He inspected sewers and cottages, attended parliament, chaired meetings and committees, supported philanthropic societies of all kinds, and personally wrote hundreds of letters seeking support for his reforms. He helped found the Ragged School Union in 1843. By 1867 it had 226 Sunday Schools, 204 weekday schools and 207 evening schools in London alone, with a total attendance of 26,000 children who without this intervention would not have received any sort of education.[4]

I will return to this point in discussing the zealotry of the fundamentalists in US politics, but it is worth stressing the link between motive, social pressure and effort. Secular reformers may work exceedingly hard, but those driven by religious concerns have a special impetus. Some may have held that God would not be so harsh as to send to hell those people who, strictly speaking, had heard the Word but whose lives were so miserable they could hardly be faulted for not paying much attention. More believed that those who died unsaved were doomed. If social improvement could save souls, then it was the Christian's highest duty to get on with it. And the resolve of any one individual was stiffened by the encouragement and example of his or her fellows. What we now call 'compassion fatigue' was regularly cured by a firm reminder of the Christian's first calling.

The evangelicals did not stop at philanthropy. They recognized that the scale of the problems of the poor were beyond individual amelioration and that efforts to persuade individual industrialists to change their ways had to be accompanied by legislation to tame those who would not voluntarily do what was right. Shaftesbury was particularly concerned about the morals of ragged children. In a speech to Parliament arguing for the regulation of the use of women and children in pits, he gave a graphic portrait of the complete absence of basic decencies: 'The girls are of all ages, from 7 to 21. They commonly work quite naked to the waist, and are dressed – as far as they are dressed at all – in a loose pair of trousers. These are seldom whole on either sex. In many of the collieries the adult colliers, whom these girls serve, work perfectly naked.'[5] Clearly those mine owners who permitted such conditions were beyond persuasion. Hence the need for legislation. And Parliament should act because, so long as it did not, then its members were responsible for permitting such a state to continue.

Although they were at heart neither rationalists nor democrats, their method of campaigning relied on the gathering of facts, the presentation of evidence and the creation of 'public opinion', often demonstrated with petitions, which could be presented to Parliament as the grounds for action. The evangelicals investigated, they surveyed, they interviewed. Their commissions of inquiry wrote detailed factual reports on the prevalence of this or that vice. Once they had proved the severity of the problem, they arranged for displays of public sentiment that would shame the government into correcting the problem.

It is now common to question the motives and effectiveness of Christian reform. Ford K. Brown said of Britain's early nineteenth-century evangelicals: 'There were societies to improve, to enforce, to reform, to benefit, to relieve, to educate, to reclaim, to encourage, to propagate, to maintain, to promote, to provide for, to support, to effect, to better, to civilize, to visit, to pressure, to mitigate, to abolish, to investigate, to publish, to aid, to extinguish. Above all there were societies to suppress.'[6] He conveys perfectly the scale of the reforming milieu and, by noting the frequency with which the reformers placed verbs in the titles of their organizations, gives some sense of their enormous energy. But the final sentence is unfair in the implication (made explicit in later Marxist and Fou-cault-inspired critiques) that what really motivated the evangelicals was the desire to stamp their own middle-class morality and sense of puritanical social order on an otherwise cheerful and liberated working class. Let us not forget that the greatest triumph was the ending of the slave trade – presumably something that Brown was happy to see suppressed. If we wish to present the regime of the modern factory as some sort of punitive discipline, we should recall what factories were like before Sir Robert Peel's factory acts. It is true that the evangelicals wished to domesticate working-class leisure activities, but it is also true that the extraordinarily high levels of gin consumption in Britain's slums were a serious threat to health and a major obstacle to improving standards of living. If we are now unimpressed by the efforts that Quakers put into making

tea and beer cheaply available, it is only because we do not appreciate the social harm that was caused by gin palaces.

It is also worth recalling that the reformers were strenuously
opposed in many quarters. Hannah More's educational goals
were not set high. She saw no point in falsely raising expectations
and educated her children to be pious and honest servants and
skilled farm workers. But, as her distant relative the novelist
E. M. Forster concluded: 'As to her work, it was good if education
is good. She taught the poor to read and wash, observe Sunday and
honour the King, and before her day no one taught them anything.'[7] For her pains she was accused of 'French' sympathies and
even of Methodism and was regularly criticized by such Tory
organs as the *Anti-Jacobin Review*.

By the 1870s evangelical reform was dead. Increasingly prosperity had removed much of its purpose. The living standards of most
Britons had improved enough to lift them above the degradation
that had moved the evangelicals. The success of reform was itself a
cause of its demise. The worst social vices that had inspired the
movement were removed. Slavery was ended. Where in 1780 there
were more gin shops than churches in London, by 1870 the ratio
was reversed. Small boys were no longer forced up chimneys. But
the evangelical reform movement was ended mainly by the extension of the franchise and the success of organized labour. For all
their sincere desire to improve the conditions of the poor, the
evangelicals were not democrats. They pursued secular improvement for a religious purpose on behalf of their clients. Once those
clients were able to determine their own desires and to pursue their
secular interests as they themselves defined them, pious philanthropy became redundant.

Promoting equality

For the next example of a religiously inspired movement to remedy
a major defect in social arrangements, we move forward more than
a century to the southern United States and the struggle for black
civil rights. In theory the subordinate status of blacks had been
ended with the victory of the Union states over the Confederacy
in the Civil War of 1861–5. The ending of the legal institution of
slavery left blacks formally free but in reality still enslaved. Drained
of their resolve by the Civil War, northerners allowed the former
Confederate states to deny blacks the right to vote, to deny them the

protection of the law, to segregate them and to provide them with only the most rudimentary public services. Slavery was replaced by 'Jim Crow'. The Jim Crow laws were named after a character in a pre-Civil War minstrel show. Thomas Dartmouth Rice, a white actor, became famous for 'blacking up', mimicking black vaudeville artists and performing a comic song-and-dance routine in which he repeatedly sang: 'Weel about and turn about and do jis so | Eb'ry time I weel about I jump Jim Crow.'

The Jim Crow laws were designed to achieve in the new urban setting the degree of segregation and subservience that informal pressures and patterns of interaction had previously maintained in the rural South. The following gives some idea of their range and purpose. In Alabama white nurses could not be asked to nurse black men; buses, toilets and restaurants were segregated; inter-racial pool and billiards games were prohibited; mixed-race marriages were void. Georgia segregated public parks, restaurants, burial grounds, barber shops and mental hospitals and required that segregated baseball grounds be two blocks apart. Mississippi not only banned inter-racial marriage but also made it an offence to print, publish or circulate arguments in favour of such mixing. And in all the southern states complex laws were used to make it difficult (if not downright impossible) for blacks to register to vote.

The courts had started to chip away at Jim Crow laws in the first part of the twentieth century, but it was direct action by southern blacks that brought legally enforced white supremacy to an end. The most influential of the early protests was the Montgomery bus boycott. On Thursday, 1 December 1955, Rosa Parks, a seamstress and member of the National Association for the Advancement of Colored People (NAACP), refused to give up her seat to a white man. She was arrested. A group of black clergy and civil rights activists called for a boycott of the buses. The boycott lasted for just over a year and ended only after the Supreme Court had ruled bus segregation illegal.

The small group of black church leaders who led the protest were at first reluctant to go beyond a token one-day boycott. E. D. Nixon, an activist in the Brotherhood of Sleeping Car Porters and a local leader of the NAACP, challenged their timidity:

> What's the matter with you people? Here you have been living off the sweat of these washerwomen all these years and you have never done anything for them. Now you have a chance to pay them back and you're too damned scared to stand on your feet and be counted!

The time has come when you men is going to have to learn to be grown men or scared boys.[8]

But once energized the black clergy provided the spine for the movement. They were unusually well placed to do so because they did not depend for their incomes on white custom or employment. Their churches provided sanctuary from white violence and meeting places where campaigns could be planned. And 'the black church supplied the civil rights movement with a collective enthusiasm generated through a rich culture consisting of songs, testimonies, oratory, and prayers that spoke directly to the needs of an oppressed group'.[9]

The main resource that the clergy could mobilize was ideological: their right to speak for Christian values. In explaining why the name 'Southern Christian Leadership' was chosen, one of the founders, Revd T. J. Jemison, made a pointed contrast with the NAACP, which had been outlawed across the South.

> Since the NAACP was like waving a red flag in front of some Southern whites, we decided we needed an organization that would do the same thing and yet be called a Christian organization. We said Southern Christian Leadership Conference so they would say, well, that's Baptist preachers so they don't fear us, but they didn't bother us.... The Negro minister only lost his place in the sun with whites when he started leading boycotts, and trying to tear down their social structure.[10]

Most prominent among those Negro ministers was Martin Luther King Jr. For those who are inclined to underestimate the power of religion, it is worth noting King's Christian names. King's father was a prominent Atlanta preacher and he named his son, as he had been named, after the leader of the Reformation.

The protests were intended to threaten. The point of large rallies is that they are large. Well-off southern whites would frequently meet Negroes, but usually only one at a time: the doorman, the nanny, the gardener. Without doing anything else, simply by gathering together in huge numbers, blacks were able to convey the potential for forced change. The concerted action of large numbers of weak people can be powerful: the boycotts seriously damaged the bus companies. And it was this economic power, not the potential for violence, that was displayed in the civil rights demonstrations. There were arguments within the movement; radical groups pressed for more damaging confrontations. But the clergy leadership and the women were determined to keep the protests peaceful. This reflected their own Christian values but it also reflected a keen awareness of the propaganda value of showing their oppressors to be bullies.

The social scientist who wishes to privilege social structure over culture could argue that the economic power of southern blacks would have been sufficient to produce civil rights and that religion was irrelevant in the pursuit of what were essentially secular rights. Given that the past is past we cannot fully refute that argument, but, in the absence of evidence to do otherwise, it seems reasonable to suppose that the persuasive work of the clergy was effective. As well as sustaining the morale of black activists and the common people whose refusal to be humiliated broke the back of segregation, the black clergy were able to call on the common value system to shame those whites who would not concede the need for change.

The Revd Bob Marsh is a poignant example of a white minister who was reluctant to recognize the merits of the civil rights case. He was the Baptist pastor of Laurel, Mississippi, a Klan stronghold and the home of Sam Bowers, the Klan boss convicted of the murder of three civil rights workers. Marsh's biographer son admits that, though the family regularly ate in the same diner as Bowers, the Klan and the Bowers trial were never discussed in the house. When a local black minister's home was bombed, Marsh joined other clergymen in a statement condemning violence, but beyond that he did little. His integration into the racist white community was pointedly exposed in early 1968, when he presented a Junior Chamber of Commerce Man of the Year award to local man Clifford Wilson. Shortly after hearing the Baptist preacher list his civic virtues, Wilson was arrested. He was one of Bowers's Klansmen who in 1966 had firebombed the home of an NAACP worker who had subsequently died of his injuries. His son reports that Marsh was severely disturbed by the discovery that his upright citizen was actually a race killer. His attempt to apologize to a black minister resulted in him being told he was a cowardly hypocrite. 'My father lost his nerve. He despaired, broke down.'[11] Humiliated he might have been, but Bob Marsh did not become active in the civil rights movement. Very few white clergy in the South did.[12]

But the civil rights activists were playing to a wider audience and they mobilized considerable support from white Christian organizations outside the South. The Quakers were especially active. The American Friends Service Committee encouraged Martin Luther King in his non-violent protests. In 1959 the committee arranged for him to tour various sites in India closely associated with Mahatma Gandhi's legacy and later nominated him for the Nobel Peace Prize, which was awarded in 1964. When King was imprisoned in Alabama in 1963, the committee arranged to publish King's 'Letter from Birmingham Jail'. This was an impassioned address to eight leading white Birmingham clergymen who had expressed some sympathy with the civil rights cause but condemned King's protest tactics. In the summer of 1964, the National Council of Churches (NCC), the federal coordinating organization for liberal and mainstream churches, spearheaded white church support for civil rights campaigns in Mississippi. The NCC recruited some 300 ministers from all over the United States to go to Mississippi to aid some 800 white college students who were engaged in a variety of local campaigns aimed at raising black political consciousness. The ministers joined civil rights workers as they 'picketed at courthouses, searched out potential registrants, taught in freedom schools and served as librarians and receptionists in freedom centres. As a result they, like the local people, were physically and emotionally intimidated'.[13] One group of clergy that were particularly prominent relative to their denomination's size were the liberal Unitarian-Universalists. In March 1965 a young black man Jimmy Lee Jackson was murdered while taking part in a voter registration drive in Selma, Alabama. Dr King called on the clergy of America to help protect the activists. On their first night in Selma, three Unitarian clergy were badly beaten by white racists and Revd James Reeb died of his injuries.

As with the British evangelicals, the final element of success was the translation of public protest into legislation. President Lyndon B. Johnson, a Texan initially selected by John F. Kennedy as his running mate to balance the appeal of a northern Catholic, was able to use his formidable political skills and his personal relationship with leading southern politicians to force the sweeping Civil Rights Act of 1964 (which outlawed discrimination in all public accommodation) through the Congress. He followed it the next year with the Voting Rights Act, which used the power of the federal state to enfranchise blacks.

Resisting state terror

The case of the Catholic Church in Latin America well illustrates the point that major religious traditions can be associated with a wide variety of political positions. Having enjoyed an unrivalled position in most Central and South American countries for centuries, the Catholic Church was deeply embedded in the social and political order. As happened earlier in revolutionary France, its position was periodically challenged in the nineteenth century by a variety of national independence movements, such as that led by Simón Bolívar in what is now Colombia, Venezuela and Ecuador. But it survived those upheavals and was often intimately involved in the various forms of right-wing dictatorships that ruled the states of Central and South America for most of the twentieth century.

> For over three hundred years following the [Spanish] conquest its fatalistic and highly spiritualized form of Christianity played an effective part in maintaining the semi-feudal structures of the old colonial order. It became locked in a symbiotic relationship with the civil authorities who granted it status, wealth and influence, particularly through the education system, in return for the church's unequivocal support.[14]

The behaviour of the Catholic hierarchy in Nicaragua is indicative. Bishop Canuto Reyes y Balladres blessed the weapons of US marines before they went into battle against the leftist guerrilla forces led by Augusto Sandino (hence 'Sandinistas'). Four bishops issued a pastoral letter calling on the guerrillas to 'abandon sterile armed struggles, return to the life of home and work and to the fulfilment of religious duties'. In 1942 Archbishop Lezcano crowned the daughter of dictator Anastasio Somoza 'Queen of the Army' with a crown borrowed from the statue of the Virgin Mary at Candelaria. Even more remarkable, when the second dictator, Somoza Garcia, was murdered in 1956, Archbishop González offered 200 days' indulgence to those Catholics who assisted with prayers for the departed dictator. However, by 1979 the attitude of the Catholic Church in Nicaragua had shifted sufficiently for the ousting of the Somoza regime to be accepted.

The previous two decades had seen Latin American politics become increasingly polarized. Half the states already had military dictatorships; the other half acquired them. Opposition became increasing radical. Inspired by the example of African liberation struggles, many left-wing movements launched guerrilla campaigns. A number of priests and Catholic intellectuals argued that the Christian had an obligation to support the poor and that, in the circumstances of Latin America, the traditional Catholic option of charity was insufficient. Camillo Torres, a former chaplain at the National University in Bogotá, joined a Marxist guerrilla group in

1966 and was killed in action by the Colombian military. In the subsequent debates about the propriety of his actions, the Conference of Latin American Bishops argued that the church should give 'effective preference to the poorest and most needy sectors'. This marked a considerable shift in the position of the institutional church. It was one thing to be a major player in a patrimonial oligarchy: as I explained in the previous chapter, the Catholic Church has long preferred deals between corporations to liberal democracy. In Brazil, for example, the Church was party to the 1930 dissolution of the Brazilian republic and the concentration of power in an authoritarian presidency. But the military regimes of the 1960s and 1970s went beyond the authoritarianism of most church leaders. They used paramilitary murder squads to 'disappear' their opponents. They tortured dissidents. They laid waste regions where guerrillas had some popular following. They gave the children of their murder victims to military personnel to raise as their own.

Peruvian priest Gustavo Gutiérrez published *A Theology of Liberation* in 1971, thus coining the expression 'liberation theology'. He argued that the economic underdevelopment and hence distress of Latin America was caused by capitalism and in particular the financial interests of US corporations. Christians were obliged to engage in class struggle in order to bring down capitalism and replace it with the social ownership of the means of production. The practical aspect of liberation theology was the establishment of 'base communities'. Rather than having a Bolshevik party that seizes power 'on behalf of' the proletariat, the radical priests brought the poor together so that they could, via Christian ideas, appreciate that they were oppressed.

Liberation theology became increasingly popular in the mid-1970s when military coups in Chile and Uruguay made the critique of US capitalism and foreign policy seem all the more relevant. Priests were active in the Sandinista movement that overthrew the Somoza dictatorship in Nicaragua. Two of them, Ferdinand Cardenal and Miguel D'Escoto, served as ministers in the first Sandinista government. In El Salvador the left wing of the Christian Democratic Party joined the Democratic Revolutionary Front, which in turn allied itself with the Faribundo Martí National Liberation Front, which began a guerrilla war in 1980.

In the 1980s the Vatican and the local church hierarchies began to rein in the movement. Concern for the poor was acceptable; Marxism was not. Base communities were fine; a radical alternative to the institutional church was unacceptable. The social conditions for liberation theology were also being eroded. The increasingly obvious failure of Communist regimes in Eastern Europe and of revolutionary movements in Africa and Latin America made Marxism increasingly unattractive. When put to the test of an election, the Sandinistas lost power in Nicaragua. Gradually the unsavoury dictatorships were replaced by elected bourgeois governments, and, after a decade of state terror, bourgeois free market capitalism no longer looked as bad as it had in 1968. Liberation theology lost its Marxist elements but retained its core message: that the Christian Church had to be on the side of the poor.

Senior churchmen were not naturally sympathetic to liberation theology, but circumstances could alter their views. El Salvadoran Archbishop Oscar Romero was appointed because it was thought he could reconcile the conservative and radical elements in the Church. However, the murder of his close friend Father Rutillo Grande by paramilitary death squads turned him into a vocal critic of the state. As a gesture of support for Grande's radical views, Romero refused to appear in public with any members of the army or government – a considerable snub in a country were even the torturers thought of themselves as good Catholics. His public campaign for human rights led to him being nominated for the Nobel Peace Prize and being shot dead by the state's assassins.[15]

In the absence of effective parliamentary opposition and the suppression of almost every opportunity to criticize the state, many church leaders (as they did in Africa) courageously took on the role of opposition. In the 1970s the Nicaraguan bishops issued a series of condemnations of government actions. Archbishop Obando memorably used a mass held to remember the victims of the Managua earthquake to criticize the regime. The President walked out and the National Guardsmen cut dead the sound equipment.

In the cases of Britain's evangelical reformers and the civil rights activists, the only internal check on the movement was the individual participants' own and shared sense of what was required or appropriate. The Catholic Church's ability to act as a vehicle for popular protest in Latin America was constrained by a characteristic of the Church itself: its preference for being, in the terms used by Max Weber and Ernst Troeltsch, a 'church' rather than a 'sect'. The Catholic Church sees itself as serving an entire people. Hence it was reluctant to take sides so completely that it would lose a large portion of the population. 'A preferential option for the poor' was one thing. Excommunicating the upper-middle-class groups, reactionary Catholics and military officers who enthusiastically

supported the right was another.[16] The Church was willing to snub
state officials and publicly to criticize regime faults, but it was not
willing to turn itself into a small sect. It was also not willing to split.
Liberation theology might have been very popular with young
Catholics in the United States and Europe. It was never accepted
by a majority of the bishops in Latin America. Hence it had to be
curbed in the interests of institutional unity.

The value of religion for political protest

These three brief case studies suggest a number of general observations about the role of religion and religious officials in political
reform and protest movements. In each case the goals were primarily secular: to tame industrialization, to end racial segregation, to
improve the lot of the poor and restore human rights. What difference did it make to have them promoted by religious people?

The moral high ground
Some people and institutions are impervious to criticism. Most are
not. Critics who can plausibly lay claim to the same ideology as
those they criticize begin with an advantage. Their interpretation of
the values or their application of them to any particular case can be
questioned but it is less easy to dismiss them entirely. In the three
examples just considered the regimes that had to be influenced
thought of themselves as Christian. To point out that they failed
to live up to their own standards was more effective than asserting
that some other body of standards was superior.

Naturally parts of the regimes in question tried to avoid being
put on the spot by denying their critics the right to the same value
territory. Hannah More's critics refused her claimed identity as a
loyal 'Church and King' conservative and tried to brand her a
subversive Methodist. The FBI tried to prove that Martin Luther
King was a communist. But the point remains: the critics would
have found a more receptive audience for such demonization if
More had been a Chartist or King had been a secular trade unionist.

After the military coup and murder of President Allende in Chile
in September 1973, Cardinal Silva set up an interdenominational
Committee for Peace to 'aid all families and persons affected by the
current situation'.[17] Mostly the committee's local branches assisted
the families of political prisoners and collated information about
torture and murder. Two years later General Pinochet forced the

committee to close down but, and this shows the power of the Church, when its functions were immediately taken over by another church-supported body, Pinochet did not close it also. Pinochet had removed Allende's government in order to protect Chile's Western and Christian values from Marxism. He could persecute the mass media and the universities but he could hardly crush the institution that embodies the ideals that he claimed motivated the coup.

Exemption

By claiming to stand above or outside mere politics, religious leaders are often able to find free social space for their criticisms of the regime when more secular forms of criticism are repressed. In July 1985, 150,000 people gathered in Velehrad, Czechoslovakia, to celebrate the 1,100th anniversary of St Methodius, one of the founders of the Christian Church in the East. The Czech Minister for Culture was spat on by a crowd that chanted 'Long Live John Paul II' and 'We want the Pope'.[18] Clearly most of the demonstrators were more interested in signalling their dissent from the Communist regime than their appreciation for church history. Equally clearly, had they been open about their primary purpose, such a demonstration would not have been permitted, even in the dog days of the Communist regime.

Even when the regime holds religion in high regard, religious leaders are not invulnerable. The state may outwardly tolerate their criticisms and either surreptitiously encourage others to do its dirty work or turn a blind eye when pro-state vigilantes take a hand. The Polish priest Jerzy Popieluszko, who had played a major part in founding the Solidarity free trade union, was murdered by two policemen in 1984. The killing of Archbishop Romero has been mentioned. But from the evidence it seems reasonable to conclude that the Ghanaian Christians who in a survey said they wanted their clergy to become involved in politics because critical clergy were safer than lay rebels were right.[19]

Drama

Even the most repressive regimes usually permit their critics to bury the dead. The funeral role of the clergy gives it enormous symbolic power. In 1987 the Catholic Church in South Korea (then a repressive oligarchy) used the Cathedral in the capital city Seoul to hold a memorial service for a young student who had died in police custody.[20] The government sent 3,000 riot police as its representative, which inadvertently but very publicly said all that needed to be said about the legitimacy of the regime. Every death of the civil rights movement was an opportunity for the clergy to denounce segregation and racism and for the laity to protest in the most dignified manner possible.

Honest brokers

Information plays a major part in many protest campaigns. With only a few exceptions, governments care enough about their reputations to seek to play down the evil they do. Hence a vital part of any protest is to collect and report information. In Brazil and Argentina and Nicaragua the surviving victims of state terror informed the local clergy, who collated details and then protested to senior authorities. They could perform this role because they were trusted to be discreet, to be honest, to be careful. Shaftesbury, with his interminable reports into this or that social vice, was regarded by many of his fellow parliamentarians as a nuisance but none doubted his honesty or sincerity.

The combination of high social status, a position above party politics and supposed personal integrity often leads to clergy being called on to perform vital but unusual roles. In the 1980s and early 1990s, when a number of African countries were trying to move from dictatorship to democracy, senior Catholic clergy were asked to preside over the transitional arrangements. The Archbishop of Cotonou played such a role in Benin, as did the Bishop of Oyem in Gabon. The Archbishop of Kisangani was asked to chair a 'national conference attempting to halt Zaire's decline into anarchy'.[21]

Networks

It is a sad but consistently observed fact of life that we find it easier to apply our high standards to others than to ourselves. Hence it is often outsiders, people somewhat removed, who initiate reform. Northern Yankees found it easier to oppose slavery than those who benefited directly from it. The London-based missionaries in southern Africa were more willing than the local Afrikaners to treat Africans as fellow human beings. For this reason a crucial feature of any protest or campaign for change is the publicizing of the problem outside its immediate area so that people and agencies that are not intimately involved can bring a more disinterested judgement to the matter. Shaftesbury's mine owners knew that they were employing children in vile conditions. His task was to bring those conditions to the attention of the widest possible audience so that the interests of the mine owners would be swamped by the opinions of the disinterested.

Church officials and religious virtuosi are often parts of national and international networks and they can use those to publicize their causes. Black clergy in Selma or Alabama were able to alert denominational colleagues elsewhere in the South. They could call on fellow ministers in other churches and in interdenominational organizations such as the National Council of Churches. Compared to the numbers of volunteers in the Student National Coordinating Committee (who bore the brunt of the racist violence), the white clergy numbers were trivial, but, because of their social status and their position as opinion-formers in their own communities, those ministers were vital in taking the civil rights movement out of the South and making it a national problem.

To summarize the above, even when it is directed to primarily secular goals, religion may have a powerful political effect because it can use its relatively privileged position 'to help keep alive a remnant of autonomy in civil society, to sustain the voice of resistance, and to prepare the grounds for a broader social-movement opposition once the authoritarian regime begins to crumble'.[22]

The New Christian Right

The first three examples concerned the role of religion in secular struggles. Their principles caused committed Christians to press for social reform, for racial equality and for social justice. That they shared a common religion with the people who obstructed those causes gave them an advantage over secular campaigners for the same goals. Church structures and ministerial leadership gave the pious protestors a head start, but they also benefited from being able to hold a mirror up to those whose behaviour they had to change. Of course, many people were never persuaded. Some industrialists and landlords never ceased to regard the God-botherers as dupes of the feckless poor. Many southerners never accepted that their treatment of blacks was unChristian. Many right-wingers remained convinced that radical priests were just communists in drag. Nevertheless, the reformers were able to use the common stock of Christianity to shame and embarrass enough people to accept their definition of what God required.

The New Christian Right (NCR) in the United States is different.[23] Although secular conservatives could support some parts of the NCR agenda, the programme as a whole appeals only to evangelical Protestants. Whereas the three previous examples can be seen as in some sense running with the tide, the NCR fights against its times. In an increasingly secular, tolerant, individualistic and permissive climate, the NCR campaigns for the return of a religious culture to the centre of public life.

The rise of the NCR

People are generally stimulated to protest by a conjunction of despair and hope: an intensification of what troubles them combines with some improvement in their circumstances to cause them to think action might be effective.

The positive roots of the NCR lie in the following. In the second half of the twentieth century the economy of the South (where conservative Protestantism was strongest) prospered while the North (with its heavy industry) declined. There was a shift of population. There was also a shift in political power. Since John F. Kennedy in 1960, every elected President has been from the South or the West. Lyndon B. Johnson was a Texan. Richard Nixon was from California. Jimmy Carter was from Georgia. Ronald Reagan was a Californian. Although a member of an old New England family, George Bush had his political base in Texas. Bill Clinton was Governor of Arkansas. George Bush Junior was Governor of Texas. Although it would be a mistake to say that the South had solved its race problem, the forced desegregation of the South had by the 1970s removed much of the stigma and made it clear that racial discrimination was not confined to the old Confederate states.

Within the sphere of religion, power had also shifted decisively to the conservative wing of Protestantism, which had been growing relative to the mainstream, especially in the 1960s. The separatist institutions established by fundamentalists in the 1920s and 1930s were bearing fruit. In particular, conservatives had made much better use than did liberals of the new technologies of radio and television to create audience networks of committed supporters of their distinctive religion and social mores. They had also mastered the organizational virtuous circle. On air they solicited donations and offered free gifts to people who phoned in. From those contacts they built computerized mailing lists that could be used to solicit funds to buy more airtime to appeal for more funds and so on. It is not easy to estimate the 'televangelism' audience, but Hadden and Swann suggest that in 1980 some twenty million people watched the top sixty-six syndicated religious TV programmes and that the top ten shows attracted fifteen million viewers (just under 7 per cent of the population) – a considerable reach by any standards and a powerful antidote to the sense of cultural inferiority that had plagued conservative Protestants since the 1920s.[24]

The negative forces can be grouped under two headings. Fundamentalists were provoked into campaigning by cultural and social forces that reminded them of their increasing marginality: black consciousness, feminism, gay rights, the anti-Vietnam War movement, the hippies, recreational drug use, mass-media portrayals of sexuality, abortion and the acceptability of divorce. All that would have been bad enough but it came with a series of changes that threatened fundamentalist isolation. The federal state expanded and deepened its reach. Before 1960 there were twenty-seven federal regulatory agencies; by 1976 there were a further fifty.[25] The federal courts imposed the will of the centre on the peripheries by, for example, ruling unconstitutional such locally accepted practices as beginning the school day with shared public prayers.[26] Local media outlets were assimilated into national networks. Local newspapers were increasingly filled by syndicated national copy. Small family firms were bought up by large corporations. And, most importantly, increased affluence made it possible for fundamentalists to join the cultural mainstream (by, for example, owning televisions and going to the movies) at a time when that culture was becoming thoroughly abhorrent.

What brought the NCR to life was the stimulus of a group of professional right-wing lobbyists who saw in the fundamentalist milieu the potential for a new right-wing movement based, not on the traditional concerns of low taxes and an assertive foreign policy, but on cultural concerns. They persuaded televangelists such as Jerry Falwell to use their television audiences and church networks to mobilize conservative Protestants in support of a series of single-issue campaigns. In the late 1970s a number of organizations such as the Moral Majority and Religious Roundtable promoted voter registration drives, raised money, targeted liberal candidates, ran advertising campaigns in support of moral conservatives, lobbied legislators, ran slates of candidates for school board and council elections, organized boycotts of media outlets that offended their values and in a variety of other ways sought to awaken a sleeping giant.

In addition to being generally right-wing on the economy, defence and foreign policy, the Christian Right was opposed to abortion, homosexuality and divorce. It was also opposed to schools teaching sex education and evolution. It was in favour of 'traditional' gender roles, public prayer in schools and the teaching of the biblical account of the divine creation of the world. It also wanted tax relief for independent 'faith' schools.

Evaluating the NCR

It is not easy to assess the impact of a diffuse movement that works on a variety of fronts, but I will summarize the impact of the NCR on the courts, on elections, on legislation and on the general cultural climate.

There are two reasons why much of the work of the NCR has been conducted through the courts: its concerns relate directly to the balance between individual freedom and social order, and the courts interpret the Constitution's references to religion. The NCR is thoroughly opposed to the notion of minority rights. It wishes to impose on the entire culture what it claims to be the views of the 'moral majority' and sees the rhetoric of minority (or in the case of women, majority) rights as a threat to its historical hegemony. Yet it is precisely when it has presented conservative Christians as a victimized minority that the NCR has had most success in the courts.[27] For example, in 1995 the Supreme Court found that the University of Virginia had been wrong to deny a Christian student group funding when non-religious groups had been funded. However, the oppressed minority appeal has worked only on very narrow ground. When a Tennessee court agreed with fundamentalist parents that their rights were infringed when their children were required to read books explaining objectionable beliefs, the Sixth Circuit Appeals Court overturned the verdict on the grounds that the lower court had not properly distinguished between knowing about something and being compelled or persuaded to embrace it. Parents could legitimately object to the latter but not to the former.

The argument that, if it was unconstitutional for the state to promote a religion, then it must also be unconstitutional for it to promote 'secular humanism', has failed. Fundamentalists initially won their claim that the Alabama State Board of Education had violated their rights by teaching their children non-Christian things. The Appeal Court overturned the judgment because it rejected the argument that all knowledge must be either Christian or secular humanist. It applied the narrower test of whether the textbooks at issue taught an identifiable philosophy of secular humanism and concluded that they did not. The courts also rejected the parity argument when they ruled that the requirement to teach divine creation was unconstitutional. The Arkansas legislature had passed an 'equal time' bill: if evolution was taught, equal time had to be given to what was now presented, not as the first twelve chapters of the Old Testament, but as 'creation science'. To establish that creation science deserved such support, its promoters had to convince the court that a non-Christian would find the special creation case as convincing as the secular alternatives. They failed to mount a coherent, let alone a persuasive, case.

The NCR has had little success in using the courts to promote its conservative socio-moral views. In one of the few decisions claimed as an NCR victory, the Supreme Court in 1986 held that the Due Process Clause of the Fourteenth Amendment to the Constitution (the basis for the general principle that the Bill of Rights applies not just to the federal government but also to state and local governments) did not protect homosexual sodomy. In so doing the Court explicitly returned the issue to the elected branches of government. There the tide has continued to run in a liberal direction, despite the NCR. As of June 2001 the anti-sodomy laws of twenty-six states had been repealed (and in eight of them the repeal came after NCR groups had started campaigning in 1978). Those of a further nine states had been struck down by the courts and in a further four court cases were pending. In the late 1980s the Supreme Court made three significant decisions on abortion, probably the NCR's most popular issue. First, it expressed unhappiness about the time-limit rules laid down in the original *Roe* v. *Wade* decision of 1973; advances in medicine had altered the life chances for premature babies. Second, the Court allowed the government to restrict public funding for abortions. Third, it permitted states to require that minors notify their parents before having abortions. However, despite having a conservative majority, the Court has very pointedly declined to outlaw abortion and it has protected the basic right to abortion where state laws have been too restrictive. Parental notification laws have been permitted only where there is a judicial 'bypass': a judge is able to waive the requirement if the minor is sufficiently mature or if telling a parent would not be in the girl's best interest. In 1997, by eight votes to one, the Court decided that a Louisiana attempt to weaken the judicial bypass was undue interference with a girl's abortion rights. In 1994, in response to violent blockades, the federal government passed the 'Freedom of Access to Clinic Entrances' Act, which allowed a picketed clinic to summon federal support. Twenty-five people appealed against a decision banning them from picketing outside a clinic. The original ban was upheld through every level of the courts and the Supreme Court refused even to hear the case.

Finally, a major part of the NCR's agenda is concerned with the public presence of Christian symbols. The NCR wants public support for acts of religious worship and for the symbols of its distinctive religious culture. Despite the appointment of five conservative justices by Ronald Reagan and his successor George Bush Senior, the Supreme Court has followed the precedents of the earlier courts in refusing to permit government support for such acts and symbols. Equally noticeable is that the lower federal courts, heavily packed with conservatives by Reagan and Bush, have proved little more sympathetic.

To summarize a large number of court cases: although the NCR was astute in presenting itself as a minority seeking only fair treatment, it actually gained very little by replacing the rhetoric of being a moral majority with that of being a persecuted minority.

As we can see from the cases that find their way to the Supreme Court, NCR organizations have succeeded in promoting bills through legislatures in areas with strong conservative traditions, but they made very little headway in Congress. They found no shortage of politicians happy to make sympathetic noises but few who would invest much political capital in promoting NCR causes. Ronald Reagan, for all his willingness to court fundamentalist voters, gave very little in return beyond such cheap gestures as declaring a 'Year of the Bible'. Even the 1994–6 Congress, with a Republican majority in both houses, failed to deliver much.

It is not easy to judge NCR impact on elections. Proponents of competing evaluations can readily list any number of contests from 1980 to 2002 to show that Christian Right support helped win or helped lose seats. On one side, we have spokesmen for the American Coalition for Traditional Values saying an Iowa conservative Republican lost his senate seat in 1984 to a liberal Democrat because he turned his back on the religious groups that had supposedly helped him win in 1978.[28] On the other side, we have reports that Virginia got its first black governor in 1990 because his white opponent was vocally anti-abortion until he discovered it was costing him the election.[29] Abortion is also thought to have delivered the Western Massachusetts seat to a Democrat for the first time in its history; the Republican was against it. Liberal Republicans blame the defeat of George Bush Senior in 1992 and Bob Dole in 1996 on the fundamentalist platform that NCR supporters foisted on the party. Movement conservatives argue that Bush and Dole lost because they showed insufficient commitment to that platform. But, whichever explanation of defeat one prefers, the fact to be explained remains defeat and not victory. In 2000, the Republican standard was carried not by Gary Bauer or Pat Buchanan or any of the other NCR favourites but by George Bush Junior, who chose to present himself as a moderate 'compassionate conservative'.

It is possible to be impressed by figures that Christian Coalition used to describe itself (and were disputed even by some insiders). In 1997 it claimed 1.9 million members, 125,000 participating churches and annual revenue exceeding $27 million.[30] But it is easier to be impressed by how little the coalition has achieved with all that money and support.

What the NCR has done best is to infiltrate the Republican Party.[31] Although Falwell and others initially promoted the movement as bipartisan, it was obviously more popular with Republicans than with Democrats, and during the 1980s many fundamentalists concentrated on taking over local branches of the party. But such entrism is of little value if the final product is rejected by the electorate as too extreme and too zealously focused on single issues. We might consider the case of the Virginia Republican Party in 1994. Virginia is a divided state. The majority of the state's population is found in the northern suburbs, which includes the fringes of Washington DC, where people are unusually affluent, socially liberal and have low levels of church involvement. But the state also has large concentrations of conservative Baptists and Methodists and is home to Falwell's Liberty University and Pat Robertson's Regent University and broadcasting empire. In the 1980s, Christian Right groups moved to infiltrate the Republican Party, something made relatively easy by the fact that party candidates are selected at a nominating convention, which, like the Iowa caucuses, gives the advantage to any group able to mobilize committed supporters. In 1994 the convention nominated as its candidate for the Senate Oliver North. North was a former Marine Corps officer who had gained notoriety for his part in the Reagan administration's covert and illegal operation to supply arms to the right-wing Contra forces in Nicaragua. North had spent years cultivating the Christian Right and the gun lobby and the support of those two groups of activists ensured him the nomination. Liberal Republican Senator John Warner was so horrified by his party's choice that he encouraged a more moderate Republican to run as an independent. Despite also being challenged by an independent, the incumbent Democrat Chuck Robb won an easy victory – one made all the more remarkable by two things. First, over the country as a whole there was a major swing to the Republicans. Second, Ollie North spent approximately $20 million (about four times Robb's budget) and

had the support of a vast army of conservative Christian volunteers.[32]

President Richard Nixon, with thirty years of winning and losing
elections, pointedly said that Republicans had to run to the right in
the primary and then to the centre in the general election.[33] NCR
activists in the party appear to have learnt only the first part of the
lesson. In many areas the effect of their zealotry was to shift the
party away from the middle ground that it needed to occupy if it
was to win major elections. The Republican Party led by George
Bush Junior appreciated that and in its first round of appointments
balanced a few NCR favourites with liberal republicans such as
Colin Powell, whose disdain for 'movement' conservatism is well
known.

The NCR can probably also claim much of the credit for a major
realignment in the US party system. One legacy of the Civil War is
the anomaly of conservative southern whites supporting the Democratic Party (or, to be more precise, rejecting the party of Abraham
Lincoln). Since the Reagan years, this constituency has been shifting
to its more natural home in the Republican Party. NCR organizations, recruiting from white fundamentalist churches strong in the
South and supporting Republican candidates in southern constituencies while denouncing liberal Democrats, have played a part in
that reorganization. It may be that, by tidying up the American
party system, the NCR has strengthened the right, but it is unlikely
that many people have changed their values or principles in the
process.

None of this is intended to deny the obvious point that, in small
political units where conservatives are numerous, the NCR can
achieve limited legislative and electoral success. However, as we
move up from the city and county to the congressional district and
the state to the federal government, we move to units of greater
cultural, social and political diversity and we see the potential for
such pressure groups as the NCR steadily diminished.

A good example of the 'small-victory – large-defeat' pattern can
be found in the battle over creationism in Kansas. Members of the
Kansas Board of Education have traditionally been elected on a
very small turnout. In 1999 the Board, dominated by fundamentalists, approved a science curriculum that made no mention of
Darwin or evolution. There was a public outcry, led by the presidents of the state's major universities and supported by editorials
in the *Washington Post* and *New York Times*. On a much higher
turnout, the fundamentalists were voted off the Board the
following year and evolution was put back on the curriculum.

One may argue, as Falwell and others have frequently done, that the NCR re-established the respectability of conservative socio-moral positions and the right of fundamentalists to be taken seriously. It is certainly the case that the 1980s saw considerable publicity given to NCR activists and their views. However, while such exposure ensures a vigorous debate, it guarantees to win that debate only if it is the case that the previous liberal hegemony was achieved by stealth. But it was not. We can take examples from a variety of levels of the political system to make the point. When the televangelist Pat Robertson ran for the Republican nomination, the early impact of his highly committed supporters brought out liberal Republicans in such numbers that, despite spending unprecedented sums, he failed to win a single primary.

Finally we can look at the big picture. How has the United States changed since the late 1970s with respect to NCR's moral agenda? The NCR is anti-homosexual, but homosexuals have not gone back into the closet. There are now openly gay congressmen and women and (an important sign of public acceptance) major US television channels air shows in which homosexuals are portrayed as normal people. The NCR is anti-abortion, but the abortion rate has declined only slightly from its peak in 1985: in 2000 it was 70 per cent higher than it was in 1972.[34] The NCR is anti-divorce. The divorce rate in 1940 among married women was 9 per cent. It rose to a high of 23 per cent in 1981 and then fell back slightly to 21 per cent in 1994. In 2000 the US Census Bureau estimated that at least 40 per cent of marriages would end in divorce. The NCR wants a return to traditional gender roles. Women made up 18 per cent of the US labour force in 1900, 30 per cent in 1950 and 46 per cent in 1997; no sign of any reverse there.[35]

To conclude this very brief review, the NCR began with a great many advantages. It had ready access to the mass media through the work of televangelists such as Falwell and Robertson. It had the mailing lists of televangelism organizations to reach its potential supporters. It was led by some extremely skilled self-publicists. It was able to make use of the excellent existing networks of conservative Protestant pastors. Nonetheless, it failed to achieve significant progress on items that were specific to its agenda (as distinct from ambitions, such as increased defence spending, which are shared with mainstream conservatives). It is always possible to argue that the NCR acted as a brake: that, without it, America would have become more liberal and permissive. But unfortunately claims for influence of this sort are untestable and have to remain in the realm of speculation. All we can do is look at the wish list, look at what was achieved and compare the two. The conclusion must be that the NCR failed to end abortion, curtail divorce, prevent mothers working, outlaw homosexuality, balance the teaching of evolution with that of creation science or restore the public primacy of conservative religion.

The advantages and disadvantages of zealotry

As political storm troopers, evangelical Protestants start with considerable advantages over secular activists. They are highly motivated. As we saw with the Clapham Sect and with the civil rights movement, they are used to giving large amounts of time, money and energy to promoting the gospel. If the cause is tinged with the millennialist expectation that we are in 'the end times' or that the return of the Messiah will be hastened by collective effort, religious zealots can deploy vast reservoirs of commitment. Once convinced that they could 'bring America back to God', the fundamentalists of the NCR brought to political campaigns the sort of effort they habitually gave to church work. Hence, where small numbers of highly committed people could swing an outcome, they had some success. For example, in his run for the Republican nomination for President in 1988, Pat Robertson won in the Iowa caucuses because that contest is decided by activists massing in a hall.

What is less often considered is that zealotry has corresponding disadvantages. The zealot divides the world into them and us, the godly and the ungodly: fine for mission or for holy war but not helpful for building the alliances that are essential for political action in a complex and pluralist democracy. First, while the NCR leaders could work with conservative Catholics, Jews and Muslims, many rank-and-file evangelicals could not sufficiently set aside their sectarian religion. An Ohio chapter of the Moral Majority memorably preceded a meeting to discuss working with conservative Catholics with a lecture on the evils of Roman Catholicism![36] Second, however much the zealots might have been willing to seek alliances, the groups they court have memories. The Catholic Church shares interests with the NCR (in the state funding for religious schools, for example, and on most socio-moral concerns), but Catholics can remember that fundamentalists used to be anti-Catholic. The black churches are conservative on moral issues but are only too well aware of the segregationist backgrounds of many older NCR supporters (such as Senators Helms and Thurmond) and are deeply suspicious of the economic liberalism of the NCR. Many Islamic groups would be at one with the NCR on gender roles, temperance and personal sexual behaviour but are excluded

by the Christian ethos of the movement and by its support for the
State of Israel. As, so it happens, are most Jews, because fundamentalists are only interested in Israel for the part they expect it to play
in hastening the Battle of Armageddon! And conservative Christians have a very long history of anti-Semitism.

Finally, many non-NCR conservatives are alienated by the 'deep'
message of the NCR. Skilled operators such as Falwell and Robertson try to confine their fundamentalist message to their core audience and speak more moderately to the wider public. But they often
fail. For example, in the aftermath of the 11 September atrocities,
Robertson on his *700 Club* show asked Falwell who was to blame.
To frequent approving 'amens' from Robertson, Falwell replied:

> throwing God out successfully with the help of the federal court
> system, throwing God out of the public square, out of the schools.
> The abortionists have got to bear some burden for this because God
> will not be mocked. The pagans and the abortionists and the femi-
> nists and the gays and lesbians; the ACLU [American Civil Liberties
> Union]; People for the American Way; all of them who have tried to
> secularize America, I point the finger in their face and say 'you
> helped this happen'.[37]

Non-fundamentalist conservatives are thus periodically reminded
of just how narrow is the NCR's core vision.

Zealots are poor at compromise. Indeed, they define themselves
against liberals by noting that liberals accept a division of the social
world into distinct spheres, each with its own values, while they,
the fundamentalists, insist on ideological consistency. The Pakistani Jama'at-I Islami was banned in 1948 because it argued that it
was wrong to swear allegiance to the Pakistan army as the new
state was not properly Islamic. In November 1986 the leadership,
aware that it was failing to recruit urban women, proposed small
changes in its view of what Islam required by way of dress code.
The majority of activists, drawn from small towns and rural areas,
refused to compromise.[38] More recently, the Jama'at-I-Islami struck
an extremely awkward position over Kashmir (the position of
which is contested by Pakistan, by India and by a Kashmiri independence movement). The Jama'at argued that, as Islam did not
permit lying, covert military operations were not acceptable. Hence
the Pakistani government had to honour its ceasefire with India
and stop supporting Kashmiri separatist groups. There was such a
hostile response, the position was quickly reversed. With some
creativity the Jama'at managed to argue that, although the govern-

ment was bound to honour its commitments, there was nothing to prevent pious Pakistani Muslims (even those who just happened to be serving soldiers) from *volunteering* to fight in Kashmir. In such ways do political necessities trip up the divinely inspired.

People driven by divine imperative are not good at trading losses in one area for gains in another. They are also not good at tolerating differences even within the camp of the faithful. The same energy that can drive an Elizabeth Fry to campaign tirelessly for a cause can also be turned inward, as fissiparousness and sectarianism.

There is also a problem with sustaining commitment. Zealots become quickly disillusioned. They are brought to politics by apocalyptic imagery that creates expectations of success every bit as unrealistic as the bogeymen that stir them to action. Hence they are ill-suited to the long haul. Religio-political mobilization thus tends to come in waves that are as short as they are intense.

Finally, there is a particular problem for religious zealots trying to win major elections in mature democracies. We see this most clearly in the United States, but it is also germane for many other polities. As politicians as diverse in ideology as Eisenhower, Kennedy, Carter, Reagan and Clinton have demonstrated, Americans do not like to elect politicians. They want to elect nice people. The key to success is to disguise ideology behind a front of almost apolitical easy-going affability. Zealots find this extremely difficult because they are not affable; they are driven obsessives. As a professional right-wing lobbyist put it to me: 'we need to look and sound like everyone's favourite uncle and instead we come across like a bunch of swivel-eyed obsessives.'

Structural advantages

Before we can draw any general lessons from the US experience, we need to note that the NCR has benefited considerably from unusual features of the US polity. There are two senses in which the NCR is a product of the open, diffuse and federal nature of the USA. First, conservative Christianity remains stronger in the United States than in any other modern industrial society, because fundamentalists have been able to construct their own subsocieties to sustain their distinctive subculture. To an extent not found in any European country, American fundamentalists are able to inhabit insulated worlds with independent Christian schools, colleges, universities and television and radio stations – worlds in which their culture is taken for granted and alternatives are seen only through the distorting prism of shared stereotypes.

Second, in the following ways, the structure of US politics allows interest groups easier entry into the political arena. In most European countries, political parties are powerful institutions that dominate the political process. The party chooses its candidates and determines its policy. Access to the mass media is free but allocated to parties not individual candidates. Spending on elections is constrained and it is paid by the parties, not the candidates. The party in power determines the legislative agenda and coerces its members to support it. The electorate recognizes the power of party by voting for parties rather than for individual legislators.

The major US parties are remarkably open. Candidates are selected locally and in diverse ways that allow small groups of activists to determine who shall represent the party. In many areas the candidate need not even be a member of the party. Hence the NCR has been able to impose its candidates on a reluctant Republican Party. With no effective cap on spending, elections can be extraordinarily expensive and candidates will need funds well beyond what the party can provide. Successful candidates will thus end up being as (if not more) beholden to special-interest groups as to their party, which makes party discipline very hard to maintain. In state legislatures and in both Houses of Congress, individual legislators are free to initiate legislation. It will not be passed unless it can command widespread support, but people can pay back debts to interest groups by promoting pet issues. The weakness of party in turn means that legislators cannot hide behind the party whip. How they vote on bills (no matter how frivolous) can be used against them at the next election. Hence the favoured NCR tactic of distributing the detailed voting records of liberals on rafts of bills that can (with varying degrees of plausibility) be construed as 'Pro-Family'. Party alignment is relevant in that there tend to be swings for and against that are based on perceptions of the effectiveness of the President but candidates can run with or against their own parties.

Ironically, the reforms to election funding that followed the scandals of the Watergate era strengthened interest groups. Although they capped the amount of money that could be spent on behalf of a particular candidate, the rules did not constrain how much could be spent on promoting general-issue positions.[39] So, rather than have individuals give money, say, to Senator Jesse Helms in North Carolina, NCR organizations could raise money to spend on advertising campaigns that promoted 'family values' in a way that made it very clear that anyone who shared those values should vote for Helms.

Many public offices that in Europe would be filled by appointment are in the United States filled by election. So there are many more elections and many of them attract very low turnouts. And major elected offices are for shorter terms than is common in Europe: congressmen and women have to face the electorate every two years. That candidates are judged more on personal record than the standing of their party gives a considerable advantage to the incumbent, who will ensure that powerful interests are well served. But the need to be personally popular encourages gesture politics and causes timidity. The Arkansas state legislature passed the pro-creation science bill because it did not involve spending taxes and there are no votes in voting against God.

In short, such success as the NCR has enjoyed owes a great deal to the structure of US politics.

Structural constraints

The NCR has failed to 'bring America back to God'. So, if the above description of opportunity structure combines with the earlier points about the advantages of zealotry to explain the successes of the NCR, what features of the opportunity structure combine with the disadvantages of zealotry to explain why, overall, it has made little headway?

The first point is simple: the Moral Majority was never a majority. As Rozell and Wilcox put it:

> The Christian Right represents 10 to 15 percent of the public, and its natural constituency among white evangelicals is an even larger segment. When this constituency is mobilized, it can swing close elections. Yet those who oppose the Christian Right are generally at least as numerous as those who support it, and if *they* are mobilized, the Christian Right usually loses.[40]

The NCR has formidable opponents. People for the American Way, for example, very effectively countered Pat Robertson's political ambitions by ensuring that what he said to his core religious audience in his role as televangelist was broadcast to the wider audience, to which he was pitching as an entrepreneur whose business just happened to be religion. Liberal pressure groups can outspend the NCR. In the 2000 elections, nearly $250 million dollars were spent on television advertising. Sixty per cent of that was spent by political parties; the rest came from special-interest groups and the ones that were not business related were the trade union organization AFL-CIO, Planned Parenthood (which promotes contraception and is pro-abortion), the League of Conservation Voters, Americans for Job Security and Emily's List, which raises money to promote women candidates.[41]

The presence of opponents is also significant in the sense that making personal morality a focus of political debate encourages others to look closely at the personal behaviour of those whose claim is to be especially virtuous. In the early 1990s the British Conservative Party under John Major ran a 'Back to Basics' campaign that stressed the Conservative commitment to fundamental values. The press took this as an invitation to examine the personal morality of leading Conservative politicians and enough of them were found to be personally corrupt thoroughly to embarrass the government. One of the most successful conservative US politicians of the 1980s, Newt Gingrich, was forced to resign from his position as Speaker of the House partly because his election strategy failed to deliver results but also because media interest in his income and his marriages threatened his claims to represent a particularly moral approach to politics. Minnesota Republican Jon Grunseth was building a strong candidacy for Congress on being pro-life and pro-family values until he was accused of sexual improprieties with teenage girls and a woman claimed to have been his mistress for nine years.[42]

While single-issue organizations are well placed to mobilize support, single-issue election candidates tend to do badly, because they are thought too narrow to be effective politicians. Even when the single issue in question is a popular one (abortion, for example), there are two obstacles to successful mobilization. The first is often overlooked when people use opinion poll data to show that this or that NCR agenda item is popular. Many people may indeed oppose abortion, but they might well accord that concern a low priority. The second obstacle is that the salience of some issue is not just a matter of how strongly people feel about it (relative to how strongly they may feel about other things). It is also a function of public agenda setting. Turning a popular sentiment into political power depends on the salience of that issue at the time when political choices are made and the NCR is not free to set public agendas. That lots of people share a position on abortion is of little use if abortion cannot be made the focus of an election. The relatively low priority that people give even to socio-moral issues about which they feel strongly is clearly illustrated by Bill Clinton's career. Despite massive negative campaigning by all the NCR organizations, he won two elections on the economy: the first because people thought he would be better than George Bush Senior at managing the economy, the second because the economy was booming. Despite Clinton's sexual and financial scandals, his approval ratings remained around 60 per cent. The 1998 elections marked the first time since 1934 that the party of the President made gains in the House in mid-term elections.[43]

One good reason for concentrating on single issues, of course, is that the single-issue movement falls apart when it strays beyond that which it has in common. In the 1930s two religious parties – Alexander Ratcliffe's Scottish Protestant League and John Cormack's Protestant Action – won seats on the local councils of Glasgow and Edinburgh on an anti-Catholic platform. But once in the council chambers the members repeatedly voted against each other because, anti-Catholicism apart, they had little in common with each other. And, as they could not determine the council agenda, the occasions on which their differences were exposed far outnumbered the times they were able to vote together. Once their inability to act successfully as a political party was exposed, both very quickly lost support. Scandinavia's Christian Democratic parties have divided over Europe.[44] Some see it as positive Christian ecumenism; others see it as a Romanist plot.[45] To put it simply, the religious party has an awkward choice: it can concentrate on the few issues that unite it (in which case it may be judged too narrow to be effective) or it can expand its agenda (in which case it risks losing what attracted its zealot core and becoming subsumed in the dominant secular conservative party).

But perhaps the greatest obstacle to the NCR has been the general reluctance of Americans to support theocracy. With varying degrees of consciousness, most Americans seem to appreciate the practical benefits of liberalism and toleration. Some have a conscious commitment to the separation of church and state; others just have a vague sense that preachers should not be telling people what they cannot do. Survey after survey has shown that most Americans distinguish between morality and law. As the Barna polling organization summarized a number of studies: 'Americans are comfortable legalizing activities – such as abortion, homosexuality, and pornography – that they feel are immoral.'[46] A 1990 review of a series of polls showed that, while three-quarters of Americans thought homosexuality immoral, a majority of those did not think that homosexual acts should be illegal.[47] A major survey sponsored by an organization in favour of greater religious influence on public life found that 58 per cent of the public thought it wrong for voters 'to seriously consider the religious affiliation of candidates'. When asked what they thought of faith-based charities receiving government funding for welfare programmes, 44 per cent were in favour, but a quarter of the sample thought it a good idea only if such programmes stayed away from religious messages. Nearly a third thought it a bad idea for the state to fund religious organizations for any purpose. Most telling were the responses to questions about public school prayers. Only 12 per cent of evangelicals thought that such prayers should be specifically Christian and 53 per cent of evangelicals (the same as for the general public) thought that a moment of shared silence was the best solution to the problem.[48]

Although the above point concerns social values, I have placed it in this section on structural constraints because it is the centripetal nature of US politics and public administration that brings this generally tolerant ethos to bear on the NCR. Although the federal structure of the USA allows far more autonomy for cities, counties and states than is common in most European countries, the USA is in the end a single state and its political structure forces the most important matters to be decided at the highest level. Any enthusiast may introduce a bill in the House of Representatives, but, to have any chance of becoming law, it must attract broad-based support. It must then pass the Senate, which, by giving two votes to every state irrespective of size, acts as a brake on regional and sectional interests. Because senators are elected by the entire state rather than by a small congressional district, they are likely to temper their preferences with thought for what most voters in the state will accept. Finally, bills have to be approved by the President, who answers to a national electorate, and they can get past his veto only with two-thirds support from Congress.

The court system is similarly centripetal. The NCR had some successes in the lower courts but then saw the victories overturned as the cases were appealed upwards. Judges always interpret the law with one eye to what they think the people want or need. Federal judges answer to a large 'imagined community' and the justices of the Supreme Court, which has the final say on most matters that concern the religiously motivated, make their judgments in the light of what they take to be the interests of America.[49]

The same general point holds true for elections and party politics; in local elections with small constituencies (such as party selection meetings) the NCR could do well but then see its preferred candidate defeated in a full primary or the full election: the examples of Pat Robertson and Ollie North have been mentioned.

What can easily be forgotten in using terms such as 'fundamentalist' to describe both Islamic Jihad in the Lebanon and Pat Robertson's Christian Coalition is that the religious zealots in the USA have accepted the essentially secular nature of public culture. They accept the rule of law. They attempt to gain their goals by conventional electoral, legislative and judicial action. They do not assert that the law of God trumps the laws of man. In arguing for their values, US fundamentalists accept secular principles. They do not tell the courts that abortion should be banned because it offends God; they argue that it infringes the basic universal human right to life. They do not campaign for public prayers in schools by asserting that such is God's will. Instead they use the language of human rights. In prosecuting the famous Scopes 'monkey trial' in Little Rock, Arkansas, William Jennings Bryan, the great populist politician of the 1920s, boldly asserted that it was better to know the Rock of Ages than to know the age of rocks. Modern creationists cannot be so dismissive; they must argue that 'Creation Science', as they now call it, fits the evidence every bit as well as the alternatives. NCR activists may privately oppose homosexuality and divorce because they think them sinful, but in promoting their views they have to argue that these vices are socially dysfunctional. Whether fundamentalists clothe their religiously inspired values in secular garb because they are genuinely committed to a separation of church and state or because they reluctantly accept that there is no alternative hardly matters. What matters is that two features of the United States place a powerful constraint on the realization in the public sphere of any distinctive religious culture: cultural diversity and egalitarianism.

Concluding thoughts on individualism

In his excellent *Culture Wars*, James Hunter is careful to point out that, behind the many specific arguments about school prayer, sex education, pornography in the arts and the like, there is a very general disagreement about the nature of authority. Though they may disagree on where it is located, conservatives share a common belief in the possibility of authoritative knowledge and guidance that transcends and constrains the individual. It may be a sacred text, a venerated tradition or the official teachings of an organization, but there is some source that allows one group of people to denounce another in what Islam calls 'Commanding what is good and forbidding what is bad'.

The problem for moral conservatives in the USA (as elsewhere) is that such certainty is being eroded. Despite being replenished by immigrants from more religiously traditional cultures, the proportion of the US population actively involved in religion is slowly declining. And within the church-, synagogue- and mosque-going population there is a visible shift from conservative, authoritarian and dogmatic faiths to increasingly individualistic and consumerist versions. Shibley documents this for new varieties of evangelicalism, which, he points out, are world affirming (rather than puritanical and ascetic), at ease with notions of individual freedom and place therapy and personal fulfilment ahead of dogma and doctrine.[50] Hunter noted a creeping relativism among the young evangelicals he studied in the 1980s.[51] Conservative Protestants are no longer as sure as their parents and grandparents that God requires the same things of all people. As the subsocieties that most strongly support fundamentalism have prospered, so their subcultures have softened. The assertive consumerism that Americans live out in other parts of their lives has come to influence religion. And, of course, the majority of Americans who are not zealous members of any religious community are even less willing to subordinate themselves to anyone else's definition of what constitutes the good life.

European observers are often struck by the apparent success of the NCR in building an influential political movement on a religiously inspired platform of socio-moral issues. In this section I have tried to draw attention to another lesson that can be drawn from the career of the NCR. Even in circumstances that are highly propitious – a very high proportion of the electorate committed to evangelical Protestantism and a remarkably open political structure – the NCR has failed in its primary purpose of reasserting the primacy of a religious culture. Understanding why it has failed is important, because it tells us a great deal about what, if we want to be formal, we can call *the functional prerequisites of a liberal democracy in a culturally diverse society with a basically egalitarian ethos*. Even many Americans who are personally committed to the religious culture that inspires the NCR appreciate that social harmony requires a division between what individuals desire and what it is right for the state to impose.

6

CONTROL

Introduction

The previous chapters were concerned with the influence of religion on regimes, nations, parties and movements. Now I want to reverse the direction of cause and consider how governments regulate religion. I will do so through three themes that correspond very roughly to time periods in the history of the Western world: obedience to God, loyalty to the community and conforming to the conventional. This simplifies enormously, but we can think of the general pattern of change since the Middle Ages as the relaxation of each of these imperatives in turn.

Most religions are not tolerant by choice. Believers have at least three good reasons to impose or maintain conformity. First, if the true God is not worshipped in the correct way, then he may punish the entire people: witness the changes in fortune of the Children of Israel in the Old Testament. Second, he will certainly punish the individual deviants. Hence, self-interest aside, true believers have a compelling desire to see their nearest and dearest also saved. Third, there is the more abstract point that our own confidence in our beliefs depends on the agreement of others. If we permit heresy, we also permit doubts to arise in our own minds. It is thus natural for a people to wish to maintain a consensus.

But that clutch of social, political and economic changes we call modernization generally weakens the ability and the impulse to enforce religious uniformity.[1] A regime may give up trying to promote obedience to the one true God beyond its boundaries but still insist that its people be uniform in religion – the position of most European states after the end of the Thirty Years War. The rise of nationalism strengthens the impetus to produce cultural uniformity. Pre-modern societies can operate with a degree of indifference to what the ordinary people think about religion because they are indifferent to ordinary people in every sense. Once political units start to think of themselves as 'fraternities', as communities of people who in some sense are of equal worth and who should all be united in loyalty to the nation, then it becomes vital that the common men and women develop a shared sense of belonging. What could be produced easily in the small tribe or clan must be engineered in the nation. Hence the nationwide systems of public education designed to produce a uniform culture and to create model citizens. Modern nation states often regard religious affiliation as an important element of social cohesion, allocate rights according to religion and, in return for the legitimation that the religious institution can offer, coerce conformity to its dictates.[2]

As we will see, the growth of religious diversity, the increase in the number of people who subscribe to no particular religion, and principles of liberal democracy together cause most Western states to scale back what is required of their citizens by way of shared identity. Ethnic nationalism, demanding common descent, language and religion, gives way to civic nationalism.[3] Most Western societies have given up vigorously promoting a national religion and have not collapsed in the process. The sphere of personal freedom has been massively extended without the anarchy so feared by political conservatives. The West's domination has been such that the rhetoric of individual human rights now prevails across almost the entire globe. Most states (and that includes those such as China that routinely infringe it) now assert the principle of religious freedom. Where the liberal democratic state is involved in policing religion, it is not because the theology of some novel religion is offensive but because the organization is construed as a threat to public order or individual rights. Modern states do not enforce orthodoxy but they do operate with a largely unexamined taken-for-granted notion of how people should be involved in 'normal' religion and hence they are mildly hostile to new religious movements that appear to infringe that consensus.

I should add that, in organizing this chapter around a rough periodization of Western evolution, I am not implying that other countries must change in similar ways. As we will see, the power of the rhetoric of human rights is such that a wide range of polities are now confronting the same problems and questions that faced the liberal democracies in the nineteenth century. This does not, however, mean that they will come to the same solutions.

Enforcing obedience to God

At our distance from such a climate it is hard to know what led people to coerce others to change religion. When the torturers of the Spanish Inquisition made a man assert faith in the Holy Catholic Church by pulling out his fingernails, did they believe that such professions represented a sincere change of heart? Or did they act more with an eye to the future: privately admitting that an allegiance produced by fear would probably not change God's view of the person recanting but hoping that to humiliate this generation of dissenters would discourage the next? Or were they thinking less of the souls of their victims and more of the pride of the faithful? If the parallel can be drawn, it certainly seems that much of the way we punish criminal offenders has less to do with their rehabilitation or even with deterrence and more to do with making the law-abiding feel better about themselves. We do know that in every age people have recognized that the essence of faith requires that it be embraced for the right reasons. Writing of the Ottoman period in Bulgaria, Maria Todorova tells the following story:

> One of the most famous episodes was when Sulyman the Magnificent went through the Maritsa Valley and whole villages of Christians came and made the sign they wanted to convert. He asked them: 'Why do you want to convert?' They answered 'Because we don't want to pay those taxes'. And he says: 'No, you're not going to do that because somebody has to be convinced in order to convert.'[4]

Taking the spread of Islam as a whole, such propriety must have been rare. People who came under its control were given three choices. They could convert and acquire the same rights as the Arab citizens. Or they could maintain their religion but lose their political, social and cultural rights. The Ottoman Empire required non-Muslims to pay a supplementary tax called *jizya*, supposedly in place of the military service that Muslims performed as a religious obligation. The Ottomans also 'taxed' the Balkan peoples of a small proportion of their boys and young men and raised them as Muslims. The third choice was to be put to the sword or expelled.

The Catholic Church, with its Roman and Spanish inquisitions of the sixteenth and seventeenth centuries, could be brutal in punishing deviation. The motives were rarely entirely theological; mundane conflicts could often stimulate a particular concern for orthodoxy. The Jews of Spain and Portugal were persecuted because they were Jews but also because their success was resented by Christian merchants. In 1492 Ferdinand and Isabella of Spain expelled all Jews who would not convert to Christianity. Alfonso, the king of Portugal, accepted many on the generous condition that they paid a large fee and promised to move on after eight months. Portugal's slightly more tolerant attitude changed abruptly when, as part of the contract for his wedding to their daughter, Alfonso's successor agreed to placate Ferdinand and Isabella's anti-Semitism. Jews were given eleven months to leave Portugal but they had to do so through Lisbon and insufficient ships had been provided to transport them. The net result was that thousands were unable to leave and were forcibly converted to Christianity. Many of those thus baptized continued to practise their Jewish faith in private and in secret, while maintaining an outward appearance of having converted. Hence their nickname: they were known as Marranos ('swine'), apparently because some maintained a fake front by cooking pork at their front doors. The Spanish Inquisition attempted to coerce real faith out of the Marranos with punishments that ranged from public confession, through the wearing of special clothes of penance, to burning at the stake. Gradually public *auto de fé* (or 'acts of faith') became less common, but the last public condemnation of Jews took place as late as 1765, the last *auto de fé* was in Mexico in 1815 and the Inquisition was not formally closed down until 1821.

By 1800 forced conversion had become rare in Europe and had largely been replaced by a system of penalties or disabilities for dissenters (of which more shortly). The only twentieth-century examples that come to mind all involve ethnic and national conflicts in which having the wrong religion is just one of a range of affronts. Above I mentioned the 1917 Serb proposal to the Croats for the removal of 'the Turks' from Bosnia. Between 1941 and 1945 the Catholic Ustaše militias in the fascist puppet state of Croatia applied the same principle to the Serbs. Thousands of Orthodox Serbs were forced to change religion on pain of death or expulsion. In one notorious case at Glina in May 1941 hundreds of Serbs were gathered in a church for what they were told was a religious service to celebrate the new constitution. Those who could produce a certificate of conversion to Catholicism were allowed to leave; the rest were slaughtered.[5] Unlike the Spanish Inquisitors, these oppressors were less interested in safeguarding or spreading the faith than in humiliating and brutalizing their opponents.

Stalin's insistence that the Ukrainian Uniates be merged into the Orthodox Church has already been mentioned. Even that, while an obvious assault on religious freedom, could be seen as a rather limited deprivation compared to the work of the Spanish Inquisition. What marked the Uniates was that they were Orthodox in ritual and in local church life but were formally attached to the Catholic Church as an institution (itself a result of a forced change of what were once Orthodox loyalties by Catholic rulers). Long term the realignment did have major consequences in that it put clergy training and appointment in the effective hands of Russian bishops determined to crush Ukrainian nationalism, which was the intention. But, if Stalin ever felt moved to defend his actions, he could claim that he was not infringing on the rights of the Uniates to practise their religion 'as such'. We might note that Stalin's attitude to religious orthodoxy was not that of the Spanish Inquisition. Torquemada cared about the true faith. Stalin was no more fond of the Orthodox Church in the Ukraine than he was of the Uniates. He forced the latter to join the former only because the former was more firmly under his thumb.

Ensuring loyalty

One of the paradoxes of the early stages of modernization is it both extended and constrained individual freedom. Industrialization brought a separation of the individual from the social roles that he or she performed and thus gradually permitted ever greater degrees of freedom outside and beyond social roles. But at the same time the rise of the nation state brought ever greater pressure for cultural uniformity. In pre-modern societies, where politics, like everything else, was a matter only for small elites, what the common people thought or felt was of little interest. With the development of competing nations and the extension of political rights to an increasing part of the population, it became important that the people thought of themselves as German or French.

In emerging nations that were based on a common religion there was considerable pressure to accept the hegemony of the putative national religion. Cardinal Richelieu was somewhat constrained in his coercion of the Huguenots because he needed the support of

European Protestant princes in his battles with rivals to French power, but he had no doubt that the strong French nation he sought to create was a Catholic nation. Gustavus Adolphus of Sweden firmly yoked the Lutheran Church to his task of nation building. Greece attained its independence only in 1829. Its position on the border between Christendom and Islam meant that its religion played an important part in a national identity that was rarely secure enough to be taken for granted. Under the dictatorship of General Iaonnis Metaxas (1936–40) the Greek government passed a variety of laws intended to bolster the Greek Orthodox Church and its claims to represent the soul of the nation. Members of other religions were denied the right to manifest their religion in public or to publish material advertising their faith. Foreigners were not permitted to evangelize. Places of worship required state permits and these were denied to non-Orthodox churches. At the end of the twentieth century, Greece was still constraining dissenters. In March 1993 four Jehovah's Witnesses were fined and imprisoned for evangelizing. For reasons discussed later, the Witnesses have often been especially persecuted, but far more conventional Christian churches have also been regarded as suspect by the Greek state. In 1993 a confidential intelligence service report on 'dangerous religions' listed over thirty Protestant churches (mostly Pentecostal and Baptist) as 'enemies of the state'. Because they were an alternative to the Greek Orthodox Church, they were a threat to Greece.

The road to freedom

Leaving aside the former Communist countries, Greece is unusual among European states. By the end of the nineteenth century most were well on the way to accepting that people should be free to choose their religion without suffering disabilities. It is important to understand how we got to this position, because it has considerable implications for how we assess the power of fundamentalists to reverse the trend. In brief, the thesis underlying what follows is that economic modernization, by producing increasing social and cultural diversity at the same time as creating a more egalitarian attitude towards a regime's subjects or citizens, created a choice between paying an ever higher price for coercing conformity or increasing the scope for individual liberty. Most states choose the latter. That is, toleration was not primarily the result of the propaganda of liberals; it was an inadvertent consequence of deep background social changes.

Without much damage to the historical record we can distinguish four roads to religious freedom. Three involved pioneering new attitudes to religion and citizenship; the fourth was merely the export of the final product to new settings. The French route involved revolutionary upheaval. The British mutation was a gradual fudge. The American model was the result of rational deliberation. The final product then became an inspiration for liberal reform.

In France the Catholic Church's close association with the old feudal order and its opposition to the social groups that led the 1789 Revolution ensured that the Revolutionaries would become anticlerical. Church lands were confiscated and the Church stripped of its public role. In his search for stability Napoleon signed a concordat with the Vatican that gave the Church the position of subsidized official state religion but gave the state considerable control over the hierarchy. In 1905 the state was again formally 'secularized'. The deep division over the power of the Church created the irony that, while religion remained more popular in France than in Britain, the French Revolution became a symbol for secular modernization of the polity.

The British route was much more gradual and informal and that owed a lot to the religious culture being Protestant rather than Catholic. In 1532, when Henry VIII announced that the Church would no longer recognize the authority of Rome and declared himself its head, there was one religion in England. The split from Rome immediately created a second one in that many English Christians refused to accept the change. Changes of regime over the next hundred years saw the Church of England become more and then less and then more Roman before settling down to become largely Protestant in doctrine and semi-Catholic in organization: it maintained the hierarchy but without the Rome connection and with lay landowners appointing the clergy.

Most British rulers (first the monarchs and later the politicians in parliament) saw the Church as an essential component of a strong nation state and sought to ensure conformity to it. Post-Reformation this became increasingly difficult. One problem for them was that two core Protestant beliefs combined to encourage factionalism and schism. On the one hand was the dogmatic certainty that there was one God and his will could be certainly known. On the other was the egalitarian idea that all believers stood in an equal relationship to God; popes and bishops were not needed to shepherd the faithful. The outcome was repeated schism from the dominant church.

A second problem for maintaining religious conformity was that Great Britain and Ireland was a multinational state. Scotland had its own national church, which was Presbyterian rather than Episcopalian and far more reformed in its doctrine and liturgy. Wales was highly receptive to dissenting movements and Ireland was divided three ways. Most natives remained Roman Catholic; the settlers divided into English Episcopalians and Scots Presbyterians. Despite strenuous attempts to constrain those who refused to conform to the national churches, the number of dissenters grew steadily until by 1851 half of those who attended church in England and Wales did so in something other than the state church.

The degree of repression varied considerably. The period of Oliver Cromwell's Protectorate was one of unprecedented liberty.[6] Episcopalian clergy were allowed to remain in those parishes where they were accepted by their people. An Order in Council of 1653 boldly rejected coercion and required 'That none be compelled to conform to the public religion by penalties or otherwise; but that endeavours be used to win them with sound doctrine, and the example of good conversation'.[7] The restoration of the monarchy in the 1660s brought the Corporation Act, which prevented dissenters holding municipal office, the Act of Uniformity, which prevented dissenters preaching, the Conventicles Act, which banned private worship meetings of more than five people who were not family members, and the Five Mile Act, which kept dissenting clergy that distance from a corporate borough. The 1673 Test Act excluded dissenters from offices of state by making the taking of communion in the parish church a qualification for holding any civil, military and naval position. Queen Anne's Toleration Act of 1688 allowed certain classes of dissenters to worship but did not free them of civil and political disabilities. It has to be said that all of these measures were more symptoms of the failing power of the national church than effective devices to strengthen it. Enforcement was always patchy and the rapid growth of the Methodist movement between 1740 and 1800 made a mockery of attempts to sustain a religious consensus. In May 1828, long after they had served any purpose other than to irritate dissenters, the Test and Corporation acts were repealed and the 1832 Reform Act so extended the franchise that dissenters became a major political power.

The important point about the British experience is that the schismatic nature of Protestantism allowed rising subordinate social groups to express their alienation by modifying the dominant religion in ways that suited their interests and their view of the world. Instead of a sharp division between those who stayed loyal to the single church and a powerful anticlerical bloc (the experience not just in France but later in Italy, Spain and Portugal), there was a more complex conflict of interests that resulted in the former established churches being gradually stripped of real power but being left with ceremonial status. Where the levels of grievance were highest, in Ireland and Wales, the Episcopalian churches were 'disestablished'. In England and Scotland, where the established churches remained the largest religious bodies, they retained some priority in state rituals but gradually lost the substance of their privileges.

An aside on necessity

It is important for our general evaluation of the contribution of Protestantism to the rise of modern liberal democracy that we appreciate how intolerant were most of the early British Protestants. The dissenters were initially no more advocates of toleration than the members of the religious establishment they left behind. The leading Elizabethan Calvinist Thomas Cartwright believed that the power of the magistrate (by which he meant what we now call 'the state') should be used against all those who did not share his faith, to 'see that they join to hear the sermons . . . and cause them to be examined how they profit, and if they profit not, to punish them'.[8] Toleration was inadvertently produced by the need to live with the diversity that Protestant schisms had unintentionally created. Only after they failed to gain the power that would have allowed them to impose their own radical and purified faith on the people did the sectarians become persuaded that diversity was actually virtuous.

I will illustrate the point with the example of national church in Scotland. The first two major schisms were thoroughly committed to theocratic rule. Until it was disbanded in 1968, the Cameronian infantry regiment had the unusual custom of mounting armed guards for its church services. This was a reminder of the regiment's origins in the Covenanting wars of the seventeenth century. The Covenanters refused to accept the settlement of the relationship between the church and the state, not because they minded a state church but because they objected to a church that was not fully committed to their radical Calvinism. When the state suppressed their rebellion, they willingly took up arms for their religious principles. In the eighteenth century the Erskine brothers broke away from the Church of Scotland to form the Secession Church, because they objected to the major landowners who funded the church imposing insufficiently godly ministers on congregations. But they had no problem at all with the notion of imposition. It was only with the third split (that of Thomas Gillespie in 1751, whose followers styled themselves the Relief Presbytery) that we find a movement opposed on principle to the state support for the church and it is a mark of the times that this third split was the *least* popular of the three and grew markedly more slowly than the Secession.

The fourth and largest split – the 1843 Disruption that led to the formation of the Free Church of Scotland – was, like the first two, rooted in the intolerant idea that the state should support the true religion. But it is important to note the new limits on what the state could do to promote the faith. In the seventeenth century it was acceptable for the government to use dragoons. By the middle of the nineteenth century, even the most zealous theocrat had given up violence and punishment; social pressure, unfair taxation and preferential access to such means of socialization as the national school system marked the limits of what was thought possible. For all that softening, there was little recognition that people had a right to choose their religion and considerable opposition to the idea of secular provision of social services.

With the exception of the Relief Presbytery, each schismatic sect aimed to impose its purified religion even more forcefully than the Church of Scotland imposed its weak and misguided version of the truth. Gradually each sect came to appreciate that it had failed in its mission and that it would remain a minority. Not surprisingly, it then began to appreciate the virtues of toleration. Initially each sect argued that its people (and grudgingly, a few others like them) should be tolerated but that others (Roman Catholics especially) should be persecuted. But gradually the sects came to accept what the state was also coming to accept: in a context of increasing religious diversity, social harmony required the state to become increasingly tolerant and finally neutral in matters of religion. And each sect gradually reduced the claims that it made for its unique access to the saving truth and came to see itself as one denomination among others.

The American route to religious freedom combined elements of the French and British: part principled formal secularity and part pragmatic acceptance of diversity. The promoters of independence were able to devise a political structure from scratch, which meant that the relationship between church and state was the subject of conscious deliberation. Although nine of the thirteen founding colonies had state churches established by law, most of those were challenged by substantial numbers of dissenters. Even if they had not been, the new country could not have had a state church because the colonies had different religions established. In order to make what the motto called *E Pluribus Unum* or 'one out of many', that one had to be very broad. The solution was the explicit assertion of two principles: the state should not support any particular religion and, equally well, the state should not constrain the religious freedoms of the individual.

The legacy of the French and the American revolutions, and of the gradual changes in the United Kingdom, was the powerful notion that a modern state that allowed its citizens to choose their government should also allow them to select their religion. The notion became so widely accepted that even countries that did not need to accommodate large bodies of dissenters gradually adopted the principle of religious freedom as part of wider packages of constitutional reforms. In 1845 Norway allowed ordinary citizens (but not civil servants) to leave the state Lutheran Church for another specified Christian organization. Complete liberty did not arrive until 1956. Denmark allowed a similar restricted right of withdrawal in 1849. Sweden followed the first part of the Norwegian example in 1860 but got to complete liberty a few years earlier: in 1951.

Catholic cultures were slow to accept the principles of liberal democracy, but the rise and fall of fascism and the radical restructuring of politics that followed the end of the Second World War in 1945 saw the Catholic Church largely abandon its corporatist approach to politics, at least in Western Europe outside the Iberian peninsula. For the rest of the twentieth century, under US hegemony, the language of individual rights became universal. It appeared in the charter of the United Nations and in almost every constitution written after 1945.

As the many examples of religious persecution presented in this study show, many states violated the rights of their citizens as much in the matter of religious freedom as in anything else. However, the political power of states committed to the principle of free choice in religion was sufficient gradually to bring others into that consensus. We can return to the example of Greece. Largely under pressure to conform to the norms of the European Union and the United Nations, in 2000 the Prime Minister, Costas Simitis, determined to remove the customary requirement to state religious identity on public documents. In particular, he decided that the new identity card should not record religion. The Orthodox Church, which is Greece's largest landowner and to which some 98 per cent of the Greek people notionally belong, announced that 'Our faith is the foundation of our ethnic identity'.[9] The Church lost the battle. In 2001 the Supreme Court decided it was unconstitutional to require religious affiliation on ID cards. The same year, the Thessaloniki District Court acquitted eleven evangelical congregations and five others of operating without a licence from the local Orthodox bishop. In a remarkable submission, the district attorney who was supposedly prosecuting the case asked the presiding judge to support a modernization of the Metaxas laws to bring them into line with the European Convention on Human Rights.

There are two major exceptions to the general history outlined above: Communist and Islamic states.

Communist repression

The history of religious freedom in Communist states can be summarized as large-scale repression, moderated only when the Party felt a need to mobilize popular sentiment in support of the state (as in the Second World War), followed by gradual thawing of relations from the 1960s. Then with the collapse of Communism in the 1990s, each country had to work out anew a relationship between the churches and the state. Those relationships are still evolving but in many countries what followed liberation was not the adoption of the laissez-faire attitude common in the West but something closer to the nineteenth-century models of limited freedom alongside an official preference for the religion of the titular nationality.

Communist states suppressed religion because they objected to it on principle and because they feared any social institutions not under party control. Most combined stick and carrot, aiming both to suppress demand for religion and to co-opt religious institutions better to serve party or national ends.

At the time of the Revolution in 1917 the Bolsheviks were sufficiently anxious to win allies for the atheism of 'scientific socialism' to be set aside. The Muslims of Central Asia were promised: 'Your beliefs and usages, your national and cultural institutions are forever free and inviolate. Know that your rights, like those of the peoples of Russia, are under the mighty protection of the revolution and its organs, the Soviet of Workers, Soldiers and Peasants.' But only two years later the policy was reversed and 'local Russians were left free to conduct antireligious campaigns during which mosques were profaned, clergy shot, religious endowment land confiscated, Shariah courts closed, and religious schools were demolished'.[10]

In the aftermath of the Second World War the Soviets became less hostile to Islam in their Eastern empire, mainly because they wanted to present themselves as the defenders of national liberation against Western (and Christian) imperialism. In the 1960s Kruschev, concerned with threats to Soviet rule, instituted a new wave of mosque closures. As the leading Muslim cleric in Tajikistan notes ruefully, at one point there were only seventeen mosques in the entire country, which was 90 per cent Muslim.[11] In the 1970s under Brezhnev the regime again relaxed in order to make political capital out of the anti-Americanism of the Vietnam War era. Then the success of the Iranian revolution in 1979 raised new fears about the loyalty of Soviet Asia and the climate became more repressive before the collapse of the Soviet Union bequeathed fears about Islamic fundamentalism to the new governments of Uzbekistan, Turkmenistan and Tajikistan.[12]

When it occupied eastern Germany after the war, the Soviet regime none too subtly tried to undermine the churches by requiring people to work on Sundays. The puppet state that the Soviets established imposed restrictions on new church building, which it regarded as a waste of scarce material as religion was due to die out shortly. It set ceilings on seminary enrolments. It used the mass media constantly to disparage religion. And it sought to replace aspects of religion by creating its own secular rites of passage. One such innovation was a coming-of-age ceremony in which young people swore allegiance to the party and to atheism. In addition to what it could do to hamstring the church as an institution, it could also punish individuals. Those who persisted in church attachments were denied membership in the Communist Party and thus access to public careers. Relations softened somewhat after the Lutheran Church in the East finally accepted the division of Germany and created its own local structure. While the Catholic Church chose to preserve itself in pious isolation, Lutheran Bishop Schönherr announced: 'We do not want to be a church against or alongside, but in socialism.'[13] The state reciprocated. Martin Luther, who had in the 1950s been denounced as the father of fascism, was rehabilitated as a proto-revolutionary, and Erich Honeker, the party boss, gave his approval by serving as the president of the committee organizing the celebrations of the quincentenary of Luther in 1983.

In Poland, where the Catholic Church was simply too powerful and too popular to be readily suppressed, the party tried to persuade the junior clergy to break the link with the Vatican and create an autonomous national church. Likewise in Czechoslovakia, restrictions on the Church's operations were accompanied by efforts to weaken the links between the Czech Church and Catholicism worldwide. *Pacem in Terris*, an association of lower clergy, was established as a counter to the hierarchy. In Russia in the 1920s, Communists encouraged junior clergy of the Orthodox Church to form the 'Living Church', an anti-hierarchy pressure group. In Bulgaria in the 1950s, the Communist government sent uncooperative priests for hard labour, encouraged a left-wing League of Orthodox Priests of Bulgaria to assert itself, stripped the Church of its lands, placed the clergy on state salaries, put the Church under control of an office within the Ministry of Foreign Affairs and reduced it to a timid spokesman for Bulgarian foreign policy initiatives. And with barely disguised contempt all the while praised the Church for its patriotism and stout defence of national culture.[14]

Of all the Communist states Albania was the most ruthless in its suppression of religion. None of the three traditions – Catholic Christianity, Orthodox Christianity and Islam – was sufficiently popular to be able convincingly to claim to represent the spirit of the Albanian people. The purges began as soon as Enver Hoxha deposed King Zog in 1945. Religion was officially abolished in 1967. The state was particularly vicious in seeking to prevent even private religious ceremonies. Father Pjeter Meshkella, a Jesuit priest, was imprisoned for twenty-five years, from 1946 to 1971. He was free for only two years before being sent back to prison for a further nine years. This time he was allowed three years of liberty before, in 1985, being arrested again for saying Christmas mass in a private house. He died in a labour camp in July 1988 having spent all but six of forty-two years of Communism in jail. Shkoder's Catholic Cathedral became a gym. The Principal Mullah of Shkoder, Sabri Koci, was arrested and imprisoned from 1967 to 1988, but he lived long enough to be able to reopen the Shkoder mosque on 16 November 1990, two months before the ban was officially lifted.

The post-soviet settlement

On matters of religion, post-soviet Russia has been liberal in rhetoric and less so in reality. The Law on Freedom of Conscience and

Religious Organizations, passed in October 1990, made 'all denominations and religions...equal under the law' and guaranteed every citizen's right to 'freedom of conscience'. The new Constitution of 1993 promised that 'all religious associations shall be separated from the state' and shall be equal before the law. This was too liberal for the Russian Orthodox Church, which mobilized its support among the members of the Duma to draft a 1993 bill that would prevent anyone without Russian citizenship engaging in any sort of missionary activity. This was, as one member of the Duma put it, 'an attempt by the Russian Orthodox Church, which has a centuries-long history as the State church, to once again gain a monopoly for itself in the country and once again claim a place near the leadership of the country'.[15] That failed but, despite massive international objections (which included a petition from the US Congress, a personal letter from the Pope and representations from the European Union), the Freedom of Conscience Bill was passed in 1997. It began with ceremonial recognition of 'Christianity, Islam, Buddhism, Judaism and other religions which constitute an inseparable part of the historical heritage of Russia's people'. It then elevated Russian Orthodoxy to a special position: 'Recognizing the special contribution of Orthodoxy to the history of Russia and to the establishment and development of Russia's spirituality and culture...' The bill distinguished between groups and organizations. A group is an association with fewer than ten participants. It can hold worship services without state registration, but it cannot have a legal personality. Hence it cannot own property, construct buildings and offer chaplaincy services in hospitals and the like. Larger bodies, 'organizations', must register with the state, and until they have been registered for fifteen years they too suffer a range of disabilities. They cannot operate seminaries or other educational institutions, print or distribute literature, affiliate with foreign bodies or even invite foreigners to preach, teach or take part in their services. And there are a wide variety of grounds for liquidating even those organizations that have been registered for the required length of time: undermining the security of the state, destroying the unity of the Russian Federation, committing disorderly acts and infringing the rights of citizens. In reality, local administrations have often been even more biased than the legislation. Many council leaders, most of them not terribly pious themselves, have taken the simple view that Russians are Orthodox and everything else should be viewed with either suspicion or disdain. Although it tried hard to comply with the new laws, the Salvation Army was ordered to close its Moscow branch in November 2001.

But, in a judgment that shows how even apparently vacuous law can become effective, the Russian Supreme Court in February 2002 ruled the Moscow ban to be illegal.[16]

In some parts of the Soviet Empire, the end of Communism brought a liberal attitude to religion. More often it resulted in a settling of scores. To restore the national integrity of their states (which had been threatened by the large numbers of Russians who had been settled in them), the leaders of repressed nations enthusiastically promoted the interests of the titular national church. In Estonia, for example, the newly independent government behaved as badly towards the Russian Orthodox Church, the religion of the colonial settlers, as the Soviet government had towards the Estonian Lutheran Church. Lithuania could be more generous than Estonia because its titular nationality had not been diluted by Russian settlement to the same extent. Its 1995 law requires religions to be recognized by the state. Eight were so recognized as 'traditional': Roman Catholic, Uniate, Russian Orthodox, Old Believer, Lutheran, Reformed, Jewish, Sunni Muslim and Karaite. Other associations could register and after twenty-five years of good conduct would be recognized by the state as valid.

In part this approach reflected the traditional European pattern of the state either directly controlling a national church or signing concordats with the major institutions. It also reflected guilt for the recent history of repression. For at least fifty years religious institutions had been ground down; it was only fair that they should be allowed to regain their former position and that meant, not the modern free market in religious goods and services but the domination of the titular national church. A third reason for wishing to maintain some control over religious activity was fear for the stability of the state. In many post-Communist states there was a serious concern about legitimacy. When a leading politician suggests that the police and religious leaders should combine to oppose sects that 'aim to undermine statehood in Russia' (as did Interior Minister Vladimir Rushailo in 2000), we might suspect a little scapegoating for the purposes of national unity, but there is a serious point.[17] By definition, all the post-Communist states are young and many are unstable. All (except Russia naturally) spent fifty years denying their own identity in the interests of the Soviet Empire. Having so recently escaped one form of colonialism, they are reluctant to acquire another and the simple fact is that most alternatives to the titular national religion are foreign imports. Hence the proposals in the Albanian Parliament that the heads of all religious communities be Albanian born. Whether it be old established Protestant churches (the Baptists, for example), nine-teenth-century sects (such as the Mormons and the Jehovah's Wit-nesses) or the new religious movements of the late twentieth century (such as Scientology), most innovations can be seen as US imperialism.

A number of times in this study I have made the point that, even though there are some common patterns of evolution, we cannot expect every country to follow the same template. There are common problems and a limited repertoire of solutions, but the circumstances in which governments have to make decisions are different. In the 1870s, when West European countries were devis-ing modern secular constitutions, religion was not a major threat to social stability. Catholic France had last tried to use British Cath-olics to destabilize the United Kingdom in 1745 and that effort had been half-hearted. The former Communist states are constructing responses to religion at a time when conflicts in the Balkans, the Caucasus, Kashmir and the Middle East offer potent examples of the force of religion within and without states. Within, religio-ethnic minorities aim to secede. Without, international Islamic fun-damentalist movements threaten the stability of any country with a sizeable Muslim population. It is not surprising, then, that even liberal groups that once campaigned for human rights are now cautious about religious liberty. In the 1980s the Albanian Helsinki Committee had promoted basic human rights against state repres-sion: in the 1990s it started to warn of the threats of religious revival. Well aware of the sensitivities of the third of the population who are Christian, the government curbed the distribution of an edition of the Qur'ān (supplied from the Middle East) that asserted that Albania was a Muslim country. Albania has also refused to permit religious political parties. The idea that the senior figures of all religions should be Albanian born is a measure designed to prevent sectarian animosity being encouraged by agents of neigh-bouring countries that would like to dismantle Albania.

In brief, the end of Communism has removed one reason why many states regulated religious organizations, but often new forms of regulation have been introduced that are inspired by the same logic as pervaded Western Europe in the early modern era: the desire to build national cohesion.

China

Prior to the success of the Chinese Communist Party in creating the People's Republic of China in 1949, China had a rich and diverse religious culture.[18] There was a widespread folk culture combining ancestor worship, various forms of divination and the worship of local deities. Buddhism was widespread by the eighth century, as were Taoism and Confucianism. Derived from the philosophical writings of Lao Zi and Zhuang Zi, Taoism is an esoteric system of belief combining alchemy, rituals, physical exercise regimes and the chanting of scriptures. Confucianism is more of a philosophy than a religion: Confucius dismissed speculation about the supernatural and instead promoted a vision of the good society based on the interlocking responsibilities of family members and of ruler and subjects. By the time it became the state orthodoxy, Confucianism concentrated on the veneration of the Emperor. Particularly in the form of the Naqshibandi Sufi Order, Islam had some considerable impact on the outlying provinces of China, and Christian missionary efforts in the late nineteenth century created substantial bodies of Chinese Christians.

The hostility to religion of the Chinese government stemmed from the usual communist concerns: an ideological commitment to atheism and a totalizing desire to remove all non-Party social institutions. But Chinese Communists also shared the development assumptions of Atatürk in Turkey and Reza Khan in Iran. The advance of economic development and the promotion of egalitarianism (especially of the sexes) required that the social inertia sustained by traditional religions be broken. The Constitution of 1954 guaranteed religious freedom but confined religion to the home and the private sphere. In the late 1950s Christian churches were attacked as local arms of Western imperialism, obliged to sever all links with sister churches outside China, and required to conduct themselves on the 'three-selves' principle: self-mission, self-funding and self-administering. All foreign missionaries were expelled. In Poland or Czechoslovakia such attempts to nationalize the Catholic Church failed because the Church had far deeper roots than the Communist Party. The relatively small number of Christians made resistance in China difficult, but many maintained secret links to the Vatican.

During the Cultural Revolution of the 1960s, the Red Guards set out to destroy religion. Almost all churches, mosques and temples were forced to close. There was some relaxation in the 1980s, especially of the controls on native Chinese religions. The earlier campaign against Confucianism was 'officially discredited under Deng Ziaoping' and the supposed residence of Confucius at Qufu has been restored.[19] This probably owes more to a desire to encourage tourism than to a new respect for the ancient religions, and the same could be said for the restoration of Buddhist temples and monasteries. What was been particularly interesting is the careful way in which Chinese Christians have tried to manage their always tense relationship with the regime. Many Catholic clergy were quite willing to join the Patriotic Catholic Association (PCA) (that is, the non-Vatican church), many refused and maintained an 'underground' church and some privately straddled the two bodies, being secretly ordained by the underground church as bishops while also serving as ordinary priests in the state-approved PCA. In the 1980s the gulf between the two churches closed. The Vatican approved many of the PCA appointments, and courageous leaders of the PCA defied the Communist regime to build close ties with their underground brethren.[20] When Bishop Odoricus Liu Ho-Teh was released from twenty years in prison in 1978, the PCA Bishop of Wuhan, Dong Guangqinq, invited him to live with him in the official residence. The authorities repeatedly exiled Ho-Teh and Dong Guangqinq repeatedly invited him back and the two worked side by side, not arguing with the Party's instructions but in practice ignoring them.

The Chinese state remains particularly at odds with four religions: Buddhism in Tibet, Islam in the western provinces, a clutch of very small Protestant sects spread all over China and Falun Gong in Beijing and the heartland.

Tibet is one of the world's few genuine theocracies.[21] Mahayana Buddhism acquired such an influence that, from the thirteenth century, the monks were the effective rulers. From 1642 the Dalai Lama, the reincarnated leader of the most powerful sect of Tibetan Buddhism, was also the effective ruler of all Tibet. The Chinese established overlordship in 1720 and ruled, at a distance, little interfering with the theocrats, until 1911. There then followed a period of autonomy, but in 1950 the Chinese regained control and began to settle Han Chinese in Tibet. Nine years later, when the Chinese brutally suppressed an uprising designed to restore clerical rule, the Dalai Lama and a large number of followers fled to India. The Chinese took control of the monasteries and stripped them of their power and wealth. In periodic outbursts of violence since, it is estimated that over one million Tibetans have died.[22]

The habit of other Communist regimes to try to suborn the clergy has been mentioned. In the case of Tibet this has taken the unusual form of manipulating reincarnation! Tibetan Buddhism is highly centralized: its two leaders are the Dalai Lama and the Panchen Lama. Tibetans believe that the soul of each is reborn and that the new avatar can be identified. The process of identifying the young boy into whom the soul of the previous Lama has been reborn is a slow one involving a variety of signs and tests, but central to it is a reciprocal arrangement in which the Dalai Lama identifies the new Panchen Lama and vice versa. The tenth Panchen Lama did not follow the Dalai Lama into exile and paid for his decision with ten years of imprisonment during the Cultural Revolution. In 1989, aged only 51, he died at the monastery of Tashilhunpo, Shigaste, Tibet, shortly after making an unusually vigorous anti-Chinese speech. It is widely believed that he was poisoned by the Chinese. In May 1995 the Dalai Lama announced that he had found the new Panchen Lama, a 6-year-old boy, in Tibet. This boy and two other leading candidates were kidnapped by the Chinese, who produced their own candidate: Gyaltsen Norbu. In June 2002 this official Panchen Lama made only his second visit to Tibet to mixed reactions. It is not yet clear if the Chinese appointment will be accepted as legitimate; the crucial test will come when the current Dalai Lama dies and his reincarnation has to be found.[23]

Muslims have often been treated better than other believers, because China has usually been keen to maintain positive relationships with Muslim states. As with other religions, Islam was severely repressed in the early period of Communist rule. Thousands of mosques were closed and whole villages were destroyed. Since the early 1980s the climate has become generally more liberal. For example, Muslims are now allowed to travel to Mecca and Islamic texts are legally published and openly distributed. But the rise of Islamic fundamentalism has created considerable anxiety in China over the stability of its western regions where there are (albeit very weak) secessionist movements. In March 2002, in the context of the war in Afghanistan, the Chinese government executed a number of Muslims leaders of the Vighur community in Xinjiang, supposedly for links with Bin Laden's Al-Qaeda network.[24]

Evangelical Protestants who form their own sects outside the state-approved churches have been persecuted. For example, in 2001 Gong Shengliang, the founder of the South China Church, was sentenced to death; other sect leaders were sentenced to between two years and life in prison.[25]

The political climate of China is very different from that of the states of Western Europe, but it is in line with the general shift from concerns about loyalty to the state to fears of the threat of the unconventional that the main object of Communist repression at the start of the twenty-first century is a new religious movement: Falun Gong. The movement was founded in 1992 by Li Hongzhi. An amalgam of the major themes from traditional Chinese religions, Buddhism and Taoism, it believes in karma and reincarnation and the existence of demonic and benign spirit forces. It uses physical movement regimes to promote spiritual well-being. Its leadership claims 100 million members; the Chinese government says two million and the true figure probably lies about seventy million, which makes it the largest organization in China outside Communist Party control.

The American industrialist J.P. Morgan once said that for every action there are two reasons – a good reason and the real reason. The good reason for government action against Falung Gong is that cited by Western governments acting against new religious movements: that they are injurious to their followers. The real reason is the classic problem of autonomous institutions. The Chinese regime is not just authoritarian; it is totalitarian. That is, it seeks to remove all social institutions, social networks and elements of civil society that it does not control. Although Falun Gong does not present any direct threat to the state (in the sense that secessionist Islamic movements do), its members refuse to accept the authority of the party.

The response has been as harsh as anything seen in the worst days of the Cultural Revolution. Since it was banned in 1999, thousands of members of Falun Gong have been incarcerated in mental institutions and imprisoned without trial. Hundreds have been tortured and murdered. The Chinese government, anxious to maintain good relations with its trading partners in the West, has justified its actions in the same language as Western governments have used in discussing supposedly dangerous new religious movements. A 2001 press release from the Chinese Embassy in the USA explained: 'the cult has destroyed the harmony of many families, as it misled a large number of obsessive followers to refuse medical services, hurt themselves or even kill innocent people.' Liu Jing, the Director of the rather directly named 'Office for Preventing and Handling Cults', said the Chinese government would try its best to educate Falun Gong practitioners so as 'to free themselves of the spiritual shackles of the cult'. He added that 'Punishments are meted out only to those who have committed crimes, endangered social stability and violated human rights of other individuals.' He further added, in a rather perplexed tone: 'It is rather difficult to liberate such followers from the addiction.'[26]

It is interesting to note that the Chinese government strategy of treating Falun Gong as a social menace seems to have been effective, even in the United States. A study of the way in which US newspapers reported religion stories found that Falun Gong was frequently referred to in the same terms as Aum, Heaven's Gate and the Solar Temple (which are discussed shortly).[27]

Islamic repression

All the major religions are ethical, in the sense that they suppose that God (or Gods or the impersonal calculus of karma) has something to say about how adherents should live. All have notions of a good life and a bad life. Commandments and precepts and principles abound. But there are certain features of Islam that give most majority Muslim states a character quite unlike countries in which Christians, Buddhists, Hindus or even Jews predominate. First, Islam is unusual in the extent to which religious precepts and principles are construed as a body of law. Muslims believe that God delivered to the Prophet very specific instructions which are to be found in the Qur'ān, the traditions of the life of the Prophet and his early followers, the consensus of the community of believers and, where those three fail, analogical reasoning.[28] The shariah (or 'clear path') has always been supplemented by secular law; as Islam expanded it did not always displace local custom. And believing that there is a single divinely ordained way of life does not, of course, tell us exactly what that is; Muslims divide as to which of a number of traditions of jurisprudence they follow.[29] Nonetheless, orthodox Muslims suppose that it is possible to construct a body of law that reflects God's instructions. A good sign of the unusual importance of the law is that the primary carrier of Islam is not, as it is in Christianity, a distinct church with a clergy. Although in some Islamic cultures there are roles that come close to that of the Catholic priest or the Protestant pastor, the primary role within Islam is that of the 'jurist' or 'juriconsult': the person who interprets the law. The more general issue of Islam's compatibility with democracy will be considered in the final chapter. Here I want to concentrate on the narrower issue of attitudes to other religions.

Islam is unusually theocratic. Its early religious leaders were also political leaders. In theory it permits no distinction between religion and other spheres of life. It rejects the division implied in Christ's injunction to 'Render unto Caesar what is Caeser's and unto God what is God's'. Pious Muslims contrast human law with the shariah. In a robust reply to criticisms of Iran's human-rights record, Ayatollah Ali Khamenei said: 'we certainly prefer the text of the Holy Qur'ān to the products of the failing minds of western lawyers. We aim toward total implementation of Qur'ānic laws.'[30]

Societies in which Muslims have the power to act as they wish are often illiberal to other religions in two general senses. First, they privilege Muslims (and in particular those with the correct brand of Islam) over other peoples. Second, they impose Islamic requirements on the entire society.

Those whom the Prophet thought decent but misguided – Christians and Jews – are usually treated as second-class citizens. They are accorded limited rights as part of a subordinate millet or dhimmi. In the Islamic republic of Iran a very small number of seats in the Parliament are allocated to the traditional Christian and Jewish communities, but adherents to these faiths may not worship in public, may not promote their beliefs in any way that might attract the attention of Muslims, and must conform outwardly to the requirements of Islam. From the constitution, which requires that the President and Vice-President be Shi'ite Muslims, to the army, which enrols Armenian and Chaldean Christians but refuses to promote them, public life privileges the Shi'ite tradition of Islam. Although it has not entirely succeeded, the religious leadership has tried to ensure that the power it acquired at the revolution is not eroded by imposing a number of institutional safeguards against future deviation. The constitution established the office of 'the Theologian Holy man' whose job it is to provide overall religious guidance to Parliament and the executive. A Council of Guardians vets all laws for conformity to the principles of Islam and vets candidates for election to Parliament. Non-Muslim religions that are not accorded dhimmi status are often accorded no rights at all and are frequently the target for repression. This is particularly so if, as in the case of the Baha'is, the religion developed after the time of the Prophet and thus violates the claim of Islam to have the final and complete revelation of God's will.[31] Halliday identifies an important vicious circle here. In order to protect their interests, fringe minorities (such as the Alevis in Turkey, the Baluchis and Pathans in Pakistan, the Kurds in Iran and the Kabyles in Algeria) tend to favour a secular state, which further compounds their deviation and makes them ready targets for the violence of Islamic fundamentalists.[32]

Islamic states deny what in liberal democracies is regarded as basic liberty. As the constitution of Pakistan puts it, the state supports religious freedom but that freedom must be exercised 'subject to law, public order and morality', and, as these are defined by Islam, that amounts to the freedom only to tread very very carefully. Islamic states impose religiously legitimated norms on the entire population; they protect Islam from challenge; they perpetuate a variety of repressive practices on the grounds that Islam mandates them; and they elide criticisms of Islam and criticisms of the state and thus treat what in other places would be legitimate disagreements as matters of treason.

Islam permits two intermediate states (the desirable and the undesirable) between the extremes of the required and the forbidden and thus allows some flexibility in behavioural codes, but whatever a particular culture of Muslims determines to be required and forbidden, in so far as it is a public matter, is applied universally. As we saw at the end of the previous chapter, in expanding the realm of human rights liberal democracies rely on people being willing to allow that others may behave immorally. For example, many Americans who share the value positions of New Christian Right organizations nonetheless allow that others should be permitted by the law to sin. It is characteristic of Islamic societies that the realm of 'immoral yet legal' is small. Saudi Arabia has a Committee for the Propagation of Virtue and Prevention of Vice. The Taliban in Afghanistan had a whole ministry for Commanding Right and Forbidding Wrong.[33] Dress codes provide one illustration of the point, as does the public fasting between dawn and sunset for the month of Ramadan. Where Muslims can enforce these requirements, they do so. Islamic requirements are obligations not just on pious individuals but on the entire society.

As well as wishing to prevent un-Islamic behaviour, most Islamic states constrain freedom of speech, especially in regard to religion. Iran's attitude to challenges to Islam was clearly expressed in its response to Salman Rushdie's *The Satanic Verses*, a novel that purportedly mocked the Prophet. In 1989 Ayatollah Khomeini announced a fatwa of death on Rushdie and offered a large reward for any Muslim who killed him. It is a useful reminder of differences between Islamic states that other Muslim countries were noticeably more circumspect in their judgement. Despite intense lobbying by the Iranian delegation, the Islamic Organization Conference in Riyadh in 1989 refused to support the death sentence and settled for merely charging Rushdie with apostasy. Iran maintained its position, despite protests from the UK and the European Union, and suffered a ten-year diplomatic rupture with the West. Less dramatically, many Muslim societies heavily restrict the freedom of non-Muslims to publish and distribute books that advertise or explain their faiths. Non-Muslims who wish to worship must do so in private. The desire to eradicate all insults to Islam was taken to the extreme by the Taliban regime in Afghanistan when in March 2001 it ordered the destruction of the two gigantic statues of the Buddha carved in solid rock at Bamiyan almost 2,000 years ago.[34] The particular challenge to the propriety of Islam of converting a

Muslim to some other faith is generally forbidden, often with the penalty of death.

One consequence of locating the template for the good society in the Qur'ān and the hadith is that a variety of social practices that are widely regarded by the rest of the world as barbaric are preserved in some Islamic societies. One pungent example is the stoning to death of adulterers – a punishment applied to the female partners in the crime but not the men. Another is the use of amputation. One whole area in which changing standards in the rest of the world has left Islamic principles thoroughly reactionary is that of gender roles. Arranged marriage at a very early age has long been recognized as one of the main causes of the subordinate and impotent position of women. The Islamic leadership in Iran when it came to power reduced the age of marriage from eighteen to thirteen. It also restored the institution of the 'temporary marriage contract', which can be binding for as little as one hour. The legal age for this kind of marriage is now nine and its critics describe it as a form of legalized prostitution that readily permits the sexual exploitation of women of poor families by wealthy men.[35] The Saudi regime restricts the lives of women in many ways, from preventing them from opening bank accounts in their own right to making their testimony as witnesses of less importance than that of men. The Taliban regime in Afghanistan was an extreme example of the repression of women. Women were required to be thoroughly veiled. They were barred from employment outside the home and thus denied any financial independence. They were banned from schools and colleges. They were not even allowed to be outside the home unless in the company of a male relative.

Finally, because Islam tends to elide the true religion and the government, religious deviation acquires a particular charge that it rarely has in non-Islamic states. Challenges to Islam can be treated not as legitimate disagreements but as treason. 'Saudi authorities consider the practice of religious beliefs and rites other than the Wahhabi interpretation of Islam as an expression of political dissent. Consequently Shia Muslims and Christians have been arrested, detained and tortured for advocating freedom of religion and thought and equal rights for members of their communities.'[36] Note that this goes considerably further than the rather petty restrictions that some post-Communist states have imposed on alternatives to the majority national faith.

As the state promotion of Islam and the suppression of alternative religions are features especially of the Middle East, it is tempting to separate political culture from religion and suppose that Saudi Arabia, for example, derives its character from the fact that it is an Arab state, a successor to the Ottoman Empire, a tribal monarchy and a place that has been overwhelmingly Muslim for ten centuries rather than from any totalizing impulses of Islam itself. It is certainly the case that the federal governments of Indonesia and Malaysia, for example, have better records of toleration than most Middle East states.[37] However, within those countries, states that have Muslim majorities have introduced the shariah and thus created the typical Muslim system of favouring citizens of one religion over those of another. Increasingly aggressive Islamist movements have caused some parts of Malaysia to be markedly less tolerant. In March 2000 Perlis state passed an Islamic faith Protection Bill that allowed officials to seek out and prosecute apostates.[38]

Pakistan

Although Pakistan was created by Indian Muslims who wished to avoid being dominated by Hindus in a state independent of Britain, its first generation of leaders (most of them British educated and not personally pious) deliberately avoided creating a theocratic state.[39] They had good reason: their own differences. Mohammad Ali Jinnah was a Shi'ite.[40] Sir Aga Khan was the spiritual head of the Ismaili sect. Sir Chaudhri Khan was an Ahmadi.[41] Like their Turkish counterparts, the generals who governed the country in the 1950s and 1960s tended to be secular modernizers. General Ayub Khan sought to curb polygamy, prevent child marriages and give women greater protection against causal divorce. However, religious parties grew in influence, and, despite his personal disdain for Muslim piety, Zulfiqar Ali Bhutto (Prime Minister from 1972 until a military coup in 1977) was forced to designate his left-wing programme 'Islamic socialism' and declare Islam the state religion of Pakistan under a new constitution. Islamization was carried further by General Zia ul-Haq, who in 1980 introduced a new legal code based on the shariah.

A consequence of making religious identity a social marker of any importance is that the state must decide just who adheres to what religion. The Ahmadis are followers of Mirza Ghulam Ahmad, a reforming Muslim who created the sect in Punjab in the 1850s. He believed that Islam becomes periodically corrupted and moribund, that God sends an inspired reformer every thousand years, and that he was that messiah or Mahdi. Because this view challenges the orthodox Muslim that the message delivered by Muhammad was final and complete in its perfection, the Ahmadis are widely regarded as apostates and are frequently treated badly. Abdus Salam, Pakistan's only Nobel prize-winner, is one of the thousands of Ahmadis who have quit the country. Fazlur Rahman, a minister in the first Pakistan government and the founder of Islamic Studies at Chicago University, is another who was driven out by the zealots. Since the 1950s Muslims had campaigned against the Ahmadis and Prime Minister Bhutto was sufficiently keen to win the Islamist vote to promote an amendment to the constitution that declared the Ahmadis not to be Muslims. The consequence of this, enshrined in a 1984 addition to the Penal Code, was that 'directly or indirectly posing' as Muslims became a serious criminal offence. As the Ahmadis think they are Muslims and do such common Muslims things as using the standard Muslim greeting and naming their children 'Muhammad', the effect of the law was to make it easy for zealots to use the state to harass them.

General Zia's Islamic laws were opposed by liberals and especially by liberal women, whose status very obviously suffered under such legislation as that asserting that the evidence of one man was worth that of two women, or that legally binding contracts had to be signed by two men or one man and two women. Other offensive items included lighter punishments for crimes where the victim was a woman. Liberals also objected to inhumane punishments such as stoning to death for adultery, flogging and hand-amputation for theft. But Zia's programme was also opposed by conservative Muslims. To decide that the state should be theocratic does not settle the arguments because Muslims themselves differ about many aspects of Islamic law. Pakistan's sizeable Shia minority follow the Jafria school of jurisprudence and bitterly resent the imposition of the main Sunni tradition of Hanafi law. The result was periodic Shia–Sunni violence.

The death of General Zia in 1988 saw a return to civilian government under Benazir Bhutto, the British-educated daughter of the last civilian Prime Minister, but the strength of popular support for an Islamic state (reinforced by the presence of very large numbers of refugees from Afghanistan) prevented her or any of her successors repealing Zia's laws.

Although a poor country, Pakistan has a large wealthy landowning class and a large professional middle class. Unlike Afghanistan or Uzbekistan, Pakistan is well integrated in the world economy and many Pakistanis are educated in the West. By and large they are not terribly orthodox Muslims and have no great liking for using the power of state to require of others what they do not practise themselves. However, the common people are conservative Muslims and the place of Islam in the national identity of Pakistan is constantly reinforced by the conflict with Hindu India. The net result is a system of law that commands little support from an elite too cautious to reform it and promotes gross inconsistencies. As with England's more punitive measures against dissenters in the eighteenth century, there is great variation according to region and local pressure. Two Christian brothers from Pakistan's Punjab province were refused ice cream by a vendor who would not serve them in bowls used by Muslims. They responded with some angry words about Islam and its Prophet. They were charged with blasphemy. During the trial Muslim prayer leaders called the faithful from Friday prayers at the nearby mosque and the mob chanted slogans demanding the death penalty. The two Christians were each sentenced to thirty-five years in prison and large fines. Most of the hundreds of people arrested for blasphemy have been released owing to lack of evidence, but 'many judges reportedly handed down guilt verdicts to protect themselves and their families from retaliation by religious extremists'.[42] The military dictator General Pervez Musharraf suggested changes to the blasphemy laws that could limit its application and constrain its use, but backed down after a series of protest rallies from conservative Muslims.

The Pakistan example is important because it draws attention to an important aspect of the state's attitude to religion that has not been directly addressed till now. This chapter is primarily concerned with legislation and with the actions of governments. But, as well as having their own direct effects, state actions, when the state cannot exercise an effective monopoly of violence, can encourage the mob. Although the government has not directly persecuted the Ahmadis and Zikris, the use of the constitution and the penal code to deny them the identity they claim allows individuals to turn personal grievances (such as disputes over land) and sleights into sectarian disputes. The combination of state dogma and impotence sets in chain a process of demonization that results in people being attacked and murdered for having the wrong religion. In many such cases, the police have sat on their hands and the courts have done little to protect minorities.

In conclusion, where Muslims predominate, they discriminate against other religions. Where they are in a minority, they form secessionist movements that seek either a redrawing of boundaries or a degree of regional autonomy that permits them to live as if they were in a Muslim state.

Tensions

In most Islamic countries there are countervailing pressures. On the one side, there are strongly traditional populations and powerful fundamentalist movements that seek rigorous implementation of the shariah. And with the modern bureaucratic nation state there is the apparatus to do it. On the other side, there are forces that lead to greater individual freedom and religious liberty. Those people who have prospered normally want the degree of choice in their cultural and social lives that they have acquired in their material lives. The outcome is often a fudge that tries to blunt the logic of Islam's impositional nature without openly challenging it. One illustration is given in the final chapter. Here I will mention the case of Nawal El Sadaawi, a well-known Egyptian campaigner for women's rights. She lost her job as Director of Public Health in the 1970s for denouncing female circumcision. She was imprisoned in 1981 for criticizing the regime of Anwar Sadat. She had recently criticized Islamic inheritance laws that a woman can inherit only half as much as her brothers: social change has seen something like a third of Egyptian households having a woman as the principal earner. In an interview with a journalist, Sadaawi rather unguardedly referred to the practice of kissing the ancient black stone at Mecca during the pilgrimage or Hajj as a 'pre-Islamic rite'. The story was reported as 'Dr Nawal El Sadaawi says Hajj is a remnant of paganism'. A notoriety-seeking lawyer invoked 'hisba' – a rule under which one person can prosecute another for insulting Islam. Had the case succeeded, she would have been forcibly divorced from her husband, for no Muslim can remain married to someone who has insulted Islam. The final result says much about the tensions in modern Islamic societies. Rather than challenge the propriety of the law, the court decided that Sadaawi had no case to answer because the proper procedures for making such a complaint had not been followed.

James Piscatori makes an important point about the intolerance of Islamic regimes but then draws a false conclusion when he says: 'Even when the political elite avows Islamic principles . . . it acts in ways which are more readily identifiable with more secular motivations. Any tyranny that exists is thus not due to the zealotry of religion in general or Islam in particular but to other political factors.'[43] It is certainly true that much of the bad behaviour of Islamic regimes has got nothing to do with Islam. But many of the intolerant features of Islamic regimes are precisely and entirely 'Islamic'. The repression of alternative religions, the persecution

of deviant Islamic sects, the punishment of apostates, the criminal-
ization of criticisms of Islam; these are all a result of Islam. That this
is the case can be immediately seen if we imagine that on Monday
every Pakistani woke up an atheist and all memory of Islam was
removed. Then no one would suggest imprisoning people for
abandoning Islam or suggest that the country's laws should conform to principles written centuries earlier.

What is correct in Piscatori's comment is that the reasons why
regimes support more or less strict versions of Islamic requirements
may be quite mundane. Prime Minister Bhutto significantly increased the power of Islam in Pakistan, not because he became
more pious, but because his previous political agenda had become unpopular. But increasing the power of Islam has the deleterious effects it does on levels of toleration only because Islam is an
intolerant religion. Distinguishing the tyranny of politicians from
the tyranny of religion is a useful reminder about the cynicism of
politicians, but it cannot allow us to imagine Islam is a religion
without content, without its own character. Does anyone imagine
that religious dissent in Saudi Arabia would be treated as it is now
if the House of Saud and its courtiers were Quakers?

What Piscatori does with the 'thus' in his second sentence is
avoid the central difference between Islam and other major religions. 'As the unalterable speech of God, the Qur'ān is deemed to
be non-negotiable: for the majority of Muslims, the spirit is firmly
achieved in the letter.'[44] Although there is widespread disagreement among Muslims about exactly what the Qur'ān requires, there
is little disagreement about the fact that it requires something that
should dominate the society. The net result is an attitude to other
religions that at the best treats their adherents as second-class
citizens. That Islamic political elites may have other interests that
are served by discriminating against religious minorities and creating a climate that encourages sectarian violence does not change
the fact that that discrimination and communal violence are
directed against *religious* minorities and justified by *religious* distinctions.

Policing religious innovation

Most states in the West are now largely indifferent to religious
identity, probably because most of their citizens are largely indifferent to religion. When in 1830 Joseph Smith claimed to have a new

revelation delivered to him by the Angel Moroni, he provoked such hostility that, after his murder by a mob in 1844, his followers, led by Brigham Young, trekked west to the open spaces of Utah to find peace.[45] In 2002 Salt Lake City, the centre of Mormonism, hosted the Winter Olympics and no one batted an eyelid. Certainly in predominantly Protestant societies such as Britain and the United States the Mormons and the other nineteenth-century innovations (such as the Jehovah's Witnesses and Christian Scientists) are largely ignored, accepted as just another slightly odd pattern on the cultural wallpaper.

In a society that rejects repression and has a basically egalitarian ethos, religious diversity gives a powerful impetus to the secularization of the state. Most Western democracies no longer claim to know which is the true religion and consequently allow considerable religious freedom to their citizens. It follows that such hostility as there is to religious innovations cannot focus on their specific theological claims; people who do not believe in any God can hardly object to the Unification Church's veneration of its leader Sun Myung Moon on the grounds that it is blasphemous.[46] Hence most hostility towards the new religions of the late twentieth century concentrated on their secondary characteristics: the way they recruited and the demands they made of their members.

To put it another way, religious innovations always provoke some hostility. That they come into being at all is an implied criticism of the prevailing culture and most new religious movements of the 1970s added some very specific criticisms. Exactly what was wrong with the nominally Christian capitalist West depended on the new religion in question. Following Max Weber and Roy Wallis, we can divide them by their orientation to the world.[47] On the puritanical world-rejecting side we have movements such as the Unification Church (or Moonies), the Divine Light Mission and The International Society for Krishna Consciousness (Hare Krishna): for them the capitalist West is decadent, indulgent, materialistic and greedy. At the other end of the axis we have world-affirming movements such as Scientology, Transcendental Meditation and Rajneeshism. These have no social critique and are largely on comfortable terms with the world, though they blame some features of our culture (bureaucratic rationality, for example) for stifling human potential. They offer ways of being happier, healthier and less repressed in the material world.[48]

Like the counter-cultural hippie movement that preceded them, these new religious movements (or NRMs) attracted a hostile press utterly out of proportion to their numbers, but it paid little attention to their core beliefs. Mostly it concentrated on their supposed recruitment tactics and the commitment of their members. This second point can be stated briefly. Most Christian churches in the West do not make any great demands on their members. Few churchgoers follow even the biblical precept of giving a tenth of their income to the church. For most, rituals are undemanding and confined to a few hours a week. At least in outward contours, the lives of most even thoroughly orthodox Christians are no different from those of others around them. Normal religion does not disrupt the social fabric. The Moonies and the Hare Krishnas were not so much the wrong religion as, in the words of the Scottish dismissal of zealotry, 'religious o'er much'.

Brainwashing

Most demands for state controls on NRMs rested on the assertion that they manipulated vulnerable young people. That most recruits were young is not a surprise. They are available. Middle-aged middle-class people have generally invested a great deal in their careers, their mortgages and their families, and, along with that, in their personalities. Most are far too set in their ways to be available for a radically different interpretation of the world. The world-rejecting NRMs largely recruited people who were between families: free from the family of birth and not yet having acquired one of their own. And they were not just metaphorically in transition. They were also in transit. Many novices were recruited in bus stations and airports. Second, there is a point about ideology. The critique of the crass materialism of bourgeois capitalism appealed to the idealism of rebellious young people.

That most recruits were young was easily taken to mean that they were not responsible for their actions. Affluent middle-class parents who could not understand why their children were throwing up their careers, giving their money to dubious swarthy foreigners and joining bizarre religions needed an explanation and a comforting one was that their children were not exercising choice; they were being 'brainwashed'. This term was first used by psychologists in descriptions of the 'thought-reform' techniques of persuasion used by Chinese guards on US servicemen captured during the Korean War.[49] Prisoners were systematically ill fed and ill treated while being given a daily diet of political education aimed at persuading them to denounce Western imperialism. Ironically, given the later popularity of the idea, the Chinese were not all that successful. Very few prisoners were converted to communism and most of those were almost certainly only conforming outwardly.

But the notion that a combination of physical and psychological pressure could forcibly convert people was on hand when the rapid growth of Hare Krishna and the like created a need for some explanation of out-of-character actions.

The popularity of the claims of brainwashing tells us more about the audience's receptivity than the intrinsic merits of the case, which were very few. Consider the following. First, the NRMs were remarkably unsuccessful at recruiting. Only a tiny fraction of those contacted became members. As a former Moonie (by then a Washington-based political consultant for right-wing Christian organizations) told me: 'So, we do our routine thousands of times a day. We get hundreds of people along to the house for a meal. We do the talks and the hard sell. And what? Maybe one person signs up for the whole week programme. And most of them split. This is not big ju-ju!' Second, the vast majority of those who stayed involved long enough to have their brains washed and blowdried still left.[50] Third, of those who left, only a small minority claimed to have been victims in any sense.[51] On close inspection many such claims seemed to consist of little more than the following: I lived with the group and we worked very hard; I broke all ties with family and previous friends and devoted myself entirely to the group; the other people were overwhelmingly nice to me.

By the middle of the 1980s, crude brainwashing explanations of NRM recruitment had been thoroughly refuted by serious scholars. Legislative attempts to regulate or prevent new religious movements had never been serious in the United States, where a long history of contentious jurisprudence provided a monument to the difficulty of trying to divide acceptable from unacceptable religion. The attempts by Bhagwan Shree Rajneesh to establish a colony in Oregon stirred the pot, but overall interest in the phenomenon waned, as did the phenomenon itself.[52] In 1968 the UK government banned foreign Scientologists from entering the country. This was of limited utility because it would only have stopped a visiting Scientologist who felt impelled to announce his religion to the airport, but it gave the impression that the government was doing something. The ban was lifted in 1980. Attempts to have the Moonies deprived of charitable status (which brings tax advantages) failed. The Charity Commissioners simply refused to act.[53]

The one clear example of state persecution was the international campaign against the Children of God, also known as the Family of Love or just the Family. Members of the movement lived communally, and, for a time in the early 1980s, female members were encouraged to engage in 'flirty fishing' as an evangelistic technique.

They would pick up men in public places and have sex with them in the hope that the relationship could be used to recruit new members. In Spain and Japan in 1990, in Australia and Venezuela in 1992 and in France in 1993, large numbers of the Family were taken into protective custody as members were investigated for charges of sexually abusing their children. In every case, the authorities concluded the charges were unfounded and the children were returned to their parents.

Religious innovations at the end of the twentieth century were far less contentious because, in their 'New Age' shape, they tended not to recruit followers or to be very demanding. Although interest in alternative spiritualities, esoteric knowledge, complementary medical techniques and various forms of bodily discipline (such as yoga, meditation and massage) is widespread, it is also shallow. People pick and mix elements of the New Age in ways that, no matter how life enhancing, are not outwardly life changing. Perhaps most important in explaining the lack of hostility to the New Age is its basic consumerism. New Age providers do not recruit excessively loyal followers. Rather, individuals buy products (tapes, books, crystals, homeopathic remedies and the like) and services (massages, training weekends and so on) and make of them what they will. Some state agencies have occasionally taken an interest in regulating what purport to be medicines. For example, there is concern that some traditional Chinese remedies may actually be more injurious than therapeutic. But by and large the consumerist orientation of the New Age allows states to remind customers of the age-old principle that 'the buyer should beware' and otherwise leave well alone.

Millennial disaster movements

This general climate of growing indifference has periodically been punctured by a number of spectacular disasters involving violent or self-destructive sects. Despite considerable differences in the supporting belief systems, they have had in common the expectation that the world is shortly to end and that the faithful are the victims of persecution.

In November 1978 the Jonestown base of the People's Temple, a communitarian sect that had moved from California to Guyana, was visited by California Congressman Leo Ryan, who wished to investigate claims that members were being held against their will. He and four others were shot dead as they were about to leave. The Temple's leader Jim Jones then led his followers to join him in a mass suicide by drinking Fla-Vor-Aid laced with potassium cyanide. Almost 1,000 people (a quarter of them children) died.[54]

In 1993 the ill-considered behaviour of the US Bureau of Alcohol, Tobacco and Firearms (or ATF) brought international notoriety to a tiny millennialist sect in Waco, Texas: the Branch Davidians.[55] This small community of former Seventh-Day Adventists believed that the end of the world was nigh and that its leader, David Koresh (formerly Vernon Howell), had a pivotal role to play in the end times. The ATF's formal interest in the Waco compound was suspicion of firearms offences, but the agents had also been led by defectors from the movement to believe that the community's children were being sexually abused. In the shooting that broke out when agents tried to arrest Koresh, four ATF officers and six Davidians died. There then followed a fifty-one-day siege that ended with the FBI storming the compound. Koresh and some seventy-two followers (including twenty-one children) died, many as a result of fires that broke out during the attack. It subsequently became clear that the initial government action was unwarranted. The group was stockpiling weapons and food in the expectation that the world might come to a violent end soon, but almost all the firearms offences were technical and trivial and the claims of child abuse were baseless. Koresh was indeed a megalomaniac who sexually exploited his female followers with the messianic claim (all too common in such movements) that the divine leader should father a new race. But it seems fairly clear that, had the FBI not fuelled the community's paranoid fantasies, the deaths would not have occurred. The specific situation aside, the Davidians were not innately violent or suicidal.

The Solar Temple was suicidal.[56] In October 1994 fifty-three members in Quebec and Switzerland killed themselves. Sixteen months later another sixteen followed suit and two years later five more adults committed suicide. Later research suggested that not all the deaths were entirely voluntary but members of the group did believe that their human forms were temporary. They were 'noble travellers' to this planet and after shedding this body would take another more noble form elsewhere.

Similar beliefs informed Heaven's Gate – a small group that started in 1975 when Marshall Herff Applewhite and Bonnie Lu Nettles, calling themselves Bo and Peep, toured the west coast of the USA preaching that a spacecraft would soon arrive to uplift the chosen few. In this early, and not very successful form, the group was closely studied by sociologist Rob Balch, who joined them while they were in Oregon.[57] Bo and Peep believed they were aliens from outer space who had come to earth to teach others about higher planes of existence. In 1976 the group disappeared from sight. It re-emerged in 1992 and began to publicize its beliefs on a web site. In 1997 thirty-nine members of the group, including Applewhite (Nettles had died in 1985), committed suicide in San Diego. The trigger seems to have been the passage close to earth of the Hale–Bopp comet, which the group believed provided 'the marker we've been waiting for – the time for the arrival of the space raft from the Level Above Human to take us home to "Their World" – in the literal heavens'.[58]

The People's Temple, the Branch Davidians, the Solar Temple and Heaven's Gate provoked a great deal of public deliberation on the nature of 'cults' (the term popularly used for what sociologists would normally call 'sects') because people found it hard to understand those who would sacrifice themselves for their religious beliefs. A rather different reaction was produced by Aum Shinrikyo, a Japanese new religion that seemed intent on sacrificing others.[59] Aum first came to attention in the 1980s when Japanese relatives began to protest that the sect's members were being asked to sever all ties with their families. When the Japanese government refused to register Aum as a valid religious corporation (a status that would allow it corporately to own property and avoid taxes), Aum responded with demonstrations and lawsuits. It founded a political party, which failed to win any seats. It then began to construct nuclear shelters to protect its members from the expected Armageddon. In 1994 Aum began to manufacture chemical weapons. In one attack in July 1994, seven people were killed in Matsumoto by sarin nerve gas. On 20 March 1995 ten members of Aum boarded five trains in the Tokyo underground and in a coordinated attack all released sarin gas. Twelve people died and thousands were injured. In addition to these attempts at mass murder, Aum was responsible for a number of separate murders of uncooperative members and public officials who were held to be persecuting the movement.

State responses

The different ways that states have responded to NRMs can be broadly summarized by the following considerations: the nature of the religion in question; the religio-ethnic composition of the state; the history of church–state relations; and the degree of democratic freedom.

First, and this is so obvious it can be overlooked, the nature of the religion itself is a primary consideration. Some religious innovations are more dangerous then others: no state has argued that we should tolerate Aum. Disputes also regularly arise when a religion encourages its members to reject some demand that the state regards as legitimate. The most common such problem concerns pacifism. Most major faiths have fringe groups that reject violence and hence refuse to serve in the armed services. By and large most stable and mature democracies have found ways of accommodating such groups; for example, by asking for some alternative peaceful form of national service. Pacifists have often found ways of making a loyal contribution within the limits of their principles: serving alongside combat units as medical orderlies and ambulance drivers, for example.[60]

But there is a more subtle point about the substance of the religion in question. The attitudes of states may vary according to rather abstract (and not always consistent) notions of the indigenous and the alien. There is no doubt that much of the hostility in the West to the Moonies, Hare Krishna, Rajneeshism and the like stemmed from the fact that these were imports from the East. The Mormons might be odd but they are odd Americans. The Moonies are arguably no further from orthodox Christianity than the Mormons or Christian Scientists, but they are followers of an odd foreigner. The same principle can be found operating in reverse, with an additional political charge. Many NRMs have found it very difficult to gain acceptance in the new nation states of the former Soviet Union because the same thing that makes them attractive to their adherents (the cachet of Western wealth and power) makes them especially suspect in the eyes of states that have just regained (or gained for the first time) their national autonomy.[61]

Second, the extent to which a state is tolerant of NRMs is usually related to its experience of religious diversity. The UK and the USA have almost two centuries of experience of maintaining stable governments that are supported by a culturally diverse but nonetheless loyal citizenry. In contrast, Greece, which is overwhelmingly Greek Orthodox Christian, is only just beginning to develop a notion of citizenship that does not suppose that a true Greek is also Orthodox and its hostility to NRMs is part and parcel of its hostility to anything not Greek Orthodox. Both dislike for Western imports and fears about loyalty have informed the Russian government's attitude to NRMs. In order to justify refusing to treat them as acceptable religions, the Russian government has exaggerated both the powers of NRMs and their size. For example, official figures estimated the White Brotherhood as having 150,000 members; Marat Shterin thinks 1,000 is nearer the mark.[62]

Third, the history of church–state relations sets the template for dealing with innovations. The Belgian government has established an official Information and Advice Centre on Harmful Sectarian Organizations.[63] In 1998 Austria created a Federal Office for Sectarian Questions. In 2001 the French National Assembly passed a law to allow the state to prevent and repress 'cults' deemed to be harmful. The Senate approved legislation that would allow the courts to dissolve sects after two complaints against them and to prevent them from operating in the neighbourhood of schools, hospitals and rest homes. France generously funds a European Federation of Centres of Research and Information on Sectarianism. In comparing these government initiatives with the lack of such action in the USA, Tom Robbins makes the interesting point that, compared to the USA, most European states have a much more paternalistic state apparatus and a longer history of welfarism.[64] While it is certainly true that libertarianism is stronger in the USA, the contrast can be refined slightly by concentrating on church–state relations. What the above countries all have in common is that they are majority Roman Catholic.[65] In all of them religion has been seen less as a matter of individual choice (and hence the rights or otherwise of religion can be dealt with as a subset of individual liberties) and more a matter of corporations negotiating a relation. As the liberal democratic state evolved in Catholic Europe, it struck concordats with the Vatican that specified the relative rights of the church and the secular state over such matters as education, marriage law, the property of the Church and such like. The German state negotiated a similar concordat with the Lutheran Church. This manner of doing business has created a general preference for the state listing what counts as a real religion. This tradition is particularly strong where there has been a church, officially supported and funded by the state (and this would include the Nordic Lutheran states). If the state is collecting taxes on behalf of the church, then it has to have an interest in exactly which ones it will support. In Denmark, a Scientology nursery in the Valby district of Copenhagen was denied state funding.[66] Whereas the growth in diversity and the expansion of individual liberty in the UK and USA took the form of abandoning state support for religion and permitting what is in effect a free for all, in the Nordic countries it initially took the form of adding new bodies to the list of what was acceptable religion. The same principle of listing, which operates against the interests of new religions, obtains in most of Eastern Europe, where, even before the interventions of Communism, there was both a strong religio-ethnic bond (the second consideration) and a tradition of the state controlling the dominant church.

The listing system is also partly derived from the millet system of the Ottomans, which, as well as ensuring the primacy of Islam, aimed to keep the peace by regulating relationships between communities. For example, the Austro-Hungarian Empire at the end of the nineteenth century permitted people to change religion but confined the right to adults and insisted on a cumbersome procedure. Converts had to seek the permission of the local official of the faith that was being left. The priest had the right to demand a second later interview (presumably, like the UK's rules about hire purchase agreements, this was intended to give the convert time to reconsider). The convert then took the permission slip to the political official and had to wait two months for the permission to become effective. The losing community had the right to insist that a supervisory committee check the seriousness of intent and the age of the convert but could not finally prevent the change. The Russian Edict of Toleration of 1905 permitted people to leave the Orthodox Church but only to join another recognized Christian Church.

As the West has become more secular, so state support for religion and the value of any benefits that result from being approved have been reduced. The listing habit now endures mainly in the negative sense that we have seen above: with governments identifying specific religions that are not acceptable. For example, Germans, for reasons that are not entirely obvious but may have something to do with the fact that it is American, have a particular dislike of Scientology. *Länder* governments have taken to warning their citizens of the dangers of Scientology. In a policy decision that is bizarre both for the narrowness of its target (why just Scientology?) and for the area of social life being protected (is selling so important?), the federal German government in 1998 introduced into its procurement guidelines the rule that any firm wanting to supply the government had to sign a form saying that it would not promote Scientology or use 'Scientology principles' in its business.[67]

It is worth pointing out that the above examples concern relatively minor (and sometimes downright trivial) restrictions on religious innovations. What is at stake are pride and principle. Some European states have allowed some organs of government to announce that they do not much like certain religions; there are no serious attempts to curtail their operations or to prevent adults joining them.

The last of the four considerations I listed that influence how states respond to religious innovations I called 'the degree of democratic freedom'. This takes us back to the examples of intolerance common in Communist and Islamic states. Put bluntly, there are authoritarian and totalitarian regimes that seek to control new religious movement as part and parcel of their general restrictions on the rights of individuals. The example of the Chinese attitude to Falun Gong has already been mentioned.

As is clear from the detailed case studies of such volumes as Boyle and Sheen's *Freedom of Religion and Belief*, most modern democracies do very little now to curtail religious freedom, and the general principle of religious liberty has (as a principle at least) become so universally accepted that even those regimes that do attempt to police religion justify their actions on such religion-neutral grounds as protecting the vulnerable from exploitation.

However, the state can have indirect effects: it may play an important part in adjudicating disputes between private individuals or agencies. As an example I would like briefly to consider one issue that frequently brings new religions to the bar of judgement: child custody cases.

New religions and children

The fate of children tests the limits of liberal toleration. Most democracies allow consenting adults an enormous degree of freedom to do what they wish in private. But that right presupposes informed choice and hence most states seek to protect those who, because of youth or incapacity, cannot be held to be making informed choices. So we allow adults to refuse life-saving medical interventions on religious grounds, but we do not permit parents to deny their children medical treatment on the same grounds. An English court convicted a Rastafarian father of manslaughter when his refusal to allow his nine-year-old daughter to be treated for diabetes led to her death.[68] In Massachusetts in 1999, Jacques and Karen Robidoux, the leaders of a tiny Protestant sect called 'The Body', were prosecuted for murder when their ten–month-old son died after they had refused him medical treatment. When another family of the same sect also lost an infant through neglect, the remaining children were taken into care and the parents prosecuted.[69]

The general notion that the state should protect children from dangerous parents underpins one area in which liberal democratic states, despite disavowing any interest in persecuting minority religions, have been drawn into judging them. Contending parents in child custody battles are able to cite the potential dangers of an arguably deviant religion as grounds for legal decisions and thus put the courts in the position of having to decide if certain religions are indeed injurious. Hence, although most modern democratic states generally avoid arbitrating the claims of competing religions, the role of the law courts in settling disputes between individuals can force them to make ad hoc decisions about the acceptability or desirability of certain religions.

Precisely because such decisions are made on the merits of individual cases, it is difficult to infer general principles, but the courts of liberal democracies such as the USA and the UK have generally been tolerant (indeed, often more tolerant than public opinion). A woman who belonged to a church that practised snake handling (not being bitten by the deadly venom is supposedly a sign of blessing) lost custody of her son in a Mississippi court case, but in 1977 the Supreme Court of Mississippi overturned the judgment. It noted that, 'although the mother belonged to a church in which snake-handling was part of the religious ritual, she did not handle the snakes; she was not qualified to handle the snakes nor was she attempting qualification to handle the snakes; and that the child was never, during the course of the religious ceremony, in proximity of the snakes or in danger of being bitten'.[70] The Supreme Court decided she had lost custody simply because she belonged to an unpopular religion and that was unacceptable. In another custody case concerning 'The Way', where an anti-cult activist who had no knowledge of the parent testified as to the deviant nature of the group, the Appellate Court overturned the decision because 'the parent's religion, rather than the parent's parental ability, had impermissibly become the focus of what should have been a hearing focused on the best interest of the child'.[71]

The current English law governing the custody of children of a failed marriage makes the welfare of the child paramount. Indeed, that is its only principle. The English courts have consistently denied an interest in the religions of the parents. For example, in 1931 a judge said: 'It is, I hope, unnecessary to say that the court is perfectly impartial in matters of religion.'[72] Nonetheless religion does enter into decisions through the back door of common-sense notions of what is good for children. The 1973 case of *Buckley* v. *Buckley* involved a Jehovah's Witness mother and a father of no religion. Despite the three girls having lived with the mother for two years after the separation, the court awarded custody to the father (in general a remarkably rare occurrence). Among other reasons given, the court noted that, if the children stayed with their mother, they would be raised differently from other children.

For example, they would not celebrate birthdays and Christmas. The 1977 case of *Hewison* v. *Hewison* resulted in custody of three children being given to their ex-Exclusive Brethren mother despite having lived with their Brethren father for six years after the separation. Again, the judgment was not that there was anything wrong with the Exclusive Brethren religion *as such*, but as Brethren the children would be raised in an unusual manner and would learn to see themselves as 'separate'. They would grow up in an environment that the court described as 'harshly limiting'.

Bradney describes a third case where a minority religion was a crucial variable. In *Re B and G* (1985), where a Scientologist father and a former Scientologist mother were contesting the custody of two children, the children had lived with the father happily for five years until the mother sought custody. The judge accepted that to move the children would be distressing but concluded it justified because 'Scientology is both immoral and socially obnoxious.... In my view it is corrupt, sinister and dangerous.'[73] Clearly the English courts were operating with a consensus of what was socially acceptable and what was not. Though they would not judge religions, they would be unsympathetic to novel and deviant religions that appeared to be demanding and unusual.

However, Bradney's review contains another case involving an unpopular new religious movement that came to a very different conclusion from the Scientology case. In *Re ST*, Lord Justice Ward was asked to consider the application of a grandmother to have her grandson made a ward of court because his mother was a member of the Family. The Family has been widely accused of encouraging sexual perversion, and medical neglect, and impairing educational development, physical abuse and the like. What made this case unlike the Scientology one was that Lord Justice Ward was presented with expert testimony from a range of academic experts on the Family (many of whose work is cited in the notes to this chapter). Their considerable body of testimony prevented the matter being decided on ill-informed and dated stereotypes of new religions. Ward concluded that the Family had changed considerably so as no longer to warrant the critical views common in the 1970s. Although he insisted on a number of concessions from the mother (such as promising to educate the child to university level if he so desired), Ward permitted the child to remain with his mother.

In essence the Ward decision represented a return to the substance of the earlier decisions: that the courts would be critical of a religion or a level of religious commitment that departed from a consensus of what was acceptable. He was prepared to temper his initial hostility to the Family once he was persuaded that it was no longer dangerously deviant and that the mother was prepared to moderate her commitment to the Family to bring her back to the consensus of what was acceptable.

Notions of what is socially acceptable can constrain religious liberty. In 1878, in *Reynolds* v. *United States*, the Supreme Court decided that Mormon polygamy, though defended on the grounds of religious freedom, could be outlawed. Congress could make laws to prohibit religiously sanctioned *practices* (not beliefs or opinions) 'which were in violation of social duties or subversive of good order'. But the limits of acceptability are now far broader than they were 200 years ago or still are outside the West. US courts have repeatedly protected the rights of individuals to practise their minority religions; for example, they have prevented Seventh-Day Adventists being forced to work on Saturdays, which they regard as the Sabbath. In 1994 a judge in Utah decided that a Mormon divorcee should lose custody of her children to their Mormon father if she left the state to marry a non-Mormon. A major consideration was the judge's belief that, if the children left the state, the mother would not raise the children as Mormons. The Utah Court of Appeals overturned the decision but on grounds that left safe the notion that a Mormon parent had a right to expect his Mormon children to be raised as Mormons. It decided that they were was no evidence that the mother would not continue her children's religious upbringing.[74]

Conclusion

The main points of this chapter can be readily summarized. The liberal democratic states of the West have largely given up policing religion, and, it must be said, this has been accepted by most Christian churches. Where in the eighteenth and nineteenth centuries nation states regarded the creation of a homogenous national culture as essential for stability, many states have learnt that they can survive perfectly well without the social cement of a shared sense of ethnic identity. Even where chauvinists wish to give pride of place to a particular ethnic or national identity, the general decline of religion in the West (combined with increasing diversity in the forms that religion may take) has meant that religion can no longer be a vital component of national identity. In largely secular states, such policing of religion as we do find is concerned primarily with groups that are patently dangerous or can be construed as threats to some very general social values.

The influence of the West has been such that religious liberty is now internationally accepted as a basic fundamental human right to which even those societies that routinely infringe it pay lip service. However, because this affects how we judge states that do police religion, it is worth noting the rise of toleration in the West had very little to do with good intentions. There are few examples of dominant churches willingly giving up the demand that the state impose the true religion on the people. Toleration was a necessary accommodation to increasing religious diversity and a growing egalitarian ethos.

Having said that, we should not underestimate the power of political ideas. It is obvious that many of the new nation states, especially those that have only recently gained their independence, put national integrity above individual freedom. But it is also clear that the work of organizations such as the United Nations has provided powerful encouragement for religious minorities to campaign for their liberty and various forms of international pressure have been effective in blunting the residual repressive tendencies of some states.

7

EXPLANATION

Introduction

This book has been written with a number of purposes in mind. First I wanted to demonstrate that religion influences politics. In retrospect that does not seem a hard task. It is always possible to argue that some of those people who claim divine inspiration for their actions are dishonest, misguided or deluded, but it would be a very curious model of human behaviour that managed to make even a fraction of the many examples discussed in the previous chapters disappear. We have the primary evidence of people asserting that they take this view rather than that because their God or Gods requires it and we have the compelling evidence of patterns of correlation. When, for example, we routinely find that regular churchgoers or people who describe themselves as religious differ systematically in their attitudes or voting preferences from people who do not engage in collective acts of worship and who do not describe themselves as religious, this seems good reason to suppose that religion matters. And religious identity remains central when we consider, not the explicit views and self-conscious actions of religiously motivated people, but more abstract patterns of group behaviour. As the many examples considered in chapter 3 show, religion is intimately implicated in the identities of tribes, ethnies and nations and the wars between them.[1]

However, to show that there are consistent links between religious beliefs and political actions seems almost trivial. Much more important is a second set of questions buried in the above: are there observable differences between Catholic, Protestant, Hindu, Buddhist, Shinto and Muslim politics? This is the issue that will be examined in this final chapter. I will begin by recapping some of the specific details presented in earlier chapters in order to establish that this is a question worth asking. I will then consider a number of general objections to the idea that religion can be a cause of politics. Having removed those obstacles to the enterprise, I will make the case that religious traditions do indeed vary in the sorts of politics they create, legitimate and sustain. In some cases this is self-evident. It is hardly a surprise that evangelical Protestants should resist being incorporated in an overwhelmingly Catholic country. However, behind such obvious connections there may be more subtle links. Many of the causal links I identify are rather unusual. They are the commonplace material of social science but the approach may be unfamiliar to both the partisan defenders and critics of certain religions. My general thesis is that the most potent connections between religion and politics are often unintended and inadvertent.

Regimes

There is at first sight a strong correlation between regime and religion. Since representative democracy became at all widespread, the vast majority of Christian countries have had democratic governments.[2] The exceptions are the Orthodox countries of Eastern Europe that fell prey to communism between 1917 and 1990; the Catholic European states that embraced fascism in the period 1922–45; and the Central American and South American countries that had a variety of military dictatorships in the twentieth century. That account suggests we can further differentiate. As I argued in Chapter 4, it was Catholic and Orthodox countries that were particularly prone to authoritarianism. The vast majority of Protestant states avoided communism and fascism.

The association of religion and regime is strengthened by the example of countries in which Muslims are in a majority. Of the 192 states in the world in 2002, 121 (that is, 63 per cent) have democratically elected governments. But, as we can see from table 7.1, less than a quarter of the forty-seven countries with an Islamic majority have democratically elected governments. There are no elective democracies at all among the sixteen Arab states of the Middle East and North Africa.

Each year an organization of academic political scientists ranks every state in the world for political rights and for civil liberties.

Table 7.1   Type of regime in Muslim countries, 2001

Type of regime	Number
Presidential-parliamentary democracies	10
Traditional monarchies	9
Authoritarian presidencies	9
Dominant party states with token opposition	7
Presidential-parliamentary with authoritarian elements	6
One-party states	3
Military ruled	1
Theocracy	1
Parliamentary democracies	1

Source: The Freedom House Survey Team, 'Freedom in the World 2002: the democracy gap'

Table 7.2   Political rights and civil liberties in Muslim and non-Muslim states, 1981 and 2001 (%)

State	Muslim		Non-Muslim	
	1981	2001	1981	2001
Free	3	2	41	59
Partly free	51	38	25	28
Not free	46	59	34	14
TOTAL	100	100	100	101
No. of states	39	47	123	145

Totals not 100 owing to rounding.
Source: The Freedom House Survey Team, 'Freedom in the World 2002: the democracy gap'

The two scores are then combined to produce a simple index of freedom. As in table 7.2, states are described as free, partially free or not free. Because the measure of civil liberties includes attention to religious freedom and gender equality, Islamic states will never do very well, but the other considerations are universally accepted as basic liberties.[3] The differences between each pair of columns, which describe the extent and direction of change between 1981 and 2001, are striking: 'while the countries of Latin America, Africa, East-Central Europe, and South and East Asia experienced significant gains for democracy and freedom over the last twenty years, the countries of the Islamic world experienced an equally significant increase in repressive regimes.'[4] The net result of the changes is that columns 2 and 4 are almost mirror images of each other.

It is possible to object to human rights being used as a universal measure. Palmiro Togliatti, the Secretary of the Italian Communist Party, derided the entire European Convention on Human Rights as a right-wing plot to protect bourgeois privilege. We could certainly make a reasonable case that freedom of speech and association, equality before the law, due process of law and the right not to be subjected to cruel and unusual punishment reflect a post-Christian individualism to which socialists and religious conservatives might object.[5] And they did. When in 1948 the United Nations proposed its Universal Declaration of Human Rights, no member state voted against, but the Soviet bloc and Saudi Arabia abstained. However, there are two good grounds for comparing regimes of very different cultures against the common yardstick. The first is that the vast majority of regimes do claim to respect and admire those standards; they may have first been articulated by Thomas Jefferson and his wealthy deist friends, but in the 200 years since they have become very widely accepted. The second point is that it does not matter if the theory of human rights is as biased as a cheap roulette wheel, because I am not making moral judgements about the quality of regimes. I am trying to make causal connections between the religious culture of a society and features of its regime, and all that matters is that both ends of the equation be accurately identified. It does not matter for my purposes here if one thinks women should be allowed or denied the vote. The political consequences that might be explained by religion need to be identified; they do not need to judged.

To return to regime comparison, such correlations do not themselves tell us much about the causes of illiberality. There are obviously many forces that shape the political history of regimes other than their religious heritage and these need to be considered. But before we too readily identify poverty or imperialism (generally the preferred candidates) as the prime causes, we should note the following. First, many of the repressive Arab regimes (Saudi Arabia, for example) have been made comparatively wealthy and powerful by oil. Second, many repressive regimes are in countries that have had two or more generations of independence in which to shape their own political fortunes. They have not been entirely free to choose their destinies. Western powers, either directly or indirectly through organizations such as the International Monetary Fund and the World Trade Organization, have continued to inter- fere around the globe, but the power differential is decreasing. In 1956 a handful of CIA operatives was able to restore the Shah of Iran to his throne after he had fled. In 1979 the USA was powerless to prevent the Islamic revolution.[6] Third, countries where the USA has most actively meddled are generally not those with the most repressive regimes; one of the biggest changes in the two decades described in table 7.2 was the shift from military dictatorship to parliamentary democracy in Central and South America.

As I noted in chapter 1, social scientific explanation of large-scale phenomena is perpetually hindered by a shortage of comparable cases. If we had a very large number of states with similar econ- omies and similarly long periods of national autonomy but differ- ent religious traditions and different sorts of governments, then we could with greater confidence draw conclusions from comparisons. But we must make do with what we have, and such contrasts as are possible certainly suggest that religion is in some way implicated in the nature of regimes.

It is worth trying to separate two closely related considerations. In one sense there is no mystery about the poor rankings of most Islamic countries on scales intended to measure the extent of dem- ocracy or individual human rights. To what extent these features stem from the countries in question being Muslim in culture is something I will consider shortly, but we can note at the outset that a number of Muslim states (the United Arab Emirates or Saudi Arabia, for example) make no pretensions to democracy and most of those that do deny the vote to women. In Kuwait, the all-male Parliament in 2000 rejected a proposal from the ruler to enfranchise women. The second consideration is slightly more subtle and it concerns what we mean by democracy. The Iranian president Mu- hammad Khatami said: 'the existing democracies do not necessar- ily follow one formula or aspect. It is possible that democracy may lead to a liberal system. It is possible that democracy may lead to a socialist system. Or it may be a democracy with the inclusion of religious norms in the government. We have accepted the third option.'[7] It is, of course, a moral matter what political regime one prefers, but in normal usage 'democracy' implies that the decisions of the people, the demos, are sovereign and final. A regime such as Iran's, which limits the choices of the people by a body of religious norms (and has those interpreted by an unelected body), is less democratic than one that does not begin with such restraints. The point becomes clear if we translate the language of choices in a language of choosers: the Iranian state discriminates in favour of conservative Shi'ite Muslims.[8]

Parties and social movements

One of the main concerns of this book has been the political actions of groups of believers, channelled through political parties, pressure groups or looser social movements. Most societies have within them people who are inspired by their faiths to seek political goals. My question is this: do Catholic, Protestant, Hindu, Buddhist and Muslim movements differ in ways that reflect differences in religion rather than differences in mundane circumstances? Although this is not my only concern, I will concentrate on violence because it is indirectly a good indicator of a range of such other important things as respect for the authority of the state and attitude to people of other views. That one group confines its attempts at expansion to handing out leaflets while another murders those who do not convert seems significant. As with regimes, there does seem to be a prima facie case to be made. But, so that the narrow focus of my remarks can be clear, some preliminary observations have to be made.

In the Poso district of Indonesia in late 1998 hundreds of Christians were killed by Muslims and vice versa. In early 2002 gangs of Christian Yoruba and Muslim Hausa youths fought street battles in Lagos in which hundreds died. In the civil wars of the 1990s in Rwanda and Burundi, Christian Hutus and Tutsis (including Catholic priests and nuns) massacred their fellow citizens. In these and similar cases it seems clear that religion plays little part in the violence, beyond forming a major social division around which people can organize their sense of grievance.

What interests me are movements that exist to make the world more godly. In every Islamic state and among every sizeable population of Muslims there are fundamentalist movements that take the requirement to engage in *jihad* or holy war literally and believe that the pursuit of God's law justifies the use of violence. Muslim Brothers, Partisans of Allah, Islamic Jihad – such movements abound in the Muslim world. The Egyptian Muslim Brotherhood sought power by assassination. It murdered two prime ministers and almost killed a third. It killed a chief of police, an interior minister, a chief justice and scores of other officials. It tried to kill President Abdul Nasser. The Brotherhood moderated, but it was replaced by other radical Islamic movements and one of those killed Nasser's successor, Anwar Sadat. The leader of Algeria's Armed Islamic Group, Antar Zouabri, said: 'There is no neutrality in this war. There are only those who are with me. All others are apostates and deserve to die.'[9]

I will consider three examples from the world of Christian fundamentalism that suggest that contemporary Christianity imposes a powerful constraint on what could be jihadi movements: Protestants in Northern Ireland; and anti-homosexuality and anti-abortion campaigners in the USA.

The conflict in Northern Ireland would seem well suited to encouraging a jihadi attitude among Protestants. When the bulk of Ireland was given its independence from Britain, the northeastern quarter, in which Protestants were a majority, was allowed to remain part of the United Kingdom. In the early 1970s Irish republicans began a campaign of terror against agents of the UK state and against Northern Irish Protestants. The evangelical Protestant cleric and politician Ian Paisley emerged as one of the leading opponents of Irish nationalism. Paisley and his evangelical followers are often blamed for the violence in Northern Ireland. As Protestants who wish to remain citizens of the United Kingdom, they strongly oppose the political demands of Irish Catholic nationalists. Their obdurate refusal to abandon their cause doubtless plays some part in the decision of some Nationalists to take up the armed struggle. What is less often noticed is that Paisley and the vast majority of his supporters have always been hostile to the use of vigilante violence by Protestants. Early on in his career Paisley used various forms of street protest and he has on occasion threatened to mobilize Ulster Protestants to prepare to defend themselves in the event of a British withdrawal from Northern Ireland. In the 1980s he memorably inspected a parade of men who, on the command, took out and waved their firearms certificates! But he has never been involved in commissioning or condoning terror. He has repeatedly and very publicly said that loyalist (that is, pro-British) killers 'besmirch the name of Protestantism'. In the 1990s, the UK government offered convicted terrorists early release from prison in return for their organizations calling a ceasefire. Paisley opposed the release of the loyalist prisoners every bit as vehemently as he opposed the release of IRA men. For thirty years Paisley's numerous enemies have been trying to find associations with violence that would blacken his reputation; to date they have failed to find (apposite metaphor) the smoking gun. This strongly suggests that his professed legalism is sincere. Since 1970 there have been about 10,000 male members of Paisley's Free Presbyterian Church who could have become involved in terrorism. I can find fewer than twenty who have been. The same point can be made even more strongly the other way round. Of some 300 or so members of loyalist paramilitary organizations whose biographies I have collected over twenty years of studying the Ulster conflict, I can think of only three who claimed to be committed Christians. The loyalist paramilitary milieu has always seen religion as a legitimate alternative to terrorism. Getting 'saved' has been widely accepted by the gunmen as a decent reason for one of their number to leave.[10] Although Paisley's evangelical Christians and the members of loyalist paramilitary groups share a common goal, they pursue it in very different ways. The Christians are not terrorists; the terrorists are not Christians.

We should note that the reluctance of Ulster's evangelical Protestants to become involved in violence comes from a setting where it would not be hard to justify it to themselves. The conflict is heavily tinged with religion. Catholic political parties try to advance 'Catholic' interests at the expense of those of 'Protestants'. Irish republican terrorists murder Protestants (and they sometimes do it in churches). The Catholic Church condemns the IRA's means but supports its ends and has consistently refused to excommunicate republican terrorists. In those circumstances, it would seem relatively easy to defend a Protestant *jihad*. But it has not happened. Among Ulster Protestants, being religious is an antidote to being involved in political violence.

In the United States, politically involved conservative Christians have, with very few exceptions, been law abiding. They have confined their attempts to achieve cultural domination to the conventional stuff of pressure groups; they petition, vote, stand for elected office and mount court cases. When televangelist Jerry Falwell, the founder of the Moral Majority, was accused by gay Christians of inadvertently encouraging anti-homosexual violence, his response was to invite leading gay Christians to a weekend conference at his Liberty University. At a joint press conference he restated his opposition to sodomy but also apologized for any anti-homosexual violence that his comments may have inadvertently encouraged. He made it as clear as possible that Christians should 'hate the sin but love the sinner'. As he said: 'There is always room for us to do things better. We have looked very carefully at and will look more carefully in the future at any kind of rhetoric in our writings or preachments or whatever, that might lead someone to have hostility toward anybody, and that includes gays and lesbians.'[11] We may, of course, be sceptical about Falwell's sincerity and see this as a publicity stunt, but it is still notable that he did not say that Sodomites were such an abomination to God that they deserved all they got.

Abortion is the most emotionally charged issue in what Hunter has called the USA's culture wars and the one item in the NCR's agenda that conservative Catholics really share with fundamentalists.[12] It has repeatedly been the focus of pressure group politics. It has also generated a considerable amount of violence. Between 1989 and 1997, in addition to thousands of pickets and protests, there were 106 bombings and arson attacks on abortion clinics. Over the same nine-year period, seven people were killed.[13] It is not easy to know what to make of that figure. In one light, as a response to adults engaging in perfectly legal consensual behaviour, it is dreadful. On the other hand, considering the strength of feeling over the issue, the frequency of abortions (there were at least 1.3 million in 1993), and the prevalence of gun-related violence in the USA, this is a remarkably small figure. More people are killed in any one year by disgruntled workers shooting their colleagues. But what is more telling are the character and status of the perpetrators of these attacks and the response of their religious institutions. Most were marginal and disturbed individuals at odds with their own faith communities. John Salvi, who was responsible for two murders, was a highly disturbed young Catholic man whose anti-abortion protests had been rejected by his own priest and Catholic congregation.[14] Michael Griffin, who killed Dr David Gunn in 1993, pleaded insanity at his trial. The only clergyman I can find personally involved in anti-abortion violence is Paul Hill, who killed a doctor and his companion in 1994. Hill was an ordained Presbyterian who had failed to find work as a clergyman. Prior to the murders he had appeared a number of times on television defending the killing of David Gunn. Despite being extremely conservative in its theology, the congregation of which he was a member excommunicated him for his radical views before he acted upon them.[15] When Father Trosch, a Catholic priest in Mobile, Alabama, said that killing doctors who performed abortions was 'justifiable homicide', his bishop immediately repudiated his views and sacked him from his parish. When Father John Earl of Rockford, Illinois, rammed an abortion clinic with his car and then took an axe to the building, he was also sacked by his bishop.

There is in the USA a very small (but always newsworthy) 'Christian Identity' movement of armed militias that reject entirely the authority of the state, but the religious inspiration for these groups is slight. They are primarily white supremacist and, though they occasionally use biblical imagery to defend their actions, they are not supported even by the most right-wing of fundamentalist churches in the USA.[16]

To repeat the assessment I made in chapter 5, it seems reasonable to conclude that even those Protestant fundamentalists and traditionalist Catholics who are inspired to campaign to restore God to the centre of Western public life confine themselves to the channels of social action that are permitted in liberal democracies. We can add, for this is a vital consideration, that most accept that there is an important difference between morality and the law; that people have a right to behave badly. They accept the basic operating principle of liberal democracy: that people have basic human rights irrespective of their religious beliefs or identities and hence that the pursuit of religious purity does not provide a warrant for infringing the rights of others.

Models of explanation

Chemists do not have to argue with their chemicals. They can pursue their explanations without the subject matter talking back. A preliminary problem in trying to tease out the connection between religious traditions and politics is that believers are themselves privy to the exercise. It is impossible to lecture about the social consequences of any religion without a partisan disputing any assertion made by insisting that the person, event, regime or organization in question is not truly representative. Mention Saudi Arabia and you will be told by someone that 'Of course, the Wahhabis are not typical Muslims'. I have been told in all seriousness that Christians have never persecuted anyone, that Muslims have never used violence to spread Islam, that Sufis have always been pacifists, as have Buddhists, and that Hindus always tolerate diversity; all claims that are readily refuted by, respectively, the Spanish Inquisition, the Arab conquest of the Middle East and North Africa, the Mahdi's Dervishes, the civil war in Sri Lanka and the attacks on Muslim communities in India.

When such discrepant evidence is raised, it is answered by a radical dualism. For the blinkered partisans, their religion causes those things they like and has nothing at all to do with the bad things. That which they admire happens *because* of the true faith; that which they dislike happens *despite* it. For example, a newspaper article by a female Muslim entitled 'Women and Islam' was subtitled 'Its culture, not Islam, to blame'.[17] Apparently the subordination of women in almost every Islamic culture has nothing to do with the teachings of the Prophet but is rather a result of un-Islamic patriarchy distorting what is really an egalitarian religion.[18]

The Pygmalion method

There is an even-handed version of this common among social scientists, which I have called the Pygmalion approach after George Bernard Shaw's play of that name (better known as the musical *My Fair Lady*). In a wager, the linguist Professor Higgins sets out to prove that he can teach the poor flower-seller Eliza Doolittle to speak like a society lady. His point is that social class is not an inherited condition but can be readily acquired and that the marks of good breeding by which some people set so much store are purely superficial. In the social sciences the Pygmalion approach takes the form of arguing that religion is epiphenomenal and circumstances are everything. Were NCR leader Jerry Falwell and the founder of the Lebanese Hezbollah, Sheikh Fadlallah, to swap places, so that the Protestant televangelist preached in the slums of southern Lebanon and Fadlallah ran a Muslim university in peaceful, stable, affluent Virginia, then their attitudes to violence would be reversed. That one is Protestant Christian and the other Muslim is irrelevant. It is the economic, political and social context that explains the different attitudes to violence (and everything else).

One justification for dismissing religion as a significant cause is that all the major religions are so broad that they can legitimate almost any course of action. Hence, what course of action is chosen cannot be explained by the faith in question. Fred Halliday, a noted political scientist and Islamic specialist, says:

> as one Iranian thinker put it, Islam is a sea in which it is possible to catch almost any fish one wants. It is, like all the great religions, a reservoir of values, symbols and ideas from which it is possible to derive a contemporary politics and social code: the answer as to why this or that interpretation was put upon Islam resides therefore, not in the religion and its texts itself, but in the contemporary needs of those articulating Islamic politics.[19]

Bruce Lawrence takes a similar line when he writes that religion's 'pervasiveness as a general condition was matched only by its malleability as a contextual variant open to limitless interpretation'.[20] Sami Zubaida similarly questions whether there is such a thing as a Muslim society.[21]

There is a Marxist version of this that supposes that what really drives the world are production, social class and class conflict.[22]

Culture is secondary; a reflection of social realities rather than a cause of them. But we can get to the same point just by recognizing that the contexts in which people have to make choices about how they interpret God's will must exert enormous influence on those interpretations. Even if US fundamentalists such as Falwell wanted to impose their vision of the godly society on their countrymen and thought any means to that end were justified, they would know that very few people would follow them. Equally well, it is easy to see that, to the people of South Lebanon, respect for individual human rights must seem like something of a luxury.

A second reason for holding to the Pygmalion position is that religions, precisely because they are embedded in what phenomenologists call 'everyday lifeworlds', have to deal with common problems and they do so with a limited repertoire of ideas. Hence it is no surprise that the same tensions and outcomes appear in a variety of religious contexts. As an illustration, consider the common reform wave pattern. With the exception perhaps of Confucianism and Hinduism, which prescribe very different patterns of life for different statuses of people, all religions in theory wish everyone to live the religious life. But too much zealotry undermines the economy. The masses are required to be 'hewers of wood and drawers of water' and cannot be permitted too much time to think on the next life or too much fussiness about how they act in this one. And, if a religion wishes to encompass more than just a small group of virtuosi sectarians, it has to tolerate considerable variation in the quality of religious observance. In turn this leads to tensions between the pragmatists and the zealots and to periodic waves of revivalism and reform.

There is a deal of good sense in the general view that social, political and economic realities often shape religions to an extent that allows us, in trying to explain this or that social change, to suppose that religion as such is peripheral. However, I cannot conclude that this prevents religion acting as a cause of some political actions.

The first objection to the Pygmalion position is a simple one. There is a crucial difference between saying that there is considerable variation in the links between any one religion and its political outcomes and saying that there is *infinite* variation and hence no possibility of contrasting religions. This is an important point, and, to clarify it, I would like to quote at length from Halliday:

> the contingency of interpretation ... is too often obscured in discussions, by both Muslims and non-Muslims alike, of the role of 'Islam'

itself in political life. The presupposition upon which much discussion of the questions rests is that there exists one, unified and clear, tradition to which contemporary believers and political forces may relate....Opponents of Islamist movements tend to reproduce this essentialist assumption in discussing such questions as whether Islamic societies can ever be democratic, or whether there is some special link between the 'Islamic mind' and terrorism. The reality is that no such essential Islam exists.[23]

It is not clear why the absence of an 'essential Islam' should preclude us from making observations about the various Islams that do exist (and Halliday does just that very well). Partisan believers may wish to have an essential Islam, but, for the rest of us, what matters is that there be enough common ground in the historical available Islams for us to consider if, as instances of a common religious tradition, they differ systematically from instances of other religious traditions. To borrow Wittgenstein's metaphor of family resemblance, we can recognize that some people look alike even though they do not all share a single characteristic that is unambiguously absent from others. Doctors do not need to identify an 'essential' form of asthma to distinguish asthma attacks from emphysema, lung cancer or pneumonia. It may be hard to discern regular differences between religions, but that does not seem like good reason to give up. To say that Islam (or any other religion) is so broad that 'it is possible to catch almost any fish one wants' or that it is open to 'limitless' interpretation is an exaggeration. There are some fish that are caught very often in certain religions and others that are found very rarely. Where is the popular Islam that denies the Prophet's divine inspiration? Where is the popular Catholicism that denies the special status of the Holy Father?

Or, to put it another way, it is useful to be reminded of the need for careful and accurate description, but the fact that there is considerable variation within any major religious tradition need not stun us into silence. Dairy cattle differ in many important respects from beef cows and no farmer would 'essentialize' cows, but we can still distinguish and compare cows and sheep. No one thinks that the Pope is a Protestant or that Ian Paisley is a Catholic.

It is worth pointing out that the assertion that the major religions are so internally diverse that we cannot impute any characteristics to them is actually more salient for Christianity, to which it is rarely applied, than it is for Islam. Since the fourth century, Christianity has been split into an Eastern wing based first on Byzantium (that is, Constantinople) and then on Moscow, and a Western wing based on Rome. The Reformation in the sixteenth century produced a three-way split in Western Christianity to give us Roman Catholicism and the Lutheran and Calvinist strands of Protestantism. Add to that the array of internal divisions and the mutation that Christianity has undergone in every distant land to which it has been transplanted and one hardly has a single uniform product. That Islam is younger and has spread less far (for example, reaching the Americas and Northern and Central Europe only in the 1960s) reduces the external sources of variation. But more important, for all its sectarian divisions, Islam retains a common list of basic requirements: the confession that there is one God and Allah is his Prophet, the standard form of worship, the requirement to give alms, the pilgrimage to Mecca and fasting at Ramadan. Alone among major religions, Islam has continued to assert that its sacred text should be read in Arabic, its original language and the language used by its founder. Christianity's sacred scriptures were written in Hebrew and Greek. The New Testament expresses the thoughts of people who spoke Aramaic and it is an amalgam of teachings that circulated in oral form in a number of languages before being written down. The lack of a single sacred language weakened objections to translating the Bible into the vernacular languages of the countries into which Christianity spread. Further cohesion is provided for Islam by the reverence for the geographical sites of the Prophet's life. Mecca has a centrality to Islam that the town and cities of Palestine have never had for Christians. One way of making the contrast is to note that, although Shi'ite Muslims prefer their mosques to Sunni ones, they can worship in them without feeling that they are offending against a basic principle of their faith. Conservative Protestants simply cannot participate in a Catholic or Orthodox mass.

My second objection to the Pygmalion method concerns its principled rejection of the reasons people give for their actions. We should never take what people say about their motives at face value, but, when people repeatedly assert that they believe that they are doing God's will, we would need powerful evidence to reject their claim and insist that, actually, religion is not important. If articulate Catholics regularly explain certain features of their society as being derived from its Catholic culture and, moreover, a number of Catholic societies have those features when a number of Protestant ones do not, then it seems perfectly sensible for us to accept, at least as a starting thesis, that those features are caused by Catholicism. This does not, of course, stop us working back a stage to argue, for example, that one reason Catholicism came to dominate that society was that it had an elective affinity with other elements of the culture or with non-cultural characteristics. Cultural innovations that do not resonate with material interests are unlikely to catch on. They will be the seed that falls on stony ground. But, to pursue the agricultural metaphor, recognizing that whether seed grows or not depends on the state of the soil does not mean that soil is the only consideration in agriculture. A farmer still needs seed.

I am guessing, but I suspect that the Pygmalion approach derives some of its popularity from contemporary cultural politics – in particular a desire to atone for imperialism. To suggest, for example, that culture plays some part in the prevalence of repressive regimes in Islamic countries is to insult people who already have enough problems. We might admire the sensitivity that underlies such reticence, but it is actually patronizing in the extreme to deny people responsibility for their actions. If, in addition to the comparative record showing that Islamic states are often repressive and authoritarian, we repeatedly find a very large number of well-qualified Islamic religious leaders such as the Egyptian Sayyid Qutb or the founder of Jama'at-I-Islami, Abu'l-A'la Mawdudi, arguing that what liberal Westerners regard as oppressive is actually divinely ordained, then I see no reason to deny Islam the right to claim its children. We cannot be partial about explanation. If it is reasonable to consider whether Catholicism played a part in the rise of fascism, it is also reasonable to consider whether characteristics of Islamic countries have something to do with Islam.

In brief, my general approach to studying the role of religion in politics is this. We should be aware that the major religions have the potential for generating and legitimating a very wide range of political movements, agendas, strategies and outcomes. But we need not take this to the extreme conclusion of supposing that religious cultures have no effects on their societies.

Orientalism

Since the publication of Edward Said's *Orientalism*, it has become common for general observations about Islam made by Westerners to be dismissed as 'orientalist'.[24] Among the putative errors of this blinkered view are the following. It takes Christianity as normal or paradigmatic and regards Islam as deviant. It treats the history and evolution of the West as normative and regards the East simply as a series of absences or failings.[25] It exaggerates the homogeneity of Christianity and Islam and the differences between them, often taking Islam to be a truncated and incomplete version of Christianity. It also imputes contrasting character types to the inhabitants of West and East; as Turner puts it: 'the rational westerner versus the unpredictable Oriental, the gentle white versus the cruel yellow man.'[26] Sardar adds that orientalists portray Orientals as lazy.[27] Finally, orientalism's apparent objectivity conceals a clear commitment to the notion that the West is superior.

The term is not useful. Its usage is too reminiscent of the habit of 1970s Marxists to dismiss everyone with whom they disagreed as 'bourgeois sociologists'.[28] And it is used for incompatible purposes. Normally it derides scholars who attribute unpleasant consequences to Islam (legitimating tribal monarchies, for example). But it is also used for the opposite purpose. Sayid describes the tendency 'to treat "Muslim" as a phenomenon of other more sturdy bases of identity formations (such as class, kinship, caste and ethnicity)' as 'the product of orientalism'.[29] If regarding Islam as a cause or as an effect can both be described as orientalist, the label is not a useful term of analysis. It may have some value in depicting the attitude of committed Christians to other faiths. It may accurately capture the arrogance of nineteenth-century British imperialists. It does not do justice to the attempts of modern social scientists to engage in accurate description and explanation.[30] Finally I might add that previous criticisms of my work as orientalist miss the point of the exercise. I am concerned not with a West–East or Christian–Muslim contrast but with systematic differences between a variety of religions (including competing varieties of Christianity).

Although they are in no sense unique to the orientalist critique, we can take three useful points from it. First, we should be accurate: ignorance is no more acceptable here than anywhere else. Second, we should be sensitive to internal variation. If it is not clear from the preceding chapters, then I will say that, in using terms such as Christianity and Islam, I am not supposing that these signify something with the consistency of set yoghurt. The obvious point is that, unless we use single terms and confine discussion of variations to places where they are germane, we will never be able to say anything.

Third, we should not exaggerate differences. There is certainly little explanatory value in thinking in terms of a 'clash of civilizations' between the Christian West and the Muslim East. Samuel Huntington's book of that title[31] is actually far more nuanced and sensitive in the contrasts it draws than its title and popularized summaries might suggest, but I would go further and stress that in what follows I am trying to disentangle what I take to be small differences. There are anthropological constants. We are born, we reproduce, we raise children, we die. There is a limited range of problems that all peoples face and hence a relatively limited repertoire of solutions. Add to that the fact that, even before the current degree of global integration and interaction, there was considerable contact between cultures and peoples and we have to conclude that there will be considerable similarities between religions.[32]

The causal nexus

In concluding these preliminary methodological observations, I want to make an important point about assigning causation to cultural phenomena: we should beware of making too much of any specific connection between any one religious idea and any one political action. For example, the World Trade Center attacks brought back to the mass media a theme from the 1980s: the willingness of Islamic fundamentalists to commit suicide. As it had been then, this fondness for martyrdom was explained by the beliefs of some Muslims that dying while engaged in holy war would result in immediate transport to the most glorious heaven. This sort of link between a religious belief and a certain action is properly vulnerable to Halliday's criticisms. First, it involves a very small number of people and hence may be unrepresentative. Second, there are enough other specific propositions in Islam about suicide, murder, violence and the appropriate ways to promote the faith to call into question the virtue of claiming this particular belief as causally effective in this circumstance. Third, it is hard to establish a clear difference between faiths on this issue. Even without the promise of virgins to attract the martyr, religions as different as Christianity and Shinto (and secular nationalisms) have produced people willing to die for the cause. In January 1884 General 'Chinese' Gordon, a staunch evangelical who had once said it was better to die violently and heroically than to go unnoticed, defied his original orders to evacuate the army from Khartoum and stayed to maintain the siege. When it was finally broken by the dervishes of the Mahdi, Gordon died a hero's death, as he knew he would, and as many suspect he wished.[33] State Shinto produced the kamikaze pilots who, for the sake of the divine Emperor, crashed their planeloads of explosives into US ships.[34] Christian Palestinians carried out suicide bombings. We may have been struck by the sight of companies of young Iranians chanting that they were ready to die for Allah as they marched off to fight Iraq in the early 1980s, but, when we allow for cultural differences in expression, we may see something similar in the solemn young British men marching past the chaplain on the way to war in 1914.

This is not to say that specific beliefs cannot have political consequences. My point is that we will be on firmer ground if, instead of examining very specific and local beliefs and actions (what difference does it make that in some schools of Islam the martyr gets virgins), we concentrate on larger and more abstract differences that are more likely to endure. For example, Protestants differ greatly about the manner in which Christ will return and the world end, but they do not differ at all in their view that religious merit cannot be transferred from one person to another and hence that we must all answer to God for ourselves. In the last half of the nineteenth century Catholics across Europe argued amongst themselves about the propriety of parliamentary democracy, but the Church as a whole maintained a fairly consistent negative attitude that is a matter of record in both word and deed. And, although the Church's attitude to any specific proposal in this or that country may have fluctuated, there is considerable consistency at the level of *general orientation* to democracy. To say this does not require a naive claim to have discovered the essential Catholicism. It merely says that, underlying the contingent variety of human experience, there are some basic socio-logics. There is an orderliness to the world.

The variables

Enough of the preliminaries: we can now move to the argument. What follows is less a general theory of politics and religion and more a listing of what seem to be the most general salient characteristics that can be extracted from the detailed case studies presented in the previous chapters. As will become clear, none of the connections is simple. Most of the relevant considerations interact with each other so that they might be better represented by a three-dimensional model than by linear exposition. But linear it must be.

The nature of the divine

The most important consideration for the political consequences of any religion is the nature of its apex. Is the divine singular or multifaceted? Is the religion monotheistic or polytheistic?

Religion is a profoundly social matter. Very rarely (and usually in the secular West) do we find individuals with their own private religions. To see why faith is normally a collective enterprise we can start from either its functions or its plausibility. As Émile Durkheim argued, religion generally acts as a form of social cement. When people worship their God (to avoid tedium I will not repeatedly add 'or Gods or non-personalized supernatural powers'; that can be assumed), they often also worship themselves. Religious rituals bring people together and often specifically include rules about personal and family disputes needing to be settled before the ritual. Rituals are often designed to bring benefits, not to individuals but to the group as a whole. Responsibilities are similarly generalized. The God of the Israelites sometimes spared the especially obedient (Lot and his family from the fate of Sodom and Gomorrah; Noah and his family from the Flood), but the Children of Israel could not avoid being punished by fingering a few of their number. We can also appreciate the social nature of religion if we start from the problem of plausibility. How do we know that this is the correct way to worship God? Tests and demonstrations are sometimes possible, but by and large we rely upon the persuasive power of the consensus. Most people believe what they believe because they were born into a culture in which everyone believes that.

Because religion is essentially social, all faiths can become enmeshed with the identity and fate of a group. And, to the extent that they are, their distinctive features will tend to get lost in the necessities of *realpolitik*. Even Buddhists, who generally find violence against others difficult to justify, can fight wars. It was never a very good one, but when Tibet was a Buddhist theocracy it had an army. Nepal and Sri Lanka have defence forces. David Martin makes the important point that the social consequences of a religion will differ depending on whether it is the official creed for a state or is free to follow its own interior logic.[35] A good example of the difference can be found in the mutation of Shinto. State Shinto, when it was the official religion of Imperial Japan, was associated with brutality, oppression and racism. When that link was forcibly broken with the reconstruction of Japan after the surrender in 1946, a very different character prevailed, and in their world survey of religious freedom Boyle and Sheen imply an explanation:

> Believing that there are many Gods and spirits in every person –
> Buddhas and *kami* – most Japanese are tolerant of other people's
> religious beliefs provided that others acknowledge and respect their

beliefs in turn. There have been no special hostilities between different religious communities and very few people are discriminated
against because of religious belief.[36]

Whether a religion is monotheistic or polytheistic is the key
consideration, because it determines the rigidity of social divisions
and the cohesion of communities. If there is just one God (and you
are sure you know his will), it is a lot easier to divide the world into
the saved and the damned, the godly and the ungodly, us and
them, than if you believe that underlying all surface differences is
a unifying cosmic consciousness and that the divine can appear in a
wide variety of forms. It is also a lot easier to suppose that the one
true God requires his believers to impose the correct religion on
everyone else.[37]

Millennialist or millenarian movements often take forms that are
overtly political. Most religious traditions periodically throw up
ecstatic movements of believers who think the world is about to
end, that the return of the saviour is imminent and that collective
action will hasten the end. Not all such movements are violent. The
Lubavitcher strand of Hasidic Judaism has become increasingly
messianic over the twentieth century, largely in reaction to the
rise of Zionism. Especially under their fifth rebbe, Shalom Dov
Baer Schneersohn, the Lubavitchers have supposed that the arrival
of the Messiah will be brought about, not by smashing down the
social order but by raising the levels of personal piety.[38] The saviour will return when we deserve him. Other movements are self-
destructive rather than destructive.

> In 1856 many Xhosa-speaking people beyond the eastern boundary
> of Cape Colony in southern Africa listened to the revelations of a
> prophet and obeyed his orders to kill all their cattle, consume their
> stored grain, and not plant new crops.... The prophet gained sup-
> port for these and other injunctions by promising that their execution
> would bring a new age in which the elderly would regain their
> youth, the ancestors would return to earth, fat cattle would again
> graze in lush pastures, people would eat from newly-filled granaries,
> and the present era of troubles would disappear.[39]

Similar movements appeared in Melanesia in the 1930s. Convinced
that the white man had stolen their 'cargo', New Guineans would
destroy their crops and homes and wait patiently for their cargo to
be delivered.[40] The members of Heaven's Gate and the People's
Temple at Jonestown destroyed themselves in anticipation of dramatic salvation. However, although such extravagant movements

are a regularly occurring phenomenon of all religions, it does seem to be the case that the ones with the greatest impact occur in monotheistic religions, because they are more likely to have a view of the world as created at one point and due to end at another. Although a polytheistic religion can have divine beings whose intervention in the world may be cataclysmic, and welcomed, and hence hastened by dramatic acts of violence, such a combination is much more likely in a monotheistic religion and more likely to involve large numbers of people. In polytheistic religions, the apocalyptic spirit tends to be confined to a local relationship with one particular deity.

Monotheism is necessary for myths of election. To imagine that we are the chosen people we need a creator God who does the choosing.[41] It is far less stimulating to be the people chosen by the tenth most important deity in a pantheon. Even without a specific election myth, monotheistic religions have a natural tendency to arrogance. If we have the true faith and everyone else is wrong, then clearly we are superior to the heathen. Hence the arrogance of Christian missionaries or the Indian Muslim Muhammad Ali who proclaimed that 'a Muslim of low character was superior to any non-Muslim be he Mahatma Gandhi himself'.[42] If the unenlightened are not just ignorant of the true faith but have actually turned down a chance to be otherwise, then they are truly beyond the pale and do not merit the basic human considerations. Hence the viciousness of the traditional Christian attitudes to the Jews (who not only rejected Christ but had him killed) and Muslim attitudes to the Baha'is, Ahmadis and Zikris.

Looked at from the other end, polytheistic religions generally find it easier than competing monotheisms to coexist. If there are many expressions of the divine and as many ways of appropriately worshipping it, the ability to impose upon others is weak. Of course, the desire to do so is never entirely absent. We must be wary, for example, of exaggerating the inclusiveness of Hinduism. It is possible by concentrating on the writings on philosophers such as Radhakhrishnan and Vivekanada to come to the following conclusion: 'Hinduism is a very tolerant religion. Hindus accept that there are many religions in the world. Each is a different way of looking for the same God. It doesn't matter which way you follow, as long as you are going to the same place.'[43] However, a moment's thought on how Hinduism drove Buddhism out of India, on Hindu–Muslim relations, or on the theocratic exploitation built into the caste system should tell us that this is public relations.[44] Adherents to a polytheistic religion such as Buddhism feel reinforced in their faith (diverse and variegated as it is) if everyone endorses it. And internal variegation can disappear in the face of external threat and the right political circumstances. Hindus may differ a great deal, but, if their villages in the Kashmir valley are being torched by Muslim separatists, they will discover a common identity. An important consideration in why many Sinhalese Buddhists have been able to overcome the inertia caused by their variegated religion and unite in defence of their culture is the shadow of their Hindu neighbour. Buddhists form 80 per cent of the population of Sri Lanka, but they are only twelve million people on a small island a short sail from the southern tip of India. The secessionist minority Tamils are a small minority in Sri Lanka, but there are seventy-five million of them across the water in Tamil Nadu. However, though competition may increase the cohesion of a polytheistic culture, peaceful coexistence is easier, and, if the faith travels (as first Hinduism and then Buddhism did into the Indian subcontinent), it will travel more by osmosis and accommodation than by conquest and suppression.

In the above paragraph I distinguished between desire and ability. This is worth spelling out. My argument does not rest on the proposition that, as a matter of personal attitude, the typical monotheist is less tolerant than the typical polytheist (though I believe that is the case). The point is that the diversity implicit in polytheism hinders the bigot. Irrespective of what any individual might wish or desire, polytheistic religions tend to create diffuse structures with a multitude of points of power. In Tibet religious officials enjoyed a great deal of economic and political power, but that power was distributed widely around a number of monasteries so that even the most senior incarnations – the Dalai Lama and the Panchen Lama – were always beholden to others. The net result was a weak social order that provided little or no resistance to the well-organized Chinese national liberation army. Huntington makes the same point on a bigger scale.[45] Of what Max Weber described as the five 'world religions', all but one are associated with major civilizations. Buddhism is not. It lost its base in India and has been assimilated as one element of the Chinese and Japanese civilizations.

The salience of this general comparison of monotheistic and polytheistic religions is reinforced by the exceptions. It is noticeable that as part of their political project Hindu nationalists have stressed, not the polytheistic Hinduism of a plurality of Gods and avatars, but a cult of Ram that comes close to Abrahamic monotheism (even to the extent of creating Abrahamic-like creation myths).

As I noted in chapter 2, one effect of British rule (and to a lesser extent Moghul rule before it) was to create a variety of Hindu sects that paid an ironic compliment to Christianity by reforming Hinduism to make it more like the faith of the imperialists.[46]

The importance of monotheism can also be seen in the consequences of it being weakened. Adherents of competing creeds find it easier to interact peacefully with each other when they move away from their orthodox dogmatic core, either to a mystical version of the faith that stresses the one-ness of everything or to a quasi-polytheism that fills the space between us and the creator with a multitude of local saints. Thus at times and places in India we find Hindus, Sikhs and Muslims performing rituals at the same shrines. The Bogomils were members of a medieval Balkan Christian sect that compromised Christian monotheism; Bogomilism was briefly the official religion of Hungary. After the Turkish conquest many Bogomils became Muslims; their more flexible version of Christianity could accommodate Allah and the Prophet. To this day there are traces of a compound Christian–Muslim faith in pockets of the Balkans. In Bulgaria in the early nineteenth century (before nationalism deepened the divisions) there was some easy mixing of Christians and Muslims, because the faith of the Muslims in question was the emotional and mystical Islam of the Sufi orders: 'They often shared the performance of offering an oblation to a common saint. There are traces on Bulgarian territory of shared sites of worship between Muslims and Christians.'[47]

The reach of religion
The extent to which religion is divisive and the consequences of the divisions it creates will depend on its reach. Tribal religions (and in this I would include Judaism) may have a single God with a unique bond to a particular people, but the political implications of this will be confined. Fundamentalist Jews may fight for greater Israel (which sets them at odds with Palestinians), but they have no desire to convert the world to their faith. Sikhs (or at least some Sikhs) seek autonomy for their homeland, but their aim is to make the Punjab thoroughly Sikh, not to convert India or the rest of the world. A tribal religion may encourage the murder and expulsion of aliens, but it cannot, as Christianity and Islam regularly have, become readily attached to imperial ambitions. In short, claiming universal application is an important consideration.

In the time of the Emperor Ashoka, the third century BC, Buddhism had universal missionary ambitions and the distinctive way an absorbing polytheistic faith spreads is fascinating, but I will

confine myself here to the two great modern universal monotheisms – Christianity and Islam – and to tension between their bound-
less reach and the magnetic pull of the nation state. For good or ill,
the autonomous nation state has for at least two centuries been the
dominant model of political organization and missionary religions
have had to come to terms with that fact.

Arabs and Pakistanis fought in Bosnia. Arabs fought in Chech-
nya. In Afghanistan the Taliban were supported by regiments of
foreign jihadis. Christendom has not shown such international
spirit since the last crusade in the fourteenth century.[48] The explanation is that Christendom fragmented into effective and powerful
nation states that were able to command the loyalty of their citizens. That the fringes of Islam can still support an international
jihad is partly explained by the fact that Muslim states, for many
reasons to do with the nature and social organization of their
economies, have remained fragile. As I will suggest shortly, Islam
has itself played a part in preventing the development of a strong
state. Nonetheless, such states now exist and they compromise
Islam's universalizing urge.[49] Even the most radical of Islamic
fundamentalisms – Khomeini's revolution in Iran – though it tried
to stimulate similar movements elsewhere, wrote into the constitution for Iran that the President had to be Iranian born. And, for
reasons of state interest, Khomeini always remained on good terms
with the Syrian regime, even though its leadership consisted of
deviant sectarians who would have been persecuted had they
been in Iran and who themselves murdered thousands of Shiʿites
in order to defuse a threat to the regime. For all its universalizing
rhetoric, once the state of Pakistan had been created, the Jamaʿat-
I-Islami became a Pakistan political party.[50] My observation is one
of small differences. Muslims are more likely than Christians (and
Hindus and Jews) to support aggressive international movements
for the promotion of the true faith.

The weakness of Muslim states aside, Islam retains a global
consistency that Christianity lacks. One characteristic that helps it
transcend national boundaries is the common language. All over
the world Muslims use the language of the religion's founder:
Arabic. Apart from Arabs, all Muslims are bilingual. They also
follow common patterns of worship and common behavioural
codes. Of course there are important divisions within Islam, but
there is also much in common.

All confess their faith with the same formula. They acknowledge one
book, and with minor differences follow one law. All pray in basic-

ally the same way and are urged to pray communally whenever possible, while the last act of prayer itself commemorates the community as the Muslim turns to his neighbour on either side in performing the salam. When Muslims give alms...it is to support the community. No one who has lived with Muslims in the month of Ramadan can fail to feel the powerful sense of community generated in the joint experience of hardship.[51]

Islam is capable of mobilizing supporters for transnational movements. Islamic fundamentalists travel across frontiers. Rather than pay taxes to the state of which they are citizens, some pious Muslims will send their alms to fund Islamic religious and political work in other states. Although analysts rightly point out that its primary goal has always been to seize control of the Arab states of the Middle East, Osama Bin Laden's al-Qaeda network unites radical Muslims of many nationalities to fight in a variety of countries.

Although universalizing, Christianity, as I noted above, is more internally varied. This had a reciprocal effect on ethnic and national groups. As we saw in the discussion of missionary activity in West Africa, because missionaries wanted to make their gospel intelligible to non-literate populations, they were often pioneers of orthography. They produced a script, a vocabulary and a grammar and in so doing they often 'fixed' linguistic groups and those divisions in turn created ethnic identities where none had previously existed or reinforced what had been only weak senses of shared identity. Those linguistic communities of faith in turn became significant political actors in the emerging nation states. So in one sense the Christian desire to spread the faith encouraged political divisions. But at the same time linguistic and ethnic divisions shaped Christianity so that its universalism was compromised by political divisions.

This is not just a matter of language and attitudes to the transmission of the sacred text. There is also a question of organization. Islam is not carried by a single institutional 'church' structure. It often develops loose networks based on schools, colleges, courts and mosque managements (and the Sufi orders have their own structure), but essentially it is carried by all Muslims as a way of life.

Christian traditions differ in the ease with which they become attached to nations and states and the relationships are not always simple. As a first set of distinctions we can distinguish the Catholic, Orthodox, Lutheran Protestant and Reformed Protestant strands and note that, compared to the other three, Catholic Christianity is unusually internationalist. Roman Catholicism is defined by a theological justification for a single universal hierarchy of authority. The theory of apostolic succession supposes that Christ bequeathed special powers to Peter, the first Bishop of Rome, who passed them on to those he ordained and so on down through the pyramid and through time. This assumption has allowed the Roman Church to retain loyalty to a transnational centre: a vital resource in sustaining opposition to communist incorporation in the countries taken over by the Soviet Empire. With less stress on such a justification, the Protestant and Orthodox strands of Christianity have been much more liable to fragment into national churches and, once so divided, for the churches to be subordinated to the state.

Now that the fragmentation is complete and every Orthodox nation state also has its autonomous Orthodox hierarchy, it is possible for these various bodies to come together in celebration of what they have in common. And a shared tradition informs certain political alliances. One reason the Greek government almost alone supported the Serbian regime of Milošević and opposed interference in the former Yugoslavia was that the Serbs were fellow Orthodox Christians. But such alliances are shallow and did not prevent the national Orthodox churches being subsumed by their respective states.

The same could be said of the Lutheran strand of Protestantism. From the first it was firmly associated with the states of which it was the official religion, and, like the Orthodox churches, the Lutheran churches were usually state enterprises, the clergy of which were employed by the state.

The thoroughly Reformed strand of Protestantism has no theological basis for sustaining any large-scale organization. Its primary unit is the congregation of the faithful: the body of believers who meet face to face to worship God and edify each other. Congregations may band together in assemblies and synods and circuits, but none of these has the justification of the Roman international hierarchy. I will shortly point to a feature of Protestantism that undermines a close association with any large political unit, but for this discussion what matters is that, of all the strands of Christianity, Catholicism has the strongest potential to transcend national boundaries. We see the political relevance of this very clearly in the different responses to communism. In Central and Eastern Europe the Catholic Church provided far more effective opposition to Soviet imperialism than did the Lutheran churches, because it was able to use its international structure to prevent national Communist Parties suborning its officials and to mobilize international action against repression.

As well as distinguishing the strands of Christianity by their ability to sustain a transnational structure, we can also note the political implications of the church/sect divide. Like the tribal religion, the church type of Christianity thinks in terms of the entire people. It supposes that religious merit can be transferred and hence that a group of virtuosi can glorify God on behalf of the people. In contrast, the sect supposes that God's promises refer only to those individuals who personally accept them and individually meet the highest standards of piety. Rather than incorporating an entire people, the sect draws the godly out of their surrounding society. Membership is not acquired simply by birth but is earned by individual conversion. The Catholic and Orthodox strands of Christianity are churchlike communal organic religions. The Reformed version of Protestantism is sectarian and individualistic and Lutheranism falls somewhere between the extremes.

The Reformed strand of Protestantism places such a very high premium on every individual's need to stand alone before God that it weakens all group bonds and makes it hard for even the most zealous believer to divide the world into us and them. Or, to be more precise, the resulting 'us' is very small. When Protestants take their religion very seriously, they fragment into competing sects, which in turn weakens their ability to sustain group identities. Protestant zealotry does not produce powerful national or international movements because the zealots become disillusioned with the lack of piety of the mass of the people. In individualistic religions the pious turn in on themselves. They also turn on their compatriots. In a basically communal religion that is well enmeshed in everyday life, that some people fail to live the required life or perform their religious duties appropriately is only a policing problem: the ungodly must be punished. But, when a basically individualistic faith is harnessed to group identity, then the failure of individuals calls into question the honesty of the faith.

Again I should stress that any observation about the effects of a religious culture needs to be qualified by consideration of circumstances. Put most simply, the tendency of a group to fragment is encouraged or depressed by external forces. A strong sense of being under threat will encourage members of any group to downplay what divides them. I have already made the point that threats to Hinduism, first from the British Raj and then from India's Muslim regional rival Pakistan, have caused many Hindus to try to overcome their internal variations to produce a coherent strong Hindu nationalism. Ian Paisley's Free Presbyterian Church of Ulster (FPCU) can provide an example on a much smaller scale. In most other settings, conservative Protestant sects have split over the expected end of the world and the propriety of baptizing infants (as opposed to adults). For forty years, the FPCU has allowed its ministers and congregations to differ over these contentious issues without dividing. This has been possible because its members feel so threatened by the overwhelming presence of Catholic Irish nationalism that, rather than weaken the conservative Protestant witness by further schism, they are prepared to relegate to matters of preference what in dominant Protestant cultures are essential matters of principle.

Although Protestantism is basically individualistic, there is one theological strand that can form the basis for asserting a religiously legitimated ethnic identity. The followers of John Calvin argued that, as God was all-powerful and all-knowing, it must be the case that whether we were saved or doomed must already be known to God even before we were born. That is, our fate was 'predestined'. The world divided into those who had been chosen – the elect – and the rest. Although strictly speaking there is no reason why election should be an inherited status, in practice Calvinists tend to think in group or ethnic terms. They are fond of the Children of Israel imagery from the Old Testament. In most settings Calvinist predestinarian thinking died out and was replaced by 'Arminianism' (so called after the sixteenth-century Dutch theologian Joseph Arminius): the notion that Christ's sacrifice was an effective atonement for all who would believe in it. That is, salvation is potentially open to all mankind.

What is important for understanding the links between conflict and religion is that the two places where Calvinism did not become superseded by a more liberal faith are southern Africa and the north-east of Ireland. In both places a small group of conservative Protestants, who were in many ways successful and privileged, found themselves surrounded by potentially overwhelming populations of people of a different faith. Calvinism provided a self-satisfying explanation of their power and of the hostility of their enemies, and a reassuring promise of eventual triumph.[52]

We can see the complexity of the political implications of the above if we return to the example of resistance to Soviet Communism. The Catholic Church was able to resist it in Slovakia, Lithuania and Poland, not just because its international structure gave it access to practical and symbolic resources but also because its organic churchlike nature allowed it to become very firmly associated with nationalism in each of these countries.[53] Because it is close to the Catholic model in its communalism, the Lutheran Church in Finland was able to perform a similar function of legitimating nationalist resistance to Soviet imperialism. General Carl Gustav Mannerheim became supreme commander and regent when Finland declared its independence in 1918. In 1939 he came out of retirement to lead the Finnish army against the Soviet Red Army in the Winter War and he remained commander-in-chief until he was elected President in 1944. It is a mark of the close ties between Finnish nationalism and the Lutheran church that there are statues of Mannerheim in the grounds of some Finnish churches. Apart from the already mentioned cases of the Boers and Ulster Protestants, there are no comparable links between Reformed Protestantism and national identity.

To summarize, though the connections are complex, we can discern some regular differences between major religious traditions in their relationship to the nation state.

The politics of orthopraxis

The issue of human rights is central to politics and high on most lists of such rights is the freedom to practise one's religion without hindrance. In previous chapters I considered the threat to such freedoms from atheistic communism and from another religion. Clearly one way in which religions may differ in their political consequences is in the way they deal with religious diversity. Even if, for the sake of argument, we suppose that all believers are similar in their desire to see their creed given pride of place in the operation of their society, what follows from that differs considerably depending on the extent to which a religion mandates a specific way of life. As with all such distinctions, this is an exaggerated abstraction, but we can distinguish religions by the extent to which they stress ritual, doctrine or social mores. The first can be dealt with very briefly. Apart from their role in legitimating the state, Shinto, Confucianism and Taoism may have few political implications: the correct performance of certain rituals at certain shrines need make little difference to those who do not take part. The one possible problem is offending relatives by ritually incorporating those who have not wanted to be so included. The Yasukuni Shinto shrine lists and deifies all the known Japanese war dead and that includes people who in their lifetime rejected Shinto on religious or political grounds. Shrine managers have steadfastly refused requests from relatives to have names removed.[54]

There are major differences in the political consequences of creeds that stress *orthodoxy* (that is, right beliefs) and *orthopraxy* (right actions). A faith that insists on a certain way of life must be concerned about dissenters and about the public status of the faith to a far greater extent than one that values orthodoxy. Christianity has some general ethical principles in the Ten Commandments of the Old Testament and the Sermon on the Mount in the New Testament of the Bible, but it does not have a body of religiously sanctioned law. For Muslims

> The Sharia is a divine law, a law given by God. It must of its nature take precedence over all other forms of law. It is theoretically immutable; if the Sharia says that such-and-such is God's law, then no earthly agency can say otherwise. If one bases the state on the Sharia, then democracy must logically be curtailed ... If the Sharia says that the punishment for highway robbery ... is crucifixion or execution by the sword ... then how can the parliament decide on another form of punishment?[55]

And what God requires, he requires of everyone. The Qur'ānic injunction to command what is right and forbid what is wrong applies universally.[56] Hence Pakistan reminds all its citizens (not just the pious Muslims) that they face three months in jail for eating, serving food or smoking in public places during Ramadan.[57]

The contrast with Christianity can be seen most clearly at the extremes. Halliday notes correctly that Islamic fundamentalism must always 'claim to determine a politics for Muslim peoples'.[58] Protestant fundamentalists in the USA divide more evenly between those who wish to 'bring America back to God' (that is, use the state to impose their view of required behaviour on everyone) and those who suppose that such imposition is not only not required but may actually prove harmful. The essence of the Protestant disagreement with Catholicism is the contrast between faith and works. For the Protestant salvation is a free gift from God to those who believe in the atoning sacrifice of God's son Jesus Christ. What saves is faith in that fact. Good behaviour should, of course, follow, but of itself it will not win salvation. If people are allowed to think that changing the laws so as to make public behaviour less offensive to God should be the main goal, they may be distracted from the need for personal faith.[59]

This crucial difference between Islam and Christianity can be seen in this simple fact of political history. Wherever they are found in significant numbers, Muslims always want either to take over the state or to secede from it – the goal being the imposition of the shariah. There is nothing comparable in the behaviour of Christians.

The role of law in Islam places a particular weight on states with majority Muslim populations. Because there is nothing very specific that Christianity mandates for governments, states with Christian peoples are able to claim divine approval without actually doing anything much. Religious legitimation can be claimed with no more than, as Ronald Reagan did, proclaiming a 'Year of the Bible' or having clergy bless the army as it marches to war. The theocratic tendencies of Islam are reinforced by the obvious role of the shariah as the touchstone of Islam. When in the 1990s rulers of Muslim states such as Tunisia wished to bolster their position against criticisms of their lack of practical accomplishments by claiming religious legitimation, they could hardly avoid implementing some aspect of the shariah.

Rule-bound religions are *inevitably* more conservative than ones that do not embed divine revelation in a legal code. This follows simply from the fact that the rules were written in the past. Islam's image of gender relations is firmly tied to the circumstances of Mecca in the time of the Prophet. There was considerable flexibility between the eighth and eleventh centuries when the four main schools of Islamic jurisprudence developed, but most Muslim authorities argue that the 'gates of interpretation' were then closed. Of course, new circumstances are constantly being created, but the general assumption that all that is required to live a godly life was known in the eleventh century means that those who wish to justify change have constantly to pull against the power of the past. There is nothing comparable in Christianity. In part this is because it is harder to find rules in the Christian tradition: only ten commandments and all of them brief! But it also follows from the separation of church and state, which I will discuss shortly. Those who do construe the Christian faith in terms of bodies of canon law are impotent to impose them on the wider society. So the Catholic Church could deny women a voice in its deliberative councils, but it could not prevent the franchise being extended to them, even in societies that were uniformly Catholic. It can prevent women from becoming priests, but it cannot prevent them from becoming police officers.

Orthoprax religions are less humane than orthodox ones. Putting it as bluntly as that may seem unnecessarily contentious, but the subject is so often evaded in scholarly writing (and crudely relished in the mass media) that it should be dealt with directly. In a nutshell, a society governed by rules written ten centuries ago will be less pleasant than a society that can evolve. I will elaborate the case.

Modern liberal democratic states have many defects but, at least in the way they treat their own citizens, in recent centuries they have encouraged and imposed an unprecedented degree of civilization. Arbitrary arrest and imprisonment are now rare. All adults now have the right to own property. Religious, sexual and political deviation is widely tolerated. The vile workplace conditions common in 1800 are rare in 2000. There is a perversely popular current of contemporary intellectual thought (represented by the work of Herbert Marcuse and Michel Foucault, for example) that seeks the grey cloud for every silver lining. In his attempt to show that liberal democratic capitalism was really bad, Marcuse was forced to argue that what looked like liberty was actually 'repressive tolerance'.[60] One might have thought that anyone able to compare the USA of the 1950s with Nazi Germany of the 1930s would have concluded that repressive tolerance was a big improvement on repressive intolerance. Likewise Foucault, especially in his comparisons of pre-modern and modern penal regimes, argued that somehow the old world of thumb screws, racks, disembowellings and the stocks was less repressive than the modern world of rational bureaucratic surveillance.[61] It may be that professionalizing punishment allows us to avoid responsibility for social control, but I find it easy to prefer imprisoning traitors to making a fond sport of disembowelling. Even if one supports the death penalty for the most serious crimes, lethal injection in private seems preferable to stoning to death and it is hard to imagine that even Foucault would think amputation of hands a more civilized punishment for theft than a fine or imprisonment. We need not get bogged down in the details of the historical comparison. To appreciate my point we need only recognize that, for almost everyone, life in Western Europe now is vastly pleasanter than it was in 1800 or, God forbid, 900. And this is not solely a matter of increased wealth. Crucial to the vastly improved quality of life has been a series of changes in ideas: in principles that govern how we should live. Women should be the equal of men; the suffering of other people and of animals should not entertain us; laws should be universal in principle and even in their application; people should not be property; speech should be free; privacy should be respected and so on. To point out that these principles are often offended against does not change the fact that very often they are not. In very many respects we have become more civilized.

If we admit that evolution, we can see the problem of taking the social teachings of the remote past and making them a template for the present. An orthoprax religion, which claims divine authority for a detailed body of rules, when those rules were compiled centuries ago, is inevitably less humane and civilized than an orthodox religion, because the vague principles of the latter do not much impede mutation. The detailed proscriptions of the former are a constant obstacle. We need mention only two facets of the shariah: the cruel punishments and the gender inequity. Which citizens in a society that has abandoned such barbaric practices would welcome a return to stoning adultresses (but not their necessary male partners) to death?

It is worth adding that, although most Muslim states are happy to defend the gender inequity of the shariah, there is considerable unease about the more medieval punishments it sometimes requires. Even those Islamic states that assert that they implement the shariah have considerable difficulty actually carrying out the hudud punishments. For example, as of late 2001 no thieves in Pakistan have actually had their hands cuts off, though many have been so sentenced. No surgeons have been willing to carry out the punishment and the state has been unwilling to find a way round that obstacle. We can detect similar unease in the case of a Sokoto, Nigerian, woman condemned to be stoned to death because she conceived a child out of wedlock. President Obasanjo objected to the sentence. The woman's supporters produced the defence that, according to Islamic law, a child can be born up to seven years after intercourse; hence the 13-month-old child could be regarded as the fruit of her previous marriage. After much international outcry, the verdict was overturned on appeal on a technicality.[62] The important point is that the ruling elites of Pakistan and the Islamic states of Nigeria have had to have recourse to technicalities, because they cannot directly challenge the shariah without also challenging the status and nature of Islam. It is not impossible, but it is harder to liberalize an orthoprax religion than an orthodox one. In defence of the Taliban, it was often said that the alternative was worse. Its treatment of women may have been medieval, but it was an improvement on their position under 'pashtunwalli', the traditions of the rural southern Afghanis. This may be so, just as it may be the case that the Prophet's invidious treatment of women was a considerable improvement on what was common in his environment. However, there is an important distinction between social rules legitimated by tradition and those justified by religion. The former can evolve more easily. Of course, people may feel strongly attached to the way they have always done things, but they will be even more strongly attached to the way they have always done things when they believe that God told them what to do.

This allows me to return to the Pygmalion objection to explaining aspects of a society by aspects of its religious culture. It may well be argued (indeed it often is) that certain deleterious features of Muslim societies (such as gender inequity or the intolerance of apostasy) are merely a consequence of their poverty or their lack of development or the absence of a democratic tradition and that in time these unfortunate features will be remedied. After all, Spain had its Inquisition in the fifteenth century and the New England states had their witch-hunting Puritans at the end of the seventeenth century. What strikes me as significant in the comparison between orthoprax and orthodox religions is that Western Christians were able to give up Inquisitors and Witchfinders-General because their faith did not give pride of place to a body of divinely ordained law. Shaped only by general principles, the orthodox religion can easily evolve with changing circumstances. To respond to the Pygmalion claim that circumstances matter more than religious ideology, I would argue that religions differ systematically in the responses to circumstances that they permit: some are more chameleon-like than others.

These observations about the political consequences of orthopraxy must be qualified by reference to universalism and power. Like Islam, the religion of the Jews mandates a certain way of life in considerable detail. But the implications are rather different, because the Jews have no ambition to convert the world or to conquer territory beyond Palestine. The second difference is that for most of their history the Jews have been dispersed in small and powerless communities that have hardly been able to impose their rules on themselves, let alone anyone else.

Another way of making the same general contrast between Christianity and Islam is to recognize that the ease with which a faith can mutate depends on the extent to which its teachings can be treated not as direct instructions but as metaphors. The more that is vague and allegorical the easier it is for every generation to alter its meaning. The centrality of the shariah to Islam does not prevent interpretation but it does restrict it. In contrast, Christianity has no choice but to be metaphorical about its teachings. It started with the revelations of a Jew and borrowed much of the Jewish tradition but rewrote it so that promises that were made to the Jews were then generalized to all human kind. Its sacred texts betray that tension.

The largest part of the Bible is taken up by the sacred scriptures of some other religion: the Old Testament. The New Testament contains new revelations but it also continues themes from the Old while giving them radically new interpretations. Christianity starts with an inconsistent attitude to its ideological base. It reprints the Old Testament but then has Christ saying 'It was written ... but I say unto you'. Islam gives some respect to Judaism and Christianity, the two major religions of the area before the Prophet's revelations, but it begins afresh. Although later generations of Muslims argued about what the Qur'ān meant, it does not start arguing with itself. We can see the same point in relationship to sacred territory. Because it remained in control of its sacred places, Islam was able to remain quite literal. Muslims still make pilgrimage to the same place that they always did. Christianity quickly dispersed from Palestine and made its home in north Africa, Asia Minor and southern Europe. There was a revival of interest in the Holy Land during the time of the Crusades, but this came too late to prevent the bonds of revelation and place being broken.

It may be argued that the above makes too much of the difference between orthodoxy and orthopraxis. John Calvin's Geneva or the Puritan towns of the early New England settlements could be cited as examples of Christian theocracies, every bit as concerned with the imposition of godly behaviour on all their citizens as any Caliphate. But I can think of very few others and even in these cases it is not clear that the theocrats had the same simple conviction that the will of God had to be embodied in civil law. Calvin was himself far more ambiguous than is often recognized. Sproxton argues that he 'thought that nothing of God's ordinance could be established by men' and that 'the justice of men and the justice of God were infinitely at odds'.[63] Perhaps the strongest evidence that the orthoprax spirit is much weaker in Christianity than in Islam is simply the historical record: Christian theocracies have been rare and short-lived.

In a number of places I have noted a major divide within Christianity. I will shortly pursue in some detail the political consequences of the individualism inherent in the Reformation. Here I want simply to note that a great deal hinges on the extent to which a religion is *communal* rather than *individualistic*. We can array the major tendencies on an axis from Catholic and Orthodox at one end, through Lutheran and Anglican, to sectarian Protestant at the other. The Catholic and Orthodox strands suppose that divine wisdom is concentrated in an elite and that merit can be transferred. Hence religion is provided by an institution that serves an entire people. This organic embrace can give protection against external tyranny (as we saw in the Catholic Church's ability to sustain national integrity against Soviet imperialism), but it can be a smothering embrace. The Catholic and Orthodox churches argued against liberal democracy while there was still an argument to be had, and, even once the argument had been lost, the general preference for organic models of association made Catholic and Orthodox cultures vulnerable to authoritarian regimes.

To summarize, whether a religion stresses correct belief or correct behaviour has considerable social and political consequences, as does how it specifies just who must obey. Finally, I have suggested whether a religious tradition sees God relating to a people jointly rather than as individuals severally is of some importance.

Religions of the powerful and the impotent

With the partial exception of Hinduism, which defines a section of the people as 'outcaste' and 'untouchable', all the major religions have been able to generate variants that appeal particularly to the poor and dispossessed. By asserting unusual piety and subjecting themselves to rigorous disciplines (for example, the medieval Christian flagellants whipped themselves till they streamed with blood), those who lack wealth and status in the eyes of the world can console themselves with imaginary inversions of hierarchies. Poor Christians could take comfort in the assertion that it was easier for a camel to pass through the eye of a needle than for a rich man to enter the kingdom of God. And, at the other end, all religions can equally find themselves comfortable in power.

But alongside that similarity there is a disparity of historical experience that reinforces the theological tendencies discussed in the previous point. Christianity began as a religion of weakness and failure. Its founder was crucified and it spent 250 years – ten generations – on the social and political margins before it became the official religion of the Roman Empire. As Cragg puts it: 'Islam did not speak from the Catacombs ... it saw the way of truth as passing always through thrones.'[64] After brief setbacks, the Prophet found himself in command of his environment: the political authority as well as the spiritual leader. 'Islam had not spent its first hundred years in the wilderness. Instead its early leaders rapidly found themselves at the head of large empires.'[65] Sometimes the role of ruler (or Sultan) became divorced in practice from that of spiritual guide (or Caliph), but it was also frequently reintegrated. As late as the nineteenth century the Ottoman Sultan declared himself also Caliph and claimed that his person was sacred.

Although it eventually came to enjoy a strong association with world domination, Christianity's long period in the wilderness gave it a very good reason to take seriously the separation of church and state that Christ had suggested when he responded to a contentious question about taxes by saying that one should render unto Caesar what belongs to Caesar and unto God what belongs to God. Even the most Caesar-like popes accepted the notion of 'two kingdoms', and the two Catholic cardinals who managed France in the seventeenth century, Richelieu and Mazarin, were perfectly clear that they were performing secular roles.

There was a much closer association of church and state in the Eastern tradition. The Emperor Constantine created a senate and a synod of bishops. The senate codified the political decrees of the emperor and was responsible for their orderly application. The synod of bishops legislated theologically for the church and the empire. Church leaders readily used the power of the state against opponents when they could. Athanasius, who had been punished by the state for his defence of Orthodoxy against the Arians, still asked the Emperor to persecute his opponents. In seventeenth-century Russia, Avvakun, the leader of the dissident Old Believers, asked the Czar to oppress his enemies. But, for all that church and state often worked closely together (and the relationship became closer with the Russian Orthodox Church under Peter being reduced to a department of state), there are still very clearly two spheres and there was no doubt which prevailed.

In Northern and Western Europe the divide was even greater. The Protestant Reformation broke Christendom into thousands of small pieces. For thirty years Catholics fought Protestants and, when eventually neither could prevail, both sides accepted that religion and politics were separate and the politics gradually became secularized

In contrast, almost every state in which Muslims are in a large majority is theocratic, and, even when necessity requires that non-Muslims be encompassed, as was the case with the Ottoman Empire, Islam is still given pride of place, rights to dissent are permitted only to the group and not to individuals, and Muslims are not permitted to depart from the true faith.

Halliday argues that in most Islamic states there is a practical division between politics and religion.

> there *is* a clear institutional difference between, say, the Sultan in the Ottoman empire and the Sheikh of Islam. And that distinction you can see today: in Saudi Arabia the al Sauds are descendants of the

Saudi monarch and the al Sheikhs are descendants of al-Wahhab [the eighteenth-century religious leader]. In Iran, the same thing. An elected president, Khatami, and then the chief religious leader who emerges from the *ulama*.[66]

What Halliday does not say is that, in each of his three examples, the political leaders operate only within the room permitted them by the religious tradition. Western monarchs used to seek the approval of the Pope. British monarchs are still crowned by the Archbishop of Canterbury, leader of the Church of England. But it is centuries since any Christian monarch paid any attention to the teachings of the Christian churches. Candidates for the Westminster Parliament (unlike those for Iran's Majlis) are not vetted by the Church of England nor, for the last 200 years, have they needed to be members of the national church. Laws passed by Parliament are not vetted to see if they accord with the bishops' view of what God requires. And the vote is not denied to non-Christians. Of course, Islamic societies have a division of labour, but they do not have a division of life-worlds, each operating with different values and attitudes.

The difference is usually put in terms of Islam not recognizing a secular sphere. Al-Banna, the founder of the Egyptian Muslim Brotherhood, said: 'if you are told you are political, answer that Islam admits no such distinction.'[67] The Algerian Front Islamique du Salut (or FIS) quotes from the Qurʾān in its programme and says: 'And his word, the most high: Do they then seek after the judgement of (the days of) ignorance? But who, for a people whose faith is assured, can give better judgement than God?'[68] For the FIS the word of God governs all. In the Soviet Union elections were confined to choosing which of an approved list of Communist Party members would best implement Marxist-Leninist principles. Likewise for the FIS the point of elections is to choose the individual Muslims best qualified to interpret Islamic law. The leader of the Ikhwan movement in the Sudan described his ideal state as 'republican and as a representative democracy'. However, he added that it would not be 'strictly speaking a direct government of and by the people; it is a government of the sharia'.[69] Mawdudi, the founder of the Jamaʿat-I-Islami, said: 'In western democracies, the people are sovereign; in Islam sovereignty vests in God ... In the former the people make their own laws ... in the latter, they have to follow and obey the laws ... given by God through the Prophet.'[70]

So far I have talked about the separation of church and state from the point of view of the religious institution and its history. Instead of asking why Islam dominates its societies more effectively than does Christianity, we can ask why Islamic states did not acquire the power and legitimacy that allowed the secular rulers of Britain, France and Sweden to dominate their churches. Part of the answer has already been given in the discussion of the tension between a universalizing religion and nationalism. Being intrinsically less universal, Christianity more easily became divided into linguistic, ethnic and national units. But there is a further consideration. Bernard Lewis has argued that Islam gave little encouragement to representative and deliberative councils:

> from the time of the Prophet until the introduction of Western insti-
> tutions in the Islamic world there was no equivalent among the
> Muslim peoples of the Athenian boule, the Roman Senate or the
> Jewish Sanhedrin, of the Icelandic Althing or the Anglo-Saxon wit-
> enagemot, or of any of the innumerable parliaments, councils,
> synods, chambers and assemblies of every kind that flourished all
> over Christendom.[71]

Such institutions did not develop in Islamic cultures because the Muslim insistence that the only law was God's law, to be inter-preted by clerics, removed the primary purpose of such bodies: the creation of legislation. Another difference Lewis notes is that Is-lamic law had little notion of corporate identities.

> almost all aspects of Muslim government have an intensely personal
> character. In principle, at least, there is no state, but only a ruler; no
> court, but only a judge. There is not even a city with defined powers,
> limits and functions, but only an assemblage of neighborhoods,
> mostly defined by family, tribal, ethnic or religious criteria, and
> governed by officials, usually military, appointed by the sovereign.[72]

Without corporate bodies there was no need for principles of repre-sentation or procedures for choosing representatives. As there was no occasion for collective decision making, there was no need for methods of arriving at agreement, other than the assertion that proper attention to the will of Allah would produce a consensus.

There is not space here for a history of the evolution of Muslim political institutions. It is enough to note that, compared to those that evolved in Western Europe, Islamic states tended to be rela-tively weak. Add to this the way that Islam is not carried by a corporate 'church' distinct from other spheres of life and we can see a very clear difference between the background to church–state relations in Christian and Islamic cultures. The separation of the two in the former allowed the development of secular politics and it permitted the evolution of a notion of the rights of the individual, distinct from whatever the dominant religion may have to say about what people should be and how they should behave.

The Burns doctrine: secularization and liberty

In the final days of the Soviet Empire, Gennadi Gerasimov, Mikhail Gorbachev's chief press spokesman, invoked a popular artist to make a point to a US television audience. He explained that, under the Brezhnev doctrine, the Soviet Union held there was only one path to socialism and the Soviet Union, as the senior partner, felt obliged to steer its Warsaw Pact neighbours. Now, he said, we recognize that no two socialist countries are identical and that each has to develop in its own way. Gerasimov called this the Sinatra doctrine: 'I did it my way!'

In the style of the admirable Gerasimov, I want to present the Burns doctrine. Two well-known lines from the eighteenth-century Scottish poet Robert Burns can exemplify much of what I want to say in this final section. The first is both the title and the chorus of his great hymn to freedom. At the end of each verse, in which he lists various vanities of class and hierarchy, he concludes: 'A man's a man for a' that' (or in English: 'A man's a man for all that'). That assertion of a common humanity underlying superficial differences of status is at the heart of liberal democracy. My second text comes from his poem 'To a mouse' and it is the line: 'The best-laid schemes of mice and men gang aft agley' (or 'often go astray'), which expresses perfectly the common sociological observation that many of the most potent changes in human affairs are unintended consequences. People set out to do one thing and achieve something very different.

In this final section I want to consider two closely related themes: the contribution of the Protestant Reformation to modern politics, particular and general. The particular I will lay out shortly; the general I can state here: its demise. If we were to single out the greatest contribution of religion to liberal democracy, it would be that the decline of religion permits the freedom of the individual.

There is no doubt that organized religion has at times confined tyranny. The success of Catholicism in opposing Soviet Communism has been mentioned a number of times. The strength of community generated by shared beliefs can block various forms of oppression. But religion is oppressive. I do not mean that dreadful things are done in the name of God (though they often are). When I say religion is an obstacle to democracy I mean something much more specific and technical.

In the Ottoman millet system, the communal violence in India and the Greek government's reluctance to uncouple citizenship and membership of the Orthodox Church, we see religious rectitude being set above everything else. Most religions have produced a liberal wing that either extends the promises supposedly made by God to his chosen people to all human kind or confines the remit of religion to only those who choose to be bound by it. But neither is orthodox. Levelling language is often used (we are all sinners in the eyes of God; we are all God's creatures), but it is always immediately qualified by a division of the world into the heathen and the godly, the righteous and the unrighteous. Even a churchlike religion that makes few demands of its members may treat harshly those who reject its authority. In the final analysis, faith is an obstacle to liberal democracy because it gives believers a trump card. Politeness and civility may make some believers cautious in the way they play the card, but in the end the people are divided into those who know the ways of God and the rest and that division is fundamentally incompatible with the basic principle of democracy: that all people are essentially of equal worth (or, as Burns puts, it: 'A man's a man for a' that'). Liberal democracy requires that human rights be equally distributed: no trumps!

Nothing in this assertion prevents people arguing for the primacy of some value other than individual liberty, reminding us that such liberty is often compromised, or asserting that the positive values of particular religions outweigh any benefits that result from its decline. I am not trying to construct a comprehensive moral balance sheet. I am arguing only that most religions taken conventionally are incompatible with liberal democracy. They cannot treat all opinion as equally valid and they cannot treat all people as equal irrespective of their religion. Hence religious societies, while they may have many pleasant features, are generally neither liberal nor democratic. If they do it in no other sphere, they restrict choice in the matter of religion.

The point can perhaps be appreciated if put like this: what most marks the political cultures of the modern industrial societies of the West from those of other countries is that the former are largely secular. To my catalogue of small differences discussed in the first part of this chapter, we can add the big difference. Liberal democracies are distinguished by having formally secular polities, their religious institutions are largely impotent except to the extent that they accept secular rules of engagement, and the majority of the population either have no religion or adhere to religions that have mutated a long way from their orthodox bases.

In this final section I want to outline one strand of an explanation of secularization[73] and I will do it by pursuing the general claim that the Protestant Reformation in Western Christianity was a vital component in the rise of liberal democracy. As we will see, this argument, like everything in the previous chapters, combines direct and indirect cause, deliberate action and inadvertent consequence, religious belief and social circumstance. Protestantism encouraged democracy in three ways. First, it played an important part in the rise of capitalism and the growth in prosperity. Second, it encouraged individualism and egalitarianism. Third, it created a context of religious diversity. All of these contributed to the development of liberal democracy, sometimes directly but mostly inadvertently. And together they weakened religion and allowed the growth of secular societies and cultures. Each part of this complex story can be sketched only briefly but each is sufficiently well known that a cursory treatment will suffice to make the argument clear.[74]

Prosperity

Max Weber has argued that a number of religious innovations had the inadvertent consequence of creating a climate that was ripe for the growth of rational capitalism.[75] Although pre-Reformation Christianity made ethical demands, it also offered to the immoral and the inattentive ways of periodically restoring themselves to good standing with the church (and, by implication, with God). Sinners could confess their sins, repent, perform the appropriate penance and receive absolution. Because the Reformers thought this system an encouragement to sin, they rejected it. With no easy way of removing the burden of sin, all people had continually to pay attention to their moral and religious life. The need to cultivate personal piety was further reinforced by removing the idea that the religious merit of pious people could be transferred by, for example, the impious leaving money in their wills to pay for masses to be said for their souls. Such changes increased the psychological and cultural pressure to be concerned about one's salvational status.

In most religions the virtuosi demonstrate their piety by retreating from the world. They shut themselves behind high walls, wander the roads begging or become hermits in the woods. Their self-denial cuts them off from normal social roles and relationships. In Weber's terms, they practise 'other-worldly asceticism'. There are two problems with making this the highest form of religious obedience. First, it can be followed by only a few people; social and economic order does not permit legions of monks. Second, that the highest form of the religious life can only ever be followed by only a small proportion of the population may cause the lay people to admire the religious virtuosi but it does not encourage them to follow a religious life. The Reformers believed that the other-worldly nature of vocation (or 'calling') that was promoted by the church depressed, rather than raised, popular levels of religiosity. In order to break down the division of religious labour that saw the few living an especially godly life while the masses plodded along, content to allow God to be placated on their behalf by the religious professionals, the Reformers argued for a new view of religious vocation. They argued that any honest occupation, engaged in diligently, glorified God. A bricklayer could attend to his soul without becoming a hermit; he could lay bricks to the glory of God. Under Luther's slogan of 'every man his own monk', this new concept of vocation allowed the common people to pursue a life of 'this-worldly asceticism'.

Weber's argument is that the religious innovations of the Reformation inadvertently created a new attitude to work at both ends of the social scale. The economic ethos of the masses was a combination of habit and sloth. They had fairly fixed notions of an expected standard of living and when that was achieved they stopped work, preferring increased leisure to capital accumulation. The wealthy tended to gamble. In the manner of Shakespeare's *Merchant of Venice*, they sank everything into high-risk speculations. If the ship came in, they were rich; if it did not, they were ruined. They tried to enrich themselves either by funding or by taking part in wars. The Puritans produced by the Reformation were neither slothful creatures of habit nor reckless freebooters and gamblers. They worked hard. Because they were anxious to avoid the temptations of the flesh, they did not indulge themselves in expensive pleasures. Instead they reinvested in their businesses and worked harder. Rather than the huge profit, they sought the unglamorous steady rate of return. More than that, they saw themselves as God's stewards, obliged to make the most of what God had given them. The result was a personality and way of life ideally suited to rational capitalism.

Individualism and egalitarianism

The Reformation also marked a major change in the relationship between the community and the individual. By rejecting the notion that the clergy possessed any particular access to divine power, the Reformers inadvertently gave an enormous boost to the autonomous individual. Where Christianity previously allowed people to be jointly responsible for their fate, the Reformers made them severally responsible.

The Reformation strengthened the individual not only against the community but also against hierarchy. The Reformers were men of their times; they were certainly not democrats. Initially it was only in the eyes of God (and not in the eyes of his creation) that we were equal and we were equal only in vice. But their attack on the authority and power of the priesthood and their insistence that all of us were equally capable of discerning the will of God (and what could be more important than that?) was, as their critics saw, a powerful blow to the very idea of hierarchy. The Reformers inadvertently laid the foundations for egalitarianism. They created a potential that subsequent economic changes would allow to be fulfilled.

The precondition for that potential being fulfilled was the fragmentation of the lifeworld. In relatively simple economies, life tends to be organized around a single social system with a single hierarchy. The elders are respected; not respected for some purposes and despised for others. The social system and its associated hierarchy change only very slowly and are understood by all those who encounter it, so that no one has any difficulty understanding who is inferior and who superior. As economies become more complex, so a variety of hierarchies are created and it becomes possible for people to occupy a number of roles that do not perfectly map on to each other and that are not all-encompassing. Ranking becomes less transparent. Change brings new occupations and new positions. Whereas the status of serf or slave specified almost everything about the person who occupied it, the role of factory labourer specified only what someone did for a part of their day and week and life. Although they did not relax their domination easily, the ruling classes gradually discovered that it was possible profitably to govern the lives of their workers *as workers* without having to dominate them entirely. It even became possible for a person to occupy a low-status role in one sphere of life and high-status role in another. The factory worker might be beneath his foreman during the working week but, as a Baptist preacher, stand above him in a pulpit on a Sunday. In a world where people occupy a number of roles or move from one to another, it becomes possible to separate the role from the person playing it. It also becomes possible for people to see themselves as something more or other than their roles. It thus becomes possible to maintain specific hierarchies of roles and relationships of power for specific purposes while also accepting in principle that all people are much of a muchness, that a man's a man for a' that.[76] My manager can command me for limited purposes and for limited times; he does not own me and cannot command my soul.

In brief, the Reformation gave a powerful boost to the notion of the individual and to egalitarianism. It took a major change in the nature of the economy and in the social relations it demanded to allow the radical implications to be played out, but eventually they were. The ruling classes opposed every single expansion of democratic rights. Each progressive step had to be hard fought, but eventually the rulers learnt that they could maintain much of their privileged position (and become accustomed to the loss of what they had to lose) without treating their social inferiors as if they were a different species. In the Western world we saw the franchise gradually extended from great men to middling men to the small man and then to great women, middling women and finally to all adults. In the late twentieth century we saw the notion of rights extended to children and even to animals.

Individualism and egalitarianism were inadvertent consequences of the Reformation. More deliberate was the new impetus to lay activism. Medieval Christianity tended to mirror the feudal structure in expecting and allowing little of the common people.[77] Protestantism demanded an active laity, mindful and diligent. Lay participation without the mediation of the clergy created a model in the sphere of religion for what later became the ethos of modern democracy. Although individualistic, Protestantism was not a lonely faith. The Protestant sects constructed themselves as self-supporting voluntary associations. Every person was responsible for his or her fate, but the Lord's people were obliged to support each other through this vale of tears. In some sects and at times, that support could be thoroughly oppressive and even unforgiving (the English Quakers of the eighteenth century would expel a bankrupt from fellowship even if he was not the author of his misfortunes), but more often mutual support and charity did a great deal to blunt the harshness of modern industrial life. As Martin has argued in his explanation of the popularity of Pentecostalism in Latin America, evangelical Protestantism offered a functionally adaptive combination of new persona suited to urban industrial capitalism (the self-reliant striving autonomous individual) and a supportive community of like-minded peers.[78]

To the extent that Protestantism thrived, the old organic feudal community of subservience, descent and fate was replaced by a series of overlapping voluntary democratic associations. Protestant sects and denominations themselves formed an important part of the network of civil society, but they also provided the organizational template for savings banks, workers' educational societies, friendly societies, trade unions, pressure groups and political parties. They also provided millions of ordinary people with training in public speaking, in committee management and in small group leadership. And they provided the personality – the autonomous and self-reliant individual – that could operate the new institutions. This was recognized by a mid-nineteenth-century historian of the Scottish Secession Churches; writing of the congregation's right to choose its minister, Thomson said:

> They insisted on the right of popular election in its full and scriptural extent – that every member of the congregation, of whatever sex or social status, should enjoy the right of choice. Called upon in this way to perform a most important duty, the people have been trained to interest themselves in their own affairs, and in attending to their own interest have acquired that habit of exercising individual judgement, which stands closely connected with the continuance of ecclesiastical and civil liberty.[79]

An important part of interesting themselves in their own affairs was learning to read and write. If people were to be held accountable for their salvation, and if that depended more on correct belief than on correct ritual performance, then they had to have access to the means of saving grace. Hearing sermons was useful, as was memorizing the questions and answers of a catechism, but reading the Bible was essential. Individual Protestants translated the scriptures into the vernacular languages and taught people to read and write. When the printing press was invented, it was used to print the Bible.[80] It is a mark of the store that Protestants set by print that, when the French Huguenots sued for peace with the Catholic majority in the Edict of Nantes in 1599, one of their conditions was that they be allowed to keep their printing presses. In many Protestant lands, the state positively encouraged the people at least to read. There was some reluctance to teach writing (Hannah More, in her Mendip schools, refused to do so). If the common people could read, they could be fed a diet of conservative and 'improving' tracts. If they could write, they might write their own not-so-conservative pamphlets. But, even with that reservation, Protestantism encouraged literacy. Post-Reformation Sweden required it: in the seventeenth century full membership of the Church was open only to those who could read. In contemporary Liberia, the Lutheran Church requires proof of literacy for baptism.[81]

In contrast the Muslims of the Ottoman Empire opposed printing, largely because they saw the mechanical reproduction of text as a threat to the traditional method of teaching Islam. They held that memorizing the Qur'ān and reciting it publicly were vital to effective religious socialization and to effective maintenance of the purity of the message as it was being spread. Foreigners in Istanbul had presses, but the only one used by Muslims was forced to close in the 1730s when pious Muslims sacked the printing works. Muslims in India embraced printing only in the nineteenth century and then only because they feared the threat of Christian missionaries. The Qur'ān was translated into Urdu to make it available to the masses, but even then there was a Catholic Church-like fear of democratic interpretation. Those who advocated printing also insisted: 'do not read any book without consulting a scholar.'[82]

We need to be cautious of claiming literacy as an especially Protestant characteristic. Religion had been associated with language long before the Reformation. In the tenth century two Greek priests with a facility with languages, the brothers Cyril and Methodius, were sent to Moravia to teach Christianity to the common people in the vernacular. They translated the liturgy and some of the Bible into Slavonic and invented a new alphabet with which to write their translations.[83] We might also note that as a response to the Reformation the Catholic Church authorities in a number of countries promoted reading as a new means to instruct the common people against the heresies of the Huguenots and other Protestants. Nonetheless, with those two qualifications, we can accept the causal connection between the Reformation and the spread of literacy. Cyril and Methodius had the rather limited interest of providing materials for the institutional Church. What distinguished the Protestant interest was its intensity (it was *very* important for people to learn to read) and its democratic reach (it was very important for *all* the people to learn to read).

Diversity

Quite inadvertently, Protestants destroyed religion's greatest source of strength: being so embedded in the life of a community and so widely accepted that it could be taken for granted. The great drawback to a democratic view of divine revelation is that people generated competing visions and, by denying the special status of the clergy, the Reformers had removed the effective mechanism for preventing schism. The result was innumerable sects. This diversity hastened the retreat of religion in two analytically separate spheres: popular consciousness and the operation of the state.

Any belief-system is most compelling when it is universal. Then it is not a set of beliefs at all; it is merely an accurate account of the world. The existence of alternative visions need not immediately undermine our conviction. We can have recourse to a wide variety of strategies for dismissing competing ideas as really being of no account. One clever strategy for reinforcing one's own beliefs when faced with large numbers of unbelievers was popularized by Christian missionaries in the nineteenth century. Borrowing the evolutionary anthropology then common, they persuaded themselves that God had created races of differing intellectual capacity and then revealed himself to peoples in a manner appropriate to their capacity for understanding. So primitive black people had been given spirits, Arabs had been given Islam, Southern Europeans had been given Catholicism and the Protestant missionaries, who represented the very pinnacle of God's creation, had been given the true faith. The problem with all such strategies is that they tend to fail when people are faced with religious dissent among their own kind. When neighbours and friends and obviously decent people start to disagree, then it is no longer so easy to be sure that what one has is indeed the absolute truth. Increased religious diversity gradually sapped the confidence of most believers, who responded by making their faiths ever more tolerant and liberal.[84] Dogmatism was replaced by relativism. By the middle of the twentieth century it was common for Christians to suppose that what was true for one person need not be true for another. Once dogmatic certainty was eroded, the most pressing reason to make sure that your children grew up in your faith was lost. If apostasy was no longer punished by eternal damnation, there was no need to indoctrinate your loved ones. With increased diversity came a steady increase in the proportion of people who had little or no religious affiliation.

Far more could be said about this, but the central point is simple. The religious pluralism inadvertently created by Protestantism gradually undermined the conviction necessary to impose on others. The same pluralism also sapped the state's enthusiasm for imposing orthodoxy.

Why did the states of the West become formally secular? The explanation lies in the restraints that egalitarian individualism places on the options for dealing with diversity. The Ottoman millet system provides an effective way to manage cultural diversity when the model of social organization allocates people to distinct communities and is comfortable with a discriminatory distribution of rights. The early British method of sending in the dragoons is available if dissenters are denied the same status as conformists. But, once dissent becomes at all common, enforcing orthodoxy becomes expensive. In an increasingly individualistic and egalitarian society, it also becomes unacceptable. I have not tried here to explain the complex interaction of public support for religion and the popularity of religious belief-systems. It is enough to note that in most Western societies modernization was accompanied by a decline in the proportion of the populace who strongly supported any particular religion. The end result was that, as the early democratic states expanded their range of activities, they increasingly did so without regard to religious orthodoxy. If the state is to command popular allegiance, and the people are divided between a number of religions and none, then the state cannot promote any particular religion.

Finally we can return to where we started: the Weber thesis. More often than not, prosperity brings tolerance and liberality and eventually secularization. Or, to turn the relationship round, had the societies of the West not prospered, then ethnic conflict would have been more common, and, as like as not, such conflict would have maintained a premium on loyalty to the traditional religion of the ethnos. Expanding economies certainly found it easier than poor countries to extend individual liberties and to be tolerant of cultural deviation. And there is a strong connection between individual prosperity and weakening commitment to a society's dominant religion. Greater personal wealth reduces our reliance on our fellows and thus weakens community bonds, which in turn allows people greater freedom to exercise choice. We see this in the history of particular religious minorities. As the English Methodists became upwardly mobile, so they became less rigorous in their Methodism; likewise Catholic migrants to Britain, the United States, Australia and New Zealand. We see it in the recent softening of white American Pentecostalism. We can also see clear evidence of it in Inglehart's massive datasets from the recurrent World Values Survey: as gross domestic product goes up, adherence to the traditional religion goes down.[85] If, as Weber does, we believe that the Reformation played a part in the rise of capitalism, then we have another inadvertent link between the rise of Protestantism and the fall of religion.

In sum, the Protestant Reformation – a change in religious culture – set in chain a variety of complex developments that played a major part in the creation of liberal democracy. Some, such as the education of the masses, can be seen as more or less deliberate, but others, such as the new importance for the individual and a general increase in egalitarianism, were accidental by-products. Far from being desired, the greatest change of all – the gradual downgrade of religion – was deeply ironic. A movement that was intended to purify the church so that its imposition on the masses could be justified ended up creating the secular state that eschewed all notions of imposing orthodoxy.

Conclusion

In this final chapter I have argued, against the current consensus of social scientists, I suspect, that religious cultures have, one way or another, contributed a great deal to modern politics and that there are important differences in the political consequences of the major world religions and strands within them. In concluding I do not want to summarize those specific connections, but I do want to repeat the underlying principles of the analysis. First, this study is intended as an exercise in social scientific explanation. It may be wrong but it is not partisan. If the proponents of any faith find themselves either flattered or insulted, then they have missed the point. Most of the causal connections I have traced between aspects of religious traditions and politics rest on unintended consequences. They are inadvertent outcomes for which nobody can claim credit.

Second, the most politically significant features of religious traditions are generally not the specific beliefs we most easily notice. For example, important though they are, the anti-Semitism of the Catholic Church in the nineteenth and early twentieth centuries, or the Shi'ite notion of the rewards for martyrdom, are of less enduring significance than the authoritarianism of the former and the legalism of the latter.

Third, nothing in the above account should be read as suggesting that religious ideas have consequences independent of the circumstances in which they are lived out. Culture and society, ideas and social realities, constantly combine. If it seems in places that too much weight is given to the Gods, it is because the current ethos of social science gives them too little attention. For all its faults, if this study has restored the balance, it will have served a useful purpose.

NOTES

CHAPTER I   RELIGION

1   A. Partington (ed.), *Oxford Dictionary of Quotations* (Oxford: Oxford University Press, 1992), 458.
2   R. S. Appleby, *The Ambivalence of the Sacred: Religion, Violence and Reconciliation* (Lanham, Md.: Rowan Littlefield, 2000), 58.
3   On this dispute, see G. Smith, V. Law, A. Wilson, A. Bohr and E. Allworth, *Nation-Building in the Post-Soviet Borderlands: The Politics of National Identities* (Cambridge: Cambridge University Press, 1998), 58–9.
4   A. Grant, *Independence and Nationhood: Scotland 1306–1469* (Edinburgh: Edinburgh University Press, 1991).
5   Smith et al., *Nation-Building in the Post-Soviet Borderlands*, 39.
6   Bob Jones III, *The Moral Majority* (Greenville, SC: Bob Jones University, 1980), 1.
7   Appleby, *The Ambivalence of the Sacred*, 85. On the details of the conflicting interpretations, see E. Kopelowitz and M. Diamond, 'Religion that strengthens democracy: an analysis of religious political struggles in Israel', *Theory and Society*, 27 (1986), 671–708.
8   Appleby, *The Ambivalence of the Sacred*, 33.
9   See the references to the Home Guard in G. Orwell, *A Patriot After All, 1940–41: The Complete Works of George Orwell*, xii (London: Secker & Warburg, 1998).
10 K. Minogue, *Politics: A Very Short Introduction* (Oxford: Oxford University Press, 1995), 7.
11 D. McLellan, *Karl Marx: Selected Writings* (Oxford: Oxford University Press, 2000).
12 J. Mullen, 'From colony to nation: the implosion of ethnic tolerance in Rwanda', in O. Igwara (ed.), *Ethnic Hatred: Genocide in Rwanda* (London: ASEAN Books, 1995), 21–33.

13   Papal correspondence quoted in D. C. Holtom, *Modern Japan and Shinto Nationalism* (Chicago: Chicago University Press, 1943), 99.
14   R. Pipes, *Russia under the Old Regime* (Harmondsworth: Penguin, 1995), 241.
15   J. P. S. Uberoi, *Religion, Civil Society and the State* (New Delhi: Oxford University Press, 1999), 91.
16   J. Sproxton, *Violence and Religion: Attitudes towards Militancy in the French Civil Wars and the English Revolution* (London: Routledge, 1995).
17   B. Y. Kunze, *Margaret Fell and the Rise of Quakerism* (London: Macmillan, 1994).
18   C. Hill, *The World Turned Upside-Down: Radical Ideas during the English Revolution* (New York: Viking, 1972).
19   H. Behrend, 'The Holy Spirit Movement and the forces of nature in the north of Uganda, 1985–87', in H. B. Hansen and M. Twaddle (eds), *Religion and Politics in East Africa*, (London: James Currey, 1995), 59–71.
20   Y.-S. Park, 'Protestant Christianity and its place in a changing Korea', *Social Compass*, 747 (2000), 514.

CHAPTER 2   EMPIRE

1   G. Dijkink, *National Identities and Geopolitical Visions* (London: Routledge, 1996), 99.
2   M. Haghayeghi, *Islam and Politics in Central Asia* (New York: St Martin's Press, 1995), 7.
3   J. J. Elias, *Islam* (London: Routledge, 1999), 33.
4   M. Roux, *Les Albanais en Yougoslavie* (Paris: Éditions de la Maison des Sciences de l'Homme, 1992), 60–1.
5   C. Cahen, *The Formation of Turkey: The Seljukid Sultanate of Rūm: Eleventh to Fourteenth Century* (London: Pearson, 2001), 125.
6   The modern system in which the state deducts tax from all people of the same 'class' at the same rate requires an effective state. In pre-modern societies, powerful individuals bid for the right to be tax collectors by promising to raise a certain amount for the ruler. Once awarded the franchise, they could raise what they liked provided they passed on the promised amount. This was 'tax farming'.
7   C. Jelavitch and B. Jelavitch, *The Establishment of the Balkan National States, 1804–1920* (Seattle: University of Washington Press, 1977), 5–6.
8   Ibid. 12.
9   Ibid. 9.
10   For an excellent account of the history of the Balkans, see T. Gallagher, *Outcast Europe: The Balkans 1789–1989* (London: Routledge, 2001).
11   Jelavitch and Jelavitch, *The Establishment of the Balkan National States*, 108.
12   G. Duijzings, *Religion and the Politics of Identity in Kosovo* (London: Hurst, 2000), 92–6.

13   Like many other small peoples of the Ottoman Empire, the Assyrians
     were promised much by Russia, France and Britain during the First
     World War and given nothing. Although less well known than the
     Kurds, the Assyrians suffered a similar fate. Those in Iraq were
     severely persecuted by both Muslim and Ba'athist regimes.

14   J. McCarthy, *The Ottoman Peoples and the End of Empire* (London:
     Arnold, 2001).

15   A. T. Embree, 'Christianity and the state in Victorian India: confron-
     tation and collaboration', in R. W. Davis and R. J. Helmstadler (eds),
     Religion and Irreligion in Victorian Society (London: Routledge), 151.

16   J. Pemble, *The Raj, the Indian Mutiny and the Kingdom of Oudh* (New
     Delhi: Oxford University Press, 1977).

17   M. Misra, 'Before the pith helmets', *New Statesman*, 8 Oct. 2001,
     pp. 31–3. See also J. Bernstein, *Dawning of the Raj: The Life and Trials
     of Warren Hastings* (London: Auram, 2001).

18   Misra, 'Before the pith helmets', 33.

19   Embree, 'Christianity and the state in Victorian India', 156.

20   Quoted in B. Porter, *The Lion's Share: A Short History of British Imperi-
     alism 1850–1995* (London: Longman, 1996), 20.

21   J. H. Morrison, *The Scottish Churches Work Abroad* (Edinburgh: T. and
     T. Clark, 1927), 36.

22   E. M. Howse, *Saints in Politics: 'The Clapham Sect' and the Growth of
     Freedom* (London: George Allen & Unwin, 1971).

23   Morrison, *The Scottish Churches Work Abroad*, 14–15.

24   Quoted in E. M. Jackson, *Red Tape and the Gospel: A Study of William
     Paton 1886–1943* (Birmingham: Phlogiston, 1980), 87.

25   Ibid. 94.

26   S. Neill, *A History of Christian Missions* (Harmondsworth: Penguin,
     1975), 456.

27   Sir D. Hawley, 'Law in the Sudan under the Anglo-Sudan Condomin-
     ium', in *The Condominium Remembered*, i. *The Making of the Sudanese
     State* (Durham: University of Durham Centre for Middle Eastern and
     Islamic Studies, Occasional Paper), quoted in The Sudan Foundation,
     'Religion in Sudan'. www.sufo.demon.co.uk/reli003.htm.

28   J. McCarthy, *The Ottoman Peoples and the End of Empire* (London:
     Arnold, 2001), 217.

29   R. S. Dunn, *The Age of Religious Wars 1559–1715* (New York:
     W.W. Norton & Co., 1979), 128.

30   J. A. Templin, *Ideology as a Frontier: The Theological Foundations of
     Afrikaner Nationalism* (Westport, Conn. Greenwood Press, 1984), 38.

31   W. A. de Klerk, *The Puritans in Africa: A Story of Afrikanerdom*
     (Harmondsworth: Penguin, 1983), 30.

32   J. Kinghorn, 'The theology of separate equality: a critical outline of the
     DRC's position on apartheid', in M. Prozesky (ed.), *Christianity Amidst
     Apartheid* (London: Macmillan, 1990), 58.

33   Ibid. 44.

34   Dunn, *The Age of Religious Wars*, 127.
35   Given the current tendency to criticize all imperialist intervention, it is worth reminding ourselves that the British 'oppression' in this area took the form of raising the age at which girls could be married off first to ten and then, in the 1890 Age of Consent Bill, to twelve.
36   G. Oommen, 'Dalit conversion and social protest in Travancore, 1854–1890', *Bangalore Theological Forum*, 28 (1996), 69–84.
37   B. D. Metcalf, *Islamic Revival in British India: Deoband 1860–1900* (Princeton: Princeton University Press, 1982).
38   A. P. Sen, *Hindu Revivalism in Bengal 1872–1905* (New Delhi: Oxford University Press, 1993). Dayananda of the Arya Samaj was much less critical of caste than R. M. Roy. He justified it, as did Gandhi and Vivekanada, by arguing that it had originally reflected merit and achievement. See S. R. Singh, *Nationalism and Social Reform in India* (New Delhi: Ranjit, 1968), and L. Roi, *A History of the Arya Samaj* (Calcutta: Orient Longmans, 1967).
39   J. Zavos, 'Defending Hindu tradition: Sanatana Dharma as a symbol of orthodoxy in colonial India', *Religion*, 31 (2001), 122.
40   A. P. Sen, *Hindu Revivalism in Bengal 1872–1905* (New Delhi: Oxford University Press, 1993), 171.
41   J. P. S. Uberoi, *Religion, Civil Society and the States* (New Delhi: Oxford University Press, 1999).
42   Ibid. 96.
43   R. A. Kapur, *Sikh Separatism: The Politics of Faith* (London: Allen & Unwin, 1986), p. xiii.
44   Ibid. 13.
45   Ibid. 25.
46   McCarthy, *The Ottoman Peoples and the End of Empire*, 2.

CHAPTER 3   NATION

1   D. Loades, 'The origins of English nationalism', in S. Mews (ed.), *Religion and National Identity* (Oxford: Blackwell, 1982), 302.
2   Gellner's theory of nationalism was initially presented in *Thought and Change* (London: Weidenfeld & Nicolson, 1965) and later elaborated in *Nations and Nationalism* (Oxford: Basil Blackwell, 1983) and *Nationalism* (London: Weidenfeld & Nicolson, 1997). For an excellent elaboration and sympathetic critique, see B. O'Leary, 'Ernest Gellner's diagnoses of nationalism...', in J. A. Hall (ed.), *The State of the Nation: Ernest Gellner and the Theory of Nationalism* (Cambridge: Cambridge University Press, 1998), 40–88.
3   On the history of Albania, see T. Gallagher, *Outcast Europe: The Balkans, 1789–1989: From the Ottomans to Milošević* (London: Routledge, 2001).
4   H. Beinin, 'Religion, legitimacy and conflict in Nigeria', *Annals of the American Academy of Political and Social Science*, 483 (1986), 50–60.

5 R. S. Dunn, *The Age of Religious Wars 1559–1715* (New York: W. W. Norton & Co., 1979), 41–2.

6 For details of the way in which the national touring of a portrait of the Black Madonna of Częstochowa as part of the Great Novena of the Millennium celebrations contributed to anti-government sentiment, see M. Osa, 'Pastoral mobilization and contention: the religious foundations of the Solidarity movement in Poland', in C. Smith, *Disruptive Religion: The Force of Faith in Social-Movement Activism* (New York: Routledge, 1996). For a general history, see B. Szajkowski, *Next to God . . . Poland: Politics and Religion in Contemporary Poland* (New York: St Martin's Press, 1983).

7 P. Michel, *Politics and Religion in Eastern Europe: Catholicism in Hungary, Poland and Czechoslovakia* (Cambridge: Polity, 1991), 132.

8 For a detailed account of the Solidarity movement, see T. G. Ash, *The Polish Revolution: Solidarity* (New York: Scribner, 1984).

9 T. Inglis, *Moral Monopoly: The Rise and Fall of the Catholic Church in Modern Ireland* (Dublin: UCD Press, 1998), esp. ch. 5.

10 A facsimile of the proclamation can be found at www/vms.utexas. edu/~jdana/history/documents.htm.

11 T. R. Dwyer, *Eamonn De Valera* (Dublin: Gill & Macmillan, 1998).

12 Gallagher, *Outcast Europe*, 100–3; I. Livezeanu, *Cultural Politics in Greater Romania* (Ithaca, NY: Cornell University Press, 1995).

13 For a good general review, see S. Alexander, 'Religion and national identity in Yugoslavia', in Mews (ed.), *Religion and National Identity*, 597–607; R. G. C. Thomas and H. R. Friman, *The South Slav Conflict: History, Religion, Ethnicity and Nationalism* (New York: Garland Publishing, 1996); S. Woodward, *Balkan Tragedy: Chaos and Dissolution after the Cold War* (Washington: Brookings Institution, 1995); P. Mojzes, *Yugoslav Inferno* (New York: Continuum, 1994); P. Mojzes (ed.), *Religion and War in Bosnia* (Atlanta, Ga.: American Academy of Religion, 1998); and G. C. Davis (ed.), *Religion and Justice in the War over Bosnia* (New York: Routledge, 1996).

14 M. Tanner, *Croatia: A Nation Forged in War* (New Haven, Conn.: Yale Nota Bene, 2001), 116.

15 Gallagher, *Outcast Europe*, 58.

16 D. Conversi, 'Violence as ethnic border: the unintended consequences of cultural assimilation in Croatian, Kurdish and Basque nationalism', in J. G. Beramendi, R. Maiz and X. M. Nunez (eds), *Nationalism in Europe: Past and Present* (Santiago de Compostela: University of Santiago Press, 1994), i. 167–98.

17 Gallagher, *Outcast Europe*, 228.

18 Tanner, *Croatia*, 219.

19 G. Duijzings, *Religion and the Politics of Identity in Kosovo* (London: Hurst, 2000), 130.

20 V. Perica, *Balkan Idols: Religion and Nationalism in Yugoslav States* (Oxford: Oxford University Press, 2002).

21   A. Rashid, *The Taliban: The Story of the Afghan Warlords* (London: Pan, 2001), 92.

22   J. Swift, *Peter the Great* (London: Hodder & Stoughton, 2000), 79. For a full account of the Russian Church in this period, see R. Pipes, *Russia under the Old Regime* (Harmondsworth: Penguin, 1995), 240.

23   This account is taken from R. Kapuściński, *Imperium* (London: Grant, 1995).

24   On the Soviet treatment of Islam, see S. Keller, *To Moscow, not Mecca: The Soviet Campaign against Islam in Central Asia, 1917–1941* (Westport, Conn.: Praeger, 2001). On Islam in the North Caucasus region, see A. Zelkina, 'Islam and Politics in the North Caucasus', *Religion, State and Society*, 21 (1993), 115–24.

25   G. V. Smith, V. Law, A. Wilson, A. Bohr and E. Allworth, *Nation-Building in the Post-Soviet Borderlands: The Politics of National Identities* (Cambridge: Cambridge University Press, 1998), 6–7.

26   The Russian Orthodox Church's website (www.xxc.ru) contains marvellous video clips of amateur film of the destruction of the original cathedral, illustrations of the various designs submitted for the intended Palace of the Soviets and photographs of the rebuilding.

27   V. Myllyniemi, 'Remarks on Russia's New Religion Law', in J. Kaplan (ed.), *Beyond the Mainstream: The Emergence of Religious Pluralism in Finland, Estonia and Russia* (Helsinki: Studia Historica, 2000), 337–40.

28   K. Kääriäinen, 'Is a shared religion possible in Russia', in Kaplan (ed.), *Beyond the Mainstream*, 347–59. For other survey data for the early 1990s, see S. White, I. McAllister and O. Kryshtanovskaya, 'Religion and politics in postcommunist Russia', *Religion, State and Society*, 22 (1994), 73–88, and L. Vorontsova and S. Filatov, 'The changing pattern of religious belief: *perestroika* and beyond', *Religion, State and Society*, 22 (1994), 89–96.

29   See E. Chmielewski, *Tribune of the Slavophiles* (Gainesville, Fla.: University of Florida Press, 1961).

30   Quoted in J. Pearce, *Solzhenitsyn: A Soul in Exile* (London: Harper-Collins, 1999), 123.

31   Quoted in P. Cockburn, 'Pope brings out joy in Catholics, suspicion in Russians', *Independent*, 27 June 2001.

32   B. R. Bociurkiw, 'The rise of the Ukrainian Autocephalous Orthodox Church, 1919–1922', in G. A. Hosking (ed.), *Church, Nation and State in Russia and Ukraine* (London: Macmillan, 1991), 228–49, and 'Soviet destruction of the Ukrainian Orthodox Church 1929–1936', *Journal of Ukrainian Studies*, 22 (1987), 3–21.

33   According to a colleague currently working in the Ukraine, the majority of Ukrainians identify themselves as Orthodox and 'Kiev Patriarchate', but 70 per cent of Orthodox congregations are Moscow Patriarchate. One possible interpretation is that Ukrainian separatist sentiment is stronger than respect for those clergy who are post-1991 nationalists.

34 W. van den Berkken, 'The Russian Orthodox Church, state and society 1991–93: the rest of the story', *Religion, State and Society*, 22 (1994), 163–8.

35 There is, of course, a positive Romantic take on this. England had the Lakeland poets; Russia had the Slavophiles.

36 D. D. Morgan, 'The essence of Welshness? Some aspects of Christian faith and national identity in Wales, *c.*1900–2000', in R. Pope (ed.), *Religion and National Identity: Wales and Scotland c.1700–2000* (Cardiff: University of Wales Press, 2001), 149.

37 M. König, 'Religion and the nation-state in South Korea', *Social Compass*, 47 (2000), 559.

38 Ibid. 562.

39 It is significant that Turkey is the only Muslim country that has had a female Prime Minister who did not inherit the post from her father or husband.

40 Turkey's secularism was always closer to the co-option method than to Stalin's outright repression. Mosques were never closed and the prayer leaders in 180,000 mosques were paid by the government's Directorate of Religious Affairs. As with Peter's treatment of the Orthodox Church, this rather neutered the institution.

41 R. Khalidi, L. Anderson, M. Muslih and R. S. Simon (eds), *The Origins of Arab Nationalism* (New York: Columbia University Press, 1991).

42 E. Wakin, *A Lonely Minority: The Modern Story of Egypt's Copts* (New York: William Morrow & Co., 1963).

43 For a history of the Muslim brotherhood in Egypt, see A. A. Ramadan, 'Fundamentalist influence in Egypt: the strategies of the Muslim Brotherhood and the Takfir groups', in M. E. Marty and R. S. Appleby (eds), *Fundamentalisms and the State* (Chicago: Chicago University Press, 1993), 152–83. On Islam generally, see G. Abdo, *No God but God: Egypt and the Triumph of Islam* (Oxford: Oxford University Press, 2000).

44 J. Beinin, 'Nasser', in J. Krieger (ed.), *The Oxford Companion to the Politics of the World* (Oxford: Oxford University Press, 193), 612–13.

45 The same story could be told of the Bourguibist regime in Tunisia. See F. Halliday, 'Fundamentalism and the state: Iran and Tunisia', in Halliday (ed.), *Nation and Religion in the Middle East* (London: Saqi, 2000), ch. 7; C. Moore, *Tunisia since Independence* (Berkeley and Los Angeles: University of California Press, 1965); and N. Salem, *Habib Bourguiba: Islam and the Creation of Tunisia* (London: Croom Helm, 1984).

46 For a general political history of modern Syria, see D. Hopwood, *Syria 1945–1986* (London: Unwin Hyman, 1988).

47 The relationship between Ba'athism and Islam has always been somewhat muddy. Although the pan-Arab socialism of Ba'athism is usually seen as an alternative to an Islamic programme, its founder Michael Aflak is reported to have said that 'Islam is to Arabism

what bones are to flesh' (W. Phares, *Lebanese Christian Nationalism: The Rise and Fall of an Ethnic Resistance* (London: Lynne Rienner Publishers, 1995), 15).

48   For some of the most insightful recent observations about Iran, see F. Halliday, *Nation and Religion in the Middle East*, and 'Iranian foreign policy since 1979: internationalism and nationalism in the Iranian revolution', in J. R. I. Cole and N. R. Keddie (eds), *Shi'ism and Social Protest* (New Haven, Conn.: Yale University Press, 1986), 88–107.

49   A. D. Smith, 'The "Golden Age" and national renewal', in G. Hosking and G. Schöpflin (eds), *Myths and Nationhood* (London: Hurst, 1997), 45.

50   S. Bakhash, *The Religion of the Ayatollahs: Iran and the Islamic Revolution* (London: Unwin, 1985), 23.

51   Ibid. 26.

52   W. M. Watt, *Islamic Fundamentalism and Modernity* (London: Routledge, 1988), 135.

53   A. Taheri, *Holy Terror: The Inside Story of Islamic Terrorism* (London: Sphere, 1987), 13.

54   E. Sivan, 'The Islamic resurgence: civil society strikes back', in L. Kaplan (ed.), *Fundamentalism in Comparative Perspective* (Amherst, Mass.: University of Massachusetts Press), 107.

55   Y.-S. Park, 'Protestant Christianity and its place in a changing Korea', *Social Compass*, 47 (2000), 517.

56   J. F. Burns, 'Hindu nationalist still proud of role in killing father of India', *New York Times on the Web*, 2 Mar. 1998.

57   R. Buultjens, 'India: religion, political legitimacy and the secular state', *Annals of the American Academy of Political and Social Science*, 483 (1986), 101.

58   A. Rajagopal, *Politics after Television: Hindu Nationalism and the Reshaping of the Public in India* (Cambridge: Cambridge University Press, 2000), 15.

59   For the details of BJP politics in the 1990s, see the essays in T. B. Hansen and C. Jaffrelot, *The BJP and the Compulsions of Politics in India* (New Delhi: Oxford University Press, 1998), and T. B. Hansen, *The Saffron Wave: Democracy and Nationalism in Modern India* (Princeton: Princeton University Press, 1999).

60   Constitutionally there are three groups that are regarded as systematically excluded: the Scheduled Castes (including the Untouchables), the Scheduled Tribes (which have always been outside the caste system) and Other Backward castes (which includes lower caste converts to other religions). It is worth noting that, although an individual cannot change caste, a whole caste can improve its relative position by 'sanscritization' – the process of imitating the manners and customs of the Brahmins.

61   A. McMillan, 'Scheduled caste voting and the BJP', paper presented at the 2001 American Political Science Association.

62 S. P. Ramet, 'Politics and religion in Eastern Europe and the Soviet Union', in G. Moyser (ed), *Politics and Religion in the Modern World* (London: Routledge, 1991), 89.

63 J. Campbell, 'Nationalism, ethnicity and religion: fundamental conflicts and the politics of identity in Tanzania', *Nations and Nationalism*, 5 (1999), 120.

64 K. Ward, 'The Church of Uganda amidst conflict', in H. B. Hansen and M. Twaddle (eds), *Religion and Politics in East Africa* (London: James Currey, 1995), 76.

65 J. Gula, 'Catholic Poles in the USSR during the Second World War', *Religion, State and Society*, 22 (1994), 10–11.

66 D. Throup, 'Render unto Caesar the things that are Caesar's: the politics of church–state conflict in Kenya, 1978–1990', in Hansen and Twaddle (eds), *Religion and Politics in East Africa*, 143–76.

67 P. Gifford, *Christianity and Politics in Doe's Liberia* (Cambridge: Cambridge University Press, 1993), 61–2.

68 G. P. Benson, 'Ideological politics and biblical hermeneutics: Kenya's Protestant churches and the nyayo state', in Hansen and Twaddle (eds), *Religion and Politics in East Africa*, 178–99.

69 P. Gifford, 'Some recent developments in African Christianity', *African Affairs*, 93 (1994), 515.

70 Ibid.

71 D. Martin, *Pentecostalism: The World their Parish* (Oxford: Blackwell, 2001), 132–52.

72 Gifford, 'Some recent developments in African Christianity', 515–16.

73 Ibid. 530.

74 D. M. Jones, *Political Development in Pacific Asia* (Oxford: Blackwell, 1997); W. T. Neill, *Twentieth-Century Indonesia* (New York: Columbia University Press, 1973).

75 K. Boyle and J. Sheen, *Freedom of Religion and Belief: A World Report* (London: Routledge, 1997), 200–8.

76 The differences between church and sect types of religion are discussed further in the final chapter and in S. Bruce, *Religion in the Modern World: From Cathedrals to Cults* (Oxford: Oxford University Press, 1990).

77 G. Smith, V. Law, A. Wilson, A. Bohr and E. Allworth, *Nation-Building in the Post-Soviet Borderlands: The Politics of National Identities* (Cambridge: Cambridge University Press, 1998), 15.

78 G. Simpson, 'The Declaration of Arbroath revitalised', *Scottish Historical Review*, 56 (1977), 11–34.

79 C. V. Wedgwood, *Richelieu and the French Monarchy* (Harmondsworth: Penguin, 1974).

80 D. Hay, *Annalists and Historians: Western Historiography from the Eighth to the Eighteenth Century* (London: Methuen, 1977).

81 R. S. Dunn, *The Age of Religious Wars 1559–1715* (New York: W. W. Norton & Co., 1979), 82.

82   R. Kapuściński, *Imperium* (London: Granta, 1993), 141.
83   A. D. Smith, 'Ethnic election and national destiny: some religious origins of nationalist ideals', *Nations and Nationalism*, 5 (1999), 331–55. See also C. C. O'Brien, *God Land* (Cambridge, Mass.: Harvard University Press, 1988).
84   B. Cauthen, 'The myth of divine election and Afrikaner ethnogenesis', in G. Hosking and G. Schöpflin (eds), *Myths and Nationhood* (London: Hurst, 1997), 107–31. For a general account of the Afrikaners, see W. A. de Klerk, *The Puritans in Africa: A Story of Afrikanerdom* (Harmondsworth: Penguin, 1983), and F. A. van Jaarsveld, *The Awakening of Afrikaner Nationalism 1868–1881* (Cape Town: Human & Rousseau, 1961).
85   On Confucianism, see J. Ching, *Chinese Religions* (London: Macmillan, 1993). On Shinto, see H. Hardacre, *Shinto and the State* (Princeton: Princeton University Press, 1991).
86   Ian McAllister, 'Political attitudes, partisanship and social structures in Northern Ireland', *Economic and Social Review*, 14 (1983), 185–202.
87   J. Manor, 'Organizational weakness and the rise of Sinhalese Buddhist extremism', in M. E. Marty and R. S. Appleby (eds), *Accounting for Fundamentalism* (Chicago: University of Chicago Press, 1994), 771.
88   R. Carwardine, 'The know-nothing party, the Protestant evangelical community and American national identity', in S. Mews (ed.), *Religion and National Identity* (Oxford: Blackwell, 1982), 449–63.
89   D. Loades, 'The origins of English nationalism', in ibid. 381.
90   M. Tanner, *Croatia: A Nation Forged in War* (New Haven, Conn.: Yale Nota Bene, 2001), 245.
91   G. C. Visser, *Ossewa Brandwag: Traitors or Patriots* (Johannesburg: Macmillan, 1976); J. H. P. Serfontein, *Brotherhood of Power: An Exposé of the Secret Afrikaner Broederbond* (London: Rex Collings, 1979).
92   J. Sproxton, *Violence and Religion: Attitudes towards Militancy in the French Civil Wars and the English Revolution* (London: Routledge, 1995), 28.
93   F. Halliday, 'The politics of Islamic fundamentalism: Iran, Tunisia and the challenge to the secular state', in A. S. Ahmed and H. Donnan (eds), *Islam, Globalization and Postmodernity* (London: Routledge, 1994), 91–113; M. Riesebrodt, *Pious Passion: The Emergence of Modern Fundamentalism in the United States and Iran* (Berkeley and Los Angeles: University of California Press, 1993); B. B. Lawrence, *Defenders of God: The Fundamentalist Revolt against the Modern Age* (London: I. B. Tauris, 1990). For a truly encyclopaedic understanding of fundamentalism, see the essays in the five volumes edited by M. E. Marty and R. S. Appleby and published by University of Chicago Press: *Fundamentalisms Observed* (1991); *Fundamentalisms and Society* (1993); *Fundamentalisms and the State* (1993); *Accounting for Fundamentalisms* (1994); *Fundamentalisms Comprehended* (1995).

94   E. Gellner, *Postmodernism, Reason and Religion* (London: Routledge, 1992), 15.
95   A. Lieven, 'Afghan statecraft', *Prospect* (Jan. 2002), 24–9.
96   J. Seabrook, *Freedom Unfinished: Fundamentalism and Popular Resistance in Bangladesh Today* (London: Zed, 2002).
97   R. H. Dekmejian, *Islam in Revolution: Fundamentalism in the Arab World* (Syracuse, NY: Syracuse University Press, 1995), 78.
98   N. Saiedi, 'What is Islamic fundamentalism', in J. K. Hadden and A. S. Shupe (eds), *Prophetic Religions and Politics* (New York: Paragon House, 1986), 193.
99   This case is made for Indonesia in J. B. Tamney, 'Islam's popularity: the case of Indonesia', *South East Asian Journal of Social Science*, 15 (1987), 53–65.
100 For a magisterial account of the rise and fall of fundamentalism, see G. Keppel, *Jihad: The Trail of Political Islam* (London: Tauris, 2002). See also the major work of another French expert on Islam: O. Roy, *Globalized Islam: Fundamentalism, De-Territorialization and the Search for a New Ummah* (London: Hurst, 2002).
101 R. Antoun, 'Sojourners abroad: migration for higher education in a post-peasant Muslim society', in Ahmed and Donnan (eds), *Islam, Globalization and Postmodernity*, 160–89.
102 A. Rashid, *Taliban: The Story of the Afghan Warlords* (London: Pan, 2001).

CHAPTER 4   PARTY

1   This section draws heavily on J. Whyte, *Catholics in Western Democracies: A Study in Political Behaviour* (Dublin: Gill & Macmillan, 1981), M. Conway, *Catholic Politics in Europe* (London: Routledge, 1997), and A. Keller, *Church and State on the European Continent* (London: Epworth Press, 1936).
2   Whyte, *Catholics in Western Democracies*, 36.
3   U. Benigni, 'Christian Democracy', in *The Catholic Encyclopaedia* (New York: Robert Appleton Co., 1908). Available online as www.newadvent.org/cathen.www
4   Whyte, *Catholics in Western Democracies*, 61.
5   Ibid. 79.
6   If space allowed I would be careful about the precise meaning of terms such as authoritarian, fascism and the like. See G. Allardyce, 'What fascism is not: thoughts on the definition of a concept', *American Historical Review*, 84 (1979), 367–88; W. Lacquer, *Fascism* (Oxford: Oxford University Press, 1996); the analytical section of R. Griffin (ed.), *Fascism* (Oxford: Oxford University Press, 1995), and J. Linz, 'Some notes towards a comparative study of fascism in sociological and historical perspective', in W. Lacquer (ed.), *Fascism: A Reader's*

Guide (Berkeley and Los Angeles: University of California Press, 1976), 3–121.

7   U. Goñi, *The Real Odessa: How Perón Brought the Nazi War Criminals to Argentina* (London: Granta Books, 2002).

8   D. Martin, *Pentecostalism: The World their Parish* (Oxford: Blackwell, 2001), 53.

9   D. Sikkink and M. Regnerus, 'For God and the Fatherland: Protestant worlds and the rise of National Socialism' in C. Smith (ed.), *Disruptive Faith: The Force of Faith in Social-Movement Activism* (Routledge: London, 1996), 148–66.

10   R. Griffin, 'Fascism', www.brookes.ac.uk/schools/humanities/roger/FASREL.htm, Feb. 2000.

11   F. Buscher and M. Phayer, 'German Catholic bishops and the holocaust, 1940–1952', *German Studies Review*, 11 (1988), 485. See also M. Phayer, *The Catholic Church and the Holocaust 1930–1965* (Bloomington, Ind.: Indiana University Press, 2000).

12   A. Stiles and A. Farmer, *The Unification of Germany 1815–1890* (London: Hodder & Stoughton, 2001).

13   M. Niemöller, *Exile in the Fatherland: Martin Niemöller's Letters from Moabit Prison* (Grand Rapids, Mich.: Eerdmans, 1986); E. Bethge, *Dietrich Bonhoeffer: A Biography* (Augsburg: Fortress Press, 2002).

14   Quoted in F. Lannon, 'Modern Spain: the project of national Catholicism', in S. Mews (ed.), *Religion and National Identity* (Oxford: Blackwell, 1982), 574.

15   R. Rémond, *Religion and Society in Modern Europe* (Oxford: Blackwell, 1999), 164.

16   Keller, *Church and State on the European Continent*, 141.

17   Conway, *Catholic Politics in Europe*, 60.

18   O. Górka, *Outline of Polish History Past and Present* (London: M. I. Kolin, 1942).

19   For details of Hungarian fascism, see G. Barany, 'The dragon's teeth: the roots of Hungarian fascism', in P. F. Sugar (ed.), *Native Fascism in the Successor States 1918–1945* (Santa Barbara: ABC-Clio, 1971), 73–82.

20   Conway, *Catholic Politics in Europe*, 83.

21   A. Rhodes, *The Vatican in the Age of Dictators, 1922–1945* (New York: Holt, Rinehart & Winston, 1973), 325.

22   R. S. Appleby, *The Ambivalence of the Sacred: Religion, Violence and Reconciliation* (Lanham, Md.: Rowan & Littlefield, 2000), 65.

23   Conway, *Catholic Politics in Europe*, 83.

24   T. Gallagher, *Outcast Europe: The Balkans, 1789–1989: From the Ottomans to Miloševic* (London: Routledge, 2001), 100.

25   T. Gallagher, 'Pluralism, tyranny and the Orthodox Church: the case of Romania', paper presented at the Political Studies Association Religion and Politics seminar, University of Sheffield, 1999.

26   Gallagher, *Outcast Europe*, 116.

27   Ibid. 117.

28   C. Callil, 'Action man', *New Statesman*, 9 Apr. 2002, p. 40.

29   Rhodes, *The Vatican in the Age of Dictators*, 103–11.

30   E. Paris, *Long Shadows: Truth, Lies and History* (London: Bloomsbury, 2002), 74–121, analyses contemporary French responses to the anti-Semitism of Vichy France.

31   As a reminder of the complexity of Catholic politics, we might note that Cardinal van Roey of Malines called on the faithful to vote against the Rexists: see Whyte, *Catholics in Western Democracies*, 79.

32   This section draws heavily on the following: J. Hiden and P. Salmon, *The Baltic Nations and Europe* (London: Longman, 1994); A. Bilmanis, *A History of Latvia* (Princeton: Princeton University Press, 1951); and R. Taagepera, *Estonia: Return to Independence* (Boulder, Colo.: Westview, 1993).

33   J. H. Jackson, *Estonia* (London: George Allen & Unwin, 1948), 237.

34   O. Chadwick, *Britain and the Vatican during the Second World War* (Cambridge: Cambridge University Press, 1986), 19. See also Rhodes, *The Vatican in the Age of the Dictators*.

35   We might note that, fifty years later and despite many Vatican pronouncements against it, the popular connection with anti-Semitism remains. A 1990 survey in Holland found Christians were more anti-Semitic than non-Christians and that Catholics were more anti-Semitic than Protestants; R. Konig, R. Eisinga and P. Scheepers, 'Explaining the relationship between Christian religion and anti-Semitism in the Netherlands', *Review of Religious Research*, 41 (2000), 373–93. Anti-Semitism remains strong in Polish Catholicism. Fr Henryk Jankowski, who was active in the Solidarity trade union, has written critically of 'international Jewry'. Former pro-democracy activist Kazimierz Swita caused great offence by erecting large crosses at the gates of Auschwitz. Radio Maryja, a Catholic radio station, regularly broadcasts anti-Semitic programmes; see S. Crawshaw, 'Hero priest touts poison and hate', *Glasgow Herald*, 14 Feb. 1999, and M. Hiller, 'Poland's new totalitarianism', *Free Inquiry*, 15 (1995), 42–5. However, we should add that anti-Semitism has also been common in some conservative evangelical Protestant circles. US government papers published in 2002 showed Billy Graham, the doyen of mass evangelists, to have expressed anti-Semitic sentiments in the 1950s.

36   Quoted in E. Campion, *Rockchoppers: Growing up Catholic in Australia* (Harmondsworth: Penguin, 1982), 26.

37   J. Bernauer SJ, 'After Christendom: the holocaust and Catholicism's current search for forgiveness', paper presented at the Forgiveness Conference, Holy Cross College, Sept. 2001.

38   R. Griffin, 'Introduction', in Griffin (ed.), *Fascism* (Oxford: Oxford University Press, 1995), 1.

39   P. F. Sugar, 'Conclusion', in Sugar (ed.), *Native Fascism in the Successor States*, 152.

40 Ibid. 151.
41 Many Orthodox countries were in a sense 'protected' from the attractions of fascism by already being under the influence of the Soviet Union, but, among those that were not, Bulgaria had an admirable record of resisting the worst aspects of fascism and comes off well in any comparison with Vichy France. Largely to placate the Germans, the National Assembly in 1943 proposed deporting Bulgarian Jews. The leaders of the Bulgarian Orthodox Church very publicly and aggressively denounced the plans and gave strong moral support to forty-three deputies of the National Assembly who blocked the scheme, which was then abandoned. See T. Todorov, *The Fragility of Goodness: Why Bulgaria's Jews Survived the Holocaust* (London: Weidenfeld & Nicolson, 2002).
42 S. W. Gilley, 'Irish Catholicism in Britain', in D. A. Kerr (ed.), *Religion, State and Ethnic Group* (Aldershot: Dartmouth, 1992), 229–60.
43 On anti-Catholicism in Scotland, see S. Bruce, *No Pope of Rome: Militant Protestants in Scotland* (Edinburgh: Mainstream, 1985).
44 M. P. Hornsby-Smith, 'English Catholics at the new millennium', in M. P. Hornsby-Smith (ed.), *Catholics in England 1950–2000* (London: Cassell, 1999), 291–306.
45 L. A. Kotler-Berkowitz, 'Religion and voting behaviour in Great Britain: a reassessment', *British Journal of Political Science*, 31 (2001), 550.
46 The strong form can also be found in Liverpool and the north-west of England. See P. J. Waller, *Democracy and Sectarianism in Liverpool: A Political and Social History of Liverpool, 1868–1939* (Liverpool: Liverpool University Press, 1981), and D. M. MacRaild, *Culture, Conflict and Migration: The Irish in Victorian Cumbria* (Liverpool: Liverpool University Press, 1998).
47 On Orangeism in Scotland, see E. McFarland, *Protestants First: Orangeism in 19th Century Scotland* (Edinburgh: Edinburgh University Press, 1990), and W. Marshall, *The Billy Boys: A Concise History of Orangeism in Scotland* (Edinburgh: Mercat Press, 1996).
48 R. Carwardine, 'Religion and politics in nineteenth-century Britain: the case against American exceptionalism', in M. A. Noll (ed.), *Religion and American Politics: From the Colonial Period to the 1980s* (New York: Oxford University Press), 241.
49 D. Morgan, 'The social and educational background of Anglican Bishops: continuities and change', *British Journal of Sociology*, 20 (1969), 295–310.
50 Quoted in A. Rossiter, ' "Between the devil and the deep blue sea": Irish women, Catholicism and colonialism', in G. Salgal and N. Yuval-Davis (eds), *Refusing Holy Orders: Women and Fundamentalism in Britain* (London: Women Against Fundamentalism, 1992), 95.
51 Appleby, *The Ambivalence of the Sacred*, 44–6.
52 On Christian Democrat parties generally, see R. E. M. Irving, *The Christian Democrat Parties of Western Europe* (London: Allen &

Unwin, 1979); M. P. Fogarty, *Christian Democracy in Western Europe 1820–1953* (Notre Dame, Ind.: University of Notre Dame Press, 1957; repr. London: Greenwood Press, 1974); D. Hanley (ed.), *Christian Democracy in Europe* (London: Pinter, 1996).

53   J. R. Montero and K. Calvo, 'Religiosity and party choice in Spain: an elusive cleavage?' in D. Broughton and H.-M. ten Napel (eds), *Religion and Mass Electoral Behaviour in Europe* (London: Routledge, 2000), 118–39.

54   C. G. A. Bryant, 'Depillarization in the Netherlands', *British Journal of Sociology*, 32 (1981), 60.

55   P. Dekker and P. Esler, 'De-pillarization, deconfessionalization and de-ideologization: empirical trends in Dutch society 1958–92', *Review of Religious Research*, 37 (1996), 325–42.

56   B. Griffin, 'The political culture of secularisation: European trends and comparative perspectives', in Broughton and ten Napel (eds), *Religion and Mass Electoral Behaviour in Europe*, 21.

57   P. Bréchon, 'Religious voting in a secular France', in Broughton and ten Napel (eds), *Religion and Mass Electoral Behaviour in Europe*, 97–117.

58   M. Donovan, 'Italy: a dramatic case of secularization?' in ibid. 140.

59   J. Madeley, 'Reading the runes: the religious factor in Scandinavian politics', in ibid. 28–43.

60   The data are discussed in detail in T. Glendinning and S. Bruce, 'The religious divide', in J. Curtice and A. Park (eds), forthcoming.

61   D. Seawright, *An Important Matter of Principle: The decline of the Scottish Conservative and Unionist Party* (Aldershot: Ashgate, 1999), and 'A confessional cleavage resurrected: the denominational vote in Britain', in Broughton and ten Napel (eds), *Religion and Mass Electoral Behaviour in Europe*, 44–60.

62   James D. Hunter, *Culture Wars: The Struggle to Define America* (New York: Basic, 1991).

63   L. A. Kellstedt, J. C. Green, C. E. Smidt and J. L. Guth, 'Faith and the vote: the role of religion in political alignments', paper presented at the 1999 annual meeting of the American Political Science Association, Atlanta.

64   L. A. Kotler-Berkowitz, 'Religion and voting behaviour in Great Britain: a reassessment', *British Journal of Political Science*, 31 (2001), 552.

65   There are, of course, important qualifications. There is certainly re-alignment in the USA. In Australia and New Zealand the shift to the right of the descendants of the Irish is partly offset by the views of more recent waves of Catholics migrants (from Croatia, for example). These later settlers are alienated from the right by its anti-immigration policy – a policy that the ex-Irish, who are now the natives, generally support. A further complication is the increasing indifference of the young to politics. If present trends to abstention continue, we will have to replace left–right voting by voting–not voting as a measure of 'conservatism'.

66 F. Fukuyama, *The End of History and the Last Man* (Harmondsworth: Penguin, 1992).

67 L. Saad, 'Public opinion about abortion', Gallup Special reports, www.gallup.com/poll/specialreports/pollsummaries.

68 B. C. Hayes, 'Religious identification and moral attitudes', *British Journal of Sociology*, 46 (1996), 457–74.

69 B. C. Hayes, 'The impact of religious identification on political attitudes: an international comparison', *Sociology of Religion* 56 (1995), 177–94.

70 J. J. M. van Holsteyn and G. A. Irwin, 'The bells toll no more: the declining influence of religion on voting behaviour in the Netherlands', in Broughton and ten Napel (eds), *Religion and Mass Electoral Behaviour in Europe*, (London: Routledge, 2000), 75–96.

CHAPTER 5   PROTEST

1 This approach underpins a whole approach to the sociological explanation of social movements. For a critical evaluation, see R. Wallis, *Salvation and Protest* (London: Francis Pinter, 1979).

2 Diary entry, Dec. 1842. Quoted in 'A Web of English History', http://dspace/dial.pipex.com/town/ terrace/adw03/peel/shaftes.htm.

3 D. Smith, *Transforming the World? The Social Impact of British Evangelicalism* (Carlisle: Paternoster Press, 1998).

4 E. Royle, 'Evangelicals and education', in J. Wolffe (ed.), *Evangelical Faith and Public Zeal: Evangelicals and Society in Britain 1780–1980* (London: SPCK, 1995), 122. See also B. Dickey, 'Going about and doing good: evangelicals and poverty c. 1815–1870', in ibid. 38–58.

5 Speeches of the Earl of Shaftesbury (1868). Quoted in 'A web of English history', http://dspace/dial.pipex.com/town/terrace/adw03/peel/shaftes.htm, 36.

6 F. K. Brown, *Fathers of the Victorians* (Cambridge: Cambridge University Press, 1961), 328.

7 J. Collingwood and M. Collingwood, *Hannah More* (Oxford: Lion, 1990), 147.

8 Quoted in 'The Montgomery bus boycott', www.watson.org/-lisa/blackhistory/civil rights-55–65/montbus.html.

9 A. Morris, 'The black church in the civil rights movement: the SCLC as the decentralized, radical arm of the black church', in C. Smith (ed.), *Disruptive Religion: The Face of Faith in Social Movement Activism* (London: Routledge, 1996), 29.

10 Ibid. 37.

11 C. Marsh, *The Last Days: A Son's Story of Sin and Segregation at the Dawn of the New South* (New York: Basic Books, 2001), 102.

12 One of the few exceptions was Earl Stallings, who in 1963 was pastor of First Baptist Church in Birmingham, Alabama. He was forced out

NOTES TO PP. 135–147   271

by segregationists in his congregation who objected to his willingness to encourage blacks to worship in the church.

13   J. Findlay, 'In keeping with the prophets: the Mississippi summer of 1964', *The Christian Century*, 8–15 June 1988, pp. 574–76.

14   A. Bradstock, *Saints and Sandinistas: The Catholic Church in Nicaragua and its Response to the Revolution* (London: Epworth Press, 1987).

15   P. Erdozain, *Archbishop Romero, Martyr of Salvador* (Maryknoll: Orbis Books, 1981). By the end of the century, outspoken clergy were in more danger from rebels than from the state. The Archbishop of Cali, Colombia, Isaias Duarte Cancino, was shot dead in March 2002 after repeatedly criticizing FARC, the Colombian left-wing guerilla movement.

16   B. Smith, 'Churches and human rights in Latin America: recent trends on the Subcontinent', in D. H. Levin (ed.), *Churches and Politics in Latin America* (Beverly Hills, Calif.; Sage, 1980), 185.

17   P. Sigmund, 'The Catholic Church in Chile', *Annals of the American Academy of Political and Social Science*, 483 (1986), 32.

18   P. Michel, *Politics and Religion in Eastern Europe: Catholicism in Hungary, Poland and Czechoslovakia* (Cambridge: Polity, 1991), 176.

19   K. Yirenkyi, 'The role of Christian churches in national politics: reflections from laity and clergy in Ghana', *Sociology of Religion*, 61 (2000), 329.

20   F. Lawson, 'Korea', in S. Mews (ed.), *Religion and Politics* (London: Longman, 1989), 153–8.

21   P. Gifford, 'Some recent developments in African Christianity', *African Affairs*, 93 (1994), 530.

22   C. Smith (ed.), *Disruptive Religion: The Force of Faith in Social Movement Activism* (London: Routledge, 1996), 21.

23   Clearly, the movement is no longer new, but, because it is the label used in all the previous studies and the usage does not create any confusion, I will stick with it.

24   J. K. Hadden and C. E. Swann, *Primetime Preachers: The Rising Power of Televangelism* (Reading, Mass.: Addison-Wesley, 1981). See S. Bruce, *Pray TV: Televangelism in America* (London: Routledge, 1990), 96–113, on audience size.

25   M. Janovitz, *The Last Half-Century: Societal Change and Politics in America* (Chicago: University of Chicago Press, 1978), 368.

26   For a thorough review of the history of church–state relations, see E. Gaustad, *Church and State in America* (New York: Oxford University Press, 1998).

27   J. Garvey, 'Fundamentalism and American law', in M. Marty and R. S. Appleby (eds), *Fundamentalisms and the State* (Chicago: University of Chicago Press, 1993), 28–48.

28   J. McLaughlin, 'The evangelical surge', *National Review*, 20 (1984), 13.

29   P. Brogan, 'Abortion issue returns to muddy political and legal waters', *Herald*, 27 July 1991.

30   J. Watson, *The Christian Coalition: Dreams of Restoration. Demands for Recognition* (London: Macmillan, 1999).

31   M. C. Moen, *The Transformation of the Christian Right* (Tuscaloosa, Ala.: University of Alabama Press, 1992).

32   M. J. Rozell and C. Wilcox, *Second Coming: The New Christian Right in Virginia Politics* (Baltimore: John's Hopkins University Press, 1996).

33   T. G. Jelen, *To Serve God and Mammon: Church–State Relations in American Politics* (Boulder, Colo.: Westview, 2000).

34   After rising from the 1972 level of 180 per 1,000 live births to 1985's 354, it fell back gently to 306 in 1997 – a change resulting mainly from better contraceptive practice (US Centers for Disease Control and Prevention, *Abortion Surveillance: Preliminary Analysis – United States 1997*, 7 Jan. 2000).

35   AFL-CIO (2001), 'Facts about working women', www.afl-cio.org/women/wwfacts.htm.

36   C. Wilcox, 'America's radical right revisited', *Sociological Analysis*, 48 (1987), 46–57.

37   Transcript of *700 Club* interview with Jerry Falwell, 13 Sep. 2001, www.pfaw.org/911/robertson_falwell.shtml.

38   S. V. R. Nasr, *The Vanguard of the Islamic Revolution: The Jama'at-I Islami of Pakistan* (Berkeley and Los Angeles: University of California Press, 1994), 93.

39   L. J. Sabato, *PAC Power: Inside the World of Political Action Committees* (New York: Norton, 1984).

40   M. J. Rozell and C. Wilcox, *God at the Grassroots: The Christian Right in the 1994 Elections* (Lanham, Md.: Rowan & Littlefield, 1995), 256.

41   Associated Press, 'Issue ad spending hit $250 million', *USA Today*, 2 Jan. 2001.

42   C. P. Gilbert and D. A. Peterson, 'Minnesota: Christians and Quistians in the GOP', in M. J. Rozell and C. Wilcox (eds), *God at the Grassroots: The Christian Right in the 1994 Elections* (Lanham, Md.: Rowan & Littlefield, 1995), 171.

43   Jelen, *To Serve God and Mammon*, 105.

44   S. Bruce, *Conservative Protestant Politics* (Oxford: Oxford University Press, 1998). See also T. Gallagher, *Glasgow: The Uneasy Peace* (Manchester: Manchester University Press, 1987), and *Edinburgh Divided* (Edinburgh: Polygon, 1987).

45   J. Madeley, 'Reading the runes: the religious factor in Scandinavian electoral politics', in D. Broughton and H.-M. ten Napel (eds), *Religion and Mass Electoral Behaviour in Europe* (London: Routledge, 2000), 37.

46   The Barna Organization, 'The year's most intriguing findings', 17 Dec. 2001, www.barna.org.

47   R. J. McKeever, *The United States Supreme Court: A Political and Legal Analysis* (Manchester: Manchester University Press, 1997), 37.

48   'It's wrong to base voting on religion, say most Americans', Pew Forum on Religion and Public Life, 2001, www. pewtrusts.com.

49 It is also the case that appointment to the Court moderates most Justices. They have a professional interest in maintaining the legitimacy of the Court and are thus reluctant to alter too drastically previous Court decisions. Richard Neely, the Chief Justice of the West Virginia Court of Appeals, pointed out to me a more mundane reason for not shifting from a clear position on a contentious matter: most Justices are sensibly reluctant to encourage a raft of appeals.

50 M. Shibley, *Resurgent Evangelicalism in the United States* (Columbia, SC: University of South Carolina Press, 1996).

51 James D. Hunter, *Evangelicalism: The Coming Generation* (Chicago: University of Chicago Press, 1987).

CHAPTER 6   CONTROL

1 For a full explanation of why this is the case, see S. Bruce, *Religion in the Modern World: From Cathedrals to Cults* (Oxford: Oxford University Press, 1996).

2 Hannah Arendt makes this point with regard to anti-Semitism: 'the breakdown of the feudal order [gave] rise to the new revolutionary concept of equality, according to which "a nation within a nation" could no longer be tolerated' (H. Arendt, *The Origins of Totalitarianism* (New York: Harcourt Brace, 1951), 11).

3 M. Ignatieff, 'Benign nationalism?', in E. Mortimer (ed.), *People, Nation and State* (London: I. B. Tauris, 1999), 141–8.

4 Quoted in www.bosnet.org/bosnia/culture/religion.shtml, 2001.

5 A. Rhodes, *The Vatican in the Age of Dictators, 1922–45* (New York: Holt, Rinehart & Winston, 1973), 327.

6 As always, one has to add qualifications; in this case 'not in Ireland'. See J. S. Wheeler, *Cromwell in Ireland* (London: Palgrave, 2001).

7 H. S. Skeats and C. S. Miall, *History of the Free Churches of England, 1688–1891* (London: Alexander & Shepheard, 1891), 44.

8 D. Little, *Religion, Order and Law: A Study in Pre-Revolutionary England* (Oxford: Basil Blackwell, 1970), 99.

9 *Observer*, 28 May 2000.

10 M. Haghaveghi, *Islam and Politics in Central Asia* (New York: St Martin's Press, 1996), 16–17.

11 Q. A. Turajonzoda, 'Religion: the pillar of society', in R. Z. Sagdeev and S. Eisenhower (eds), *Central Asia: Conflict, Resolution and Change* (Washington: Center for Political and Strategic Studies, 1995), ch. 18; www.cpss.org/casiabk/chap18.

12 On Soviet policy towards religion generally, see A. Luukkanen, *The Party of Unbelief: The Religious Policy of the Bolshevik Party 1917–1929* (Helsinki: Studia Historica, 1994); N. S. Timasheff, *Religion in Soviet Russia 1917–1942* (Westport, Conn.: Greenwood, 1980); A. Benningsen and M. Broxup, *The Islamic Threat to the Soviet State* (London: Croom Helm, 1983); P. Mojzes, *Religious Liberty in Eastern Europe and the*

USSR: Before and After the Great Transformation (New York: Oxford University Press, 1992); and G. N. Shuster, *Religion behind the Iron Curtain* (Westport, Conn.: Greenwood, 1978).

13 Quoted in S. Bruce, *Choice and Religion: A Critique of Rational Choice* (Oxford: Oxford University Press, 1999), 110.

14 S. P. Ramet, 'Politics and religion in Eastern Europe and the Soviet Union', in G. Moyser (ed.), *Politics and Religion in the Modern World* (London: Routledge, 1991), 86.

15 D. H. David, 'Editorial: Russia's new law on religion: progress or regress', *Journal of Church and State*, 39 (1997), 128.

16 On the original ban, see *Christianity Today*, 12 Nov. 2001. On the Supreme Court decision, see I. Traynor, 'Russian court lifts Salvation Army ban', *Herald*, 8 Feb. 2002.

17 *Mormon News*, 13 Oct. 2000.

18 J. Ching, *Chinese Religions* (London: Macmillan, 1993); S. Feuchtwang, *The Imperial Metaphor: Popular Religion in China* (London: Routledge, 1992).

19 K. Boyle and J. Sheen, *Freedom of Religion and Belief: A World Report* (London: Routledge, 1997), 182.

20 B. Leung, 'Communist party–Vatican interplay over the training of church leaders in China', *Journal for the Scientific Study of Religion*, 40 (2001), 657–73.

21 F. Michael, *Rule by Incarnation: Tibetan Buddhism and its Role in Society and State* (Boulder, Colo.: Westview, 1982).

22 Boyle and Sheen, *Freedom of Religion and Belief*, 186.

23 A very detailed account of the story can be found in I. Hilton, *The Search for the Panchen Lama* (Harmondsworth: Penguin, 2001).

24 *Guardian*, 23 Mar. 2002.

25 Associated Press, 'China sentences Christian sect leader to death', 31 Dec. 2001.

26 Embassy of the People's Republic of China in the United States of America, Press release 0104, 28 Feb. 2001.

27 H. Hill, J. Hickman and J. McClendon, 'Cults and sects and doomsday groups', *Review of Religious Research*, 43 (2001), 24–38.

28 Much of what Muslims casually call 'Qurʾānic law' actually postdates the Qurʾān by some considerable time. Halliday and Zubaida make this observation both to challenge theocratic Muslims and to challenge analysts who believe Islam is unusually theocratic ('Roundtable', *Prospect*, Nov. 2001). These seem rather different projects. As I argue in the final chapter, what matters for social explanation is not what Islam 'really' requires but what Muslims believe to be the case. My case is that Islam is unusually theocratic, not that it *should* be so.

29 Details can be found in J. J. Elias, *Islam* (London: Routledge, 1999), M. Ruthven, *Islam in the World* (Harmondsworth: Penguin, 1984), B. Lewis, *The Political Language of Islam* (Chicago: University of

Chicago Press, 1988), and D. Waines, *An Introduction to Islam* (Cambridge: Cambridge University Press, 1995).

30 Boyle and Sheen, *Freedom of Religion and Belief*, 416–17.

31 Far worse is the position of religions that have rejected the Prophet. The Baha'i community in Iran (once thought to number 300,000) has largely been eradicated. Baha'is have been tortured and murdered. The leadership has been completely removed and many of the remaining Baha'is in Iran hide their identity (by, for example, recording themselves as Zoroastrians). As an aside, it is worth noting that, in a fine illustration of the common strategy of blackening dissenters with as wide a range of vices as possible, Iranian mullahs also accuse Baha'is of being traitorous. In 1943 a clumsy forgery was published in Mashhad that purported to be the memoirs of Count Dolgoruki, Russian envoy to Tehran from 1845 to 1854. This document showed that Bâbîsm, the precursor to Baha'ism, was invented by the Russians to divide and thus weaken Islam. See D. M. MacEoin, 'Changes in charismatic authority in Qajar Shi'ism', in F. Bosworth and C. Hillenbrand (eds), *Qajar Iran: Social, Economic and Political Change* (Edinburgh: Edinburgh University Press, 1984), 148–76.

32 F. Halliday, *Nation and Religion in the Middle East* (London: Saqi Books, 2000), 185.

33 For a magisterial philosophical and historical examination of the concept, see M. Cook, *Commanding Right and Forbidding Wrong in Islamic Thought* (Cambridge: Cambridge University Press, 2001).

34 A number of British commentators drew invidious comparisons between Western concerns for these statues and indifference over the suffering of Afghan civilians. Such carping both underestimates the importance of material artefacts for the survival of a culture and misses the point that a regime that is willing to destroy all physical evidence of alternative religions is also likely to destroy their adherents.

35 Boyle and Sheen, *Freedom of Religion and Belief*, 426.

36 Ibid. 454.

37 The constitution establishes Islam as the religion of the Malay Federation but allows that 'other religions may be practised in peace and harmony'. The shariah applies only to Muslims in personal matters. However, non-Muslims are not permitted to promote their religions. See ibid. 218–21.

38 It is worth noting that tolerance of diversity and violence are not opposite ends of a single scale. A crucial intervening variable is the power of the state. Although the culture is profoundly intolerant, Saudi Arabia and Iran have relatively little vigilante violence (compared with parts of Indonesia, for example), because they have powerful centralized state control systems that prevent spontaneous acts of communal violence.

39   H. Alavi, 'Pakistan and Islam: ethnicity and ideology', in F. Halliday and H. Alavi (eds), *State and Ideology in the Middle East and Pakistan* (New York: Monthy Review Press, 1988), 64–111.

40   S. Wolpert, *Jinnah of Pakistan* (New York: Oxford University Press, 1984).

41   S. V. R. Nasr, *The Vanguard of the Islamic Revolution: The Jamaʿat-I Islami of Pakistan* (Berkeley and Los Angeles: University of California Press, 1994), 106.

42   2001 Annual Report on International Religious Freedom, excerpts from United Sates Commission on International Religious Freedom, released by the Bureau of Democracy, Human Rights and Labor, US Department of State, 26 Oct. 2001, 'Pakistan'.

43   J. P. Piscatori, *Islam in a World of Nation-States* (Cambridge: Cambridge University Press, 1988), 148.

44   M. Ruthven, *Islam: A Very Short Introduction* (Oxford: Oxford University Press, 2000), 75.

45   N. Anderson, *Desert Saints: The Mormon Frontier in Utah* (Chicago: University of Chicago Press, 1942).

46   For a general study of the Moonies, see E. Barker, *The Making of a Moonie* (Oxford: Blackwell, 1984).

47   For an insightful analysis of NRMs (new religious movements) in terms of orientation to the world, see R. Wallis, *The Elementary Forms of the New Religious Life* (London: Routledge, 1984).

48   Useful surveys of new religions can be found in J. G. Melton, *Encyclopedic Handbook of Cults in America* (New York: Garland, 1992), and E. Arweck and P. B. Clarke (eds), *New Religious Movements in Western Europe: An Annotated Bibliography* (Westport, Conn.: Greenwood Press, 1997). See also J. Beckford, *Cult Controversies* (London: Tavistock, 1985).

49   The term was introduced into English by Hunter as a translation for *hsi nao* ('cleansing the mind'); see E. Hunter, *Brainwashing in Red China* (New York: Vanguard Press, 1951). Other early works in this tradition were E. H. Schein, 'The Chinese indoctrination program for prisoners of war', *Psychiatry*, 19 (1956), 149–72; R. J. Lifton, ' "Thought reform" of western civilians in Chinese communist prisons', *Psychiatry*, 19 (1956), 173–95, and R. Lifton, *Chinese Thought Reform and the Psychology of Totalism* (New York: Norton, 1961). The idea that disruption of the central nervous system could make people unusually credulous and susceptible to ideas they would not normally accept was popularized by W. Sargant, *The Battle for the Mind: A Physiology of Conversion and Brainwashing* (London: Heinemann, 1957). See also E. H. Schein, L. Schneier and C. Barker, *Coercive Persuasion* (New York: Norton, 1961). For a critical discussion, see J. T. Richardson (ed.), *The Brainwashing–Deprogramming Controversy* (New Brunswick, NJ: Transaction, 1980).

50   Detailed analysis of the effectiveness of Moonie recruitment can be found in Barker, *The Making of a Moonie*.

51 J. T. Richardson, 'Apostates, whistleblowers, law and social control', in D. Bromley (ed.), *The Politics of Religious Apostasy* (Westport, Conn.: Praeger, 1998), 171–89; E. Barker, 'Defection from the Unification Church: some strategies and distinctions', in D. Bromley (ed.), *Falling from the Faith* (Newbury Park, Calif.: Sage, 1998), 75–93.

52 L. F. Carter, *Charisma and Control in Rajneeshpuram* (Cambridge: Cambridge University Press, 1990).

53 On the UK treatment of NRMs, see E. Barker, 'Tolerant discrimination: church, state and the new religions' in P. Badham (ed.), *Religion, State and Society in Modern Britain* (Lampeter: Edwin Mellen Press, 1988), 185–208.

54 J. R. Hall, *Gone from the Promised Land: Jonestown in American Cultural History* (New Brunswick, NJ: Transaction Books); D. Chidester, *Salvation and Suicide: An Interpretation of Jim Jones, the People's Temple and Jonestown* (Bloomington, Ind.: Indiana University Press, 1988); R. Moore, *A Sympathetic History of Jonestown: The Moore Family Involvement in People's Temple* (Lewiston, Me.: Edwin Mellen Press, 1985).

55 D. Anthony and T. Robbins, 'Religious totalism, exemplary dualism and the Waco tragedy', in T. Robbins and S. J. Palmer (eds), *Millennium, Messiahs and Mayhem* (New York: Routledge, 1997), 261–84; D. Bromley and E. D. Silver, 'The Branch Davidians: a social profile and organizational history' in T. Miller (ed.), *America's Alternative Religions* (Albany, NY: SUNY Press, 1995), 149–58; S. A. Wright (ed.), *Armageddon in Waco: Critical Perspectives on the Branch Davidian Conflict* (Chicago: University of Chicago Press, 1995).

56 J. R. Hall and P. Schulyer, 'The mystical apocalypse of the Solar Temple', in Robbins and Palmer (eds), *Millennium, Messiahs and Mayhem*, 285–311; M. Introvigne, 'Ordeal by fire: the tragedy of the Solar Temple', *Religion*, 25 (1995), 267–83; S. J. Palmer, 'Purity and danger in the Solar Temple', *Journal of Contemporary Religion*, 11 (1996), 303–18.

57 R. Balch, 'Looking behind the scenes in a religious cult: implications for the study of conversion', *Sociological Analysis*, 41 (1980), 137–43; 'When the light goes out, darkness comes: a study of defection from a totalistic cult', in R. Stark (ed.), *Religious Movements: Genesis, Exodus and Numbers* (New York: Paragon House, 1985), 11–63; 'Waiting for the ships: disillusionment and the revitalization of faith in Bo and Peep's flying saucer cult', *Syzygy: Journal of Alternative Religion and Culture*, 3 (1994), 95–116.

58 G. Niebuhr, 'On the furthest fringes of millennialism', *New York Times*, 28 Mar. 1997.

59 I. Reader, *A Poisonous Cocktail? Aum Shinrikyo's Path to Violence* (Copenhagen: NIAS Publications, 1997), and *Religious Violence in Contemporary Japan: The Case of Aum Shinrikyo* (Honolulu: University of Hawaii Press, 2000); M. R. Mullins, 'Aum Shinrikyo as an apocalyptic movement', in Robbins and Palmer (eds), *Millennium, Messiahs*

and Mayhem, 313–24; R. J. Kisala and M. R. Mullins, *Religion and Social Crisis in Japan: Understanding Japanese Society through the Aum Affair* (New York: Palgrave, 2001); R. J. Kisala, 'The AUM Spiritual Truth Church in Japan', in A. Shupe (ed.), *Wolves within the Fold: Religious Leadership and Abuses of Power* (New Brunswick, NJ: Rutgers University Press, 1998), 33–48.

60 On pacifism generally, see D. Martin, *Pacifism* (London: Routledge & Kegan Paul, 1965). On the tensions between sects and the state, see B. R. Wilson, *Sects and Society* (London: Heinemann, 1961; repr. London: Greenwood Press, 1978).

61 On NRMs in Armenia, see E. Barker, 'The opium wars of the new millennium: religion in Eastern Europe and the former Soviet Union', in M. Silk (ed.), *Religion on the International News Agenda* (Hartford: Pew Program on Religion and the News Media, 2000), 39–59; 'But who's going to win? National and minority religion in post-communist society', in I. Borowik (ed.), *New Religions in Central and Eastern Europe* (Cracow: Nomos, 1997), and 'Quo vadis? The pursuit of understanding church-state relationships in Central and Eastern Europe', in I. Borowik (ed.), *Church–State Relations in Central and Eastern Europe* (Cracow: Nomos, 1999), 99–118.

62 E. Borenstein, 'Articles of faith: the media response to Maria Devi Christos', *Religion* 25 (1995), 249–66; M. Shterin, 'New religions and the changes in religious legitimation in Russia', in J. Kaplan (ed.), *Beyond the Mainstream* (Helsinki: Finnish Literature Society, 2001), 361–71.

63 In response to criticisms from a very large number of church and civil-rights groups, and representations from the US government, the United Nations and others, the Belgian government has clarified its position. In a lengthy response to the Special Rapporteur on Religious Tolerance of the UN Commission on Human Rights, it argued that its designation of a wide range of Christian organizations as 'sectes' did not, as critics supposed, of itself carry any negative connotations! See UN Commission on Human Rights, 55th Session, 1999, Item 11(*e*), paras 41–3.

64 T. Robbins, 'Combating "cults" and "brainwashing" in the United States and Western Europe: a comment on Richardson's and Intro-vigne's report', *Journal for the Scientific Study of Religion* 40 (2001), 172–3.

65 J. C. Soper, 'Tribal instinct and religious persecution: why do Western European states behave so badly?', *Journal for the Scientific Study of Religion* 40 (2001), 177–85, correctly points out that French secularism has a peculiarly Catholic tone to it.

66 *Jylands Posten*, 26 Feb. 2000.

67 In May 2000 the Office of the US Trade Representative officially added Germany to its list of states guilty of discriminatory trade practices. In June 2000 the German Ambassador made an official statement to the US Congress defending his country's policy: see 'Written statement

of the Ambassador of Germany, Jürgen Chrobog, for inclusion in the official record of the hearing of the House of Representatives International Relations Committee Treatment of Religious Minorities in Western Europe', www.house.gov/international_relations/full/relminor/germany.htm. For a good account of the dispute, see J. Joffe, 'Germany vs. the Scientologists', *New York Review of Books*, 24 Apr. 1997, pp. 16–21.

68 *Herald*, 6 Nov. 1993.

69 W. Kaminer, 'Sectual discrimination', *American Prospect*, 13 (11 Mar. 2002). Kaminer tries to present The Body as a victim of state persecution by comparing its treatment with the more generous treatment afforded Christian Science, which neatly reminds us that one century's dangerous deviants may become the next century's respectable denomination.

70 C. Wah, 'Jehovah's Witnesses and child custody cases in the United States, 1996–98', *Review of Religious Research*, 42 (2001), 373.

71 Ibid.

72 Quoted in A. Bradney, 'Children of a newer God: the English courts, custody disputes and new religious movements', in S. J. Palmer and C. Hardman (eds), *Children in New Religions* (New Brunswick, NJ: Rutgers University Press, 1995), 211.

73 The full text of the Appeal Court judgment is online at www.demon.co.uk/castle/audit/appeal.html.

74 M. W. Homer, 'The precarious balance between freedom of religion and the best interests of the child', in Palmer and Hardman (eds), *Children in New Religions*, 188.

CHAPTER 7   EXPLANATION

1 Huntington goes further and argues that culture (which is dominated by religion) is the main division in modern geopolitics; S. P. Huntington, *The Clash of Civilizations and the Remaking of the World Order* (London: Simon & Schuster, 1996).

2 We should note, however, that even the most apparently democratic regimes may have very large blind spots. There is a case for saying that the USA was not a democracy until the late 1960s because many of the southern states cynically disenfranchised blacks.

3 There can, of course, be legitimate disagreements between scholars about some of the judgements that make up these scales. However, the difference between Islamic and non-Islamic states is so great that we can be confident they reflect a genuine difference and not just US social science prejudice.

4 The Freedom House Survey Team, 'Freedom in the World 2002: the democracy gap', www.freedomhouse.org/ratings/index.htm.

5 For an insightful discussion of the origins of modern notions of human rights, see A. W. B. Simpson, *Human Rights and the End of*

Empire: Britain and the Genesis of the European Convention (Oxford: Oxford University Press, 2001), and C. Gearty's review of it: 'Airy-Fairy', *London Review of Books*, 29 Nov. 2001, pp. 9–12. For an interesting but finally unsuccessful attempt to set human rights on some transcendent basis, see M. Ignatieff, *Human Rights as Politics and Idolatry* (Princeton: Princeton University Press, 2001).

6 Huntington, *The Clash of Civilizations*, ch. 4.

7 Quoted in J. Esposito and J. O. Voll, 'Islam and democracy', www.neh.gov/news/humanities/2000–11/islam.html.

8 As we saw in ch. 3, it was common for West European countries to insist on the head of state being a member of the state church. When, as part of a general democratization, power was transferred from the monarch to an elected politician, the religious requirement was not. Thus, for example, the British monarch is nominally the head of the Church of England and is prevented by the Act of Settlement from being a Catholic, but the British throne has been impotent for two centuries and none of these restrictions apply to the Prime Minister.

9 R. Grieve, 'Caught between the hammer and the nail', *Herald*, 1 Feb. 1995.

10 The issue of Paisley's responsibility for terrorism, and the links between evangelicals and terrorists, are examined in great detail in S. Bruce, 'Fundamentalism and political violence: the case of Paisley and Ulster evangelicals', *Religion*, 31 (2001), 387–405.

11 Reuters, 'Falwell vows to tone down rhetoric on gays', Reuters press release, 22 Oct. 1999.

12 J. D. Hunter, *Culture Wars: The Struggle to Define America* (New York: Basic Books, 1991).

13 Figures compiled by the National Abortion Federation and available at www.religioustolerance.org/abo_viol.htm, 2002.

14 C. Berlet, 'John Salvi, abortion clinic violence and Catholic right conspiricism', *Public Eye*, www.publiceye/rightist/salvi.html, 2002.

15 K. Sawyer, 'Turning from "weapon of the spirit" to shotgun', *Washington Post*, 7 Aug. 1994.

16 Like the two leaders of the tiny and short-lived Orange Volunteers paramilitary group in Northern Ireland, many members of the militias are inspired by British-Israelism: the belief that the white Anglo-Saxons are not just metaphorically the Chosen People but are actually descended from the lost tribes of Israel. On the militias, see M. Durham, *The Christian Right, The Far Right and the Boundaries of American Conservatism* (Manchester: Manchester University Press, 2000); M. Barkun, *Religion and the Racist Right: The Origins of the Christian Identity Movement* (Chapel Hill, NC: University of North Carolina Press, 1994); and H. Bushart, J. Craig and M. Barnes, *Soldiers of God: White Supremacists and their Holy War for America* (New York: Pinnacle Books, 1998).

17 R. W. Maqsood, 'Women and Islam', *Daily Telegraph*, 15 Nov. 2001.
18 There is an equally myopic vision from the other side. Richard Dawkins argues that Christianity is responsible for most bad things; for a discussion and reply, see D. Martin, *Does Christianity Cause War?* (Oxford: Oxford University Press, 1997).
19 F. Halliday, *Nation and Religion in the Near East* (London: Saqi Books, 2000), 134.
20 B. B. Lawrence, *Defenders of God: The Fundamentalist Revolt against the Modern Age* (London: I. B. Tauris, 1990), 46.
21 S. Zubaida, 'Is there a Muslim society?', *Economy and Society*, 24 (1995), 151–88.
22 For a good discussion of the effects of Marxism on the study of nationalism, see P. Worsley, 'Models of the modern world-system', *Theory, Culture and Society*, 7 (1990), 83–95.
23 F. Halliday, *Nation and Religion in the Middle East* (London: Saqi Books, 2000).
24 E. Said, *Orientalism* (London: Routledge, 1978).
25 B. S. Turner, *Orientalism, Postmodernism and Globalism* (London: Routledge, 1994), 39–40.
26 Ibid. 44.
27 Z. Sardar, *Orientalism* (Buckingham: Open University Press, 1999), 60–2.
28 For an example of pointless name calling in which the great polymath Ernest Gellner is dismissed as a 'neo-orientalist', see P. Glavanis, 'Political Islam within Europe: a contribution to the analytical framework', *Innovation*, 11 (1998), 391–410. For a useful critique of orientalism, see E. Burke III, 'Orientalism and world history: representing Middle Eastern nationalism and Islamism in the twentieth century', *Theory and Society*, 27 (1998), 489–507.
29 S. Sayid, 'Beyond Westphalia: nations and diasporas – the case of the Muslim umma', in B. Hess (ed.), *Unsettled Multiculturalisms: Diasporas, Entanglements and Transruptions* (London: Zed Books), 33–49.
30 Although this point is slightly tangential, it is worth noting that the British ruling classes have usually preferred Muslims to Jews in the Middle East and to Hindus in India. The highly experienced foreign correspondent James Cameron notes this in *The Making of Israel* (London: Secker & Warburg, 1976) and *An Indian Summer* (London: Macmillan, 1975).
31 Huntington, *The Clash of Civilizations*.
32 For an extremely sensitive analysis of interactions, see F. Robinson, *Islam and Muslim History in South Asia* (New Delhi: Oxford University Press, 2000).
33 B. Thompson, *Imperial Vanities: The Adventures of the Baker Brothers and Gordon of Khartoum* (London: HarperCollins, 2002).
34 A. Axell, *Kamikaze: Japan's Suicide Gods* (London: Longman, 2002).
35 Martin, *Does Christianity Cause War?*, 37: 'where societies exhibit a relatively low level of differentiation and where religion provides

the modality of integration, the consequence must be a vigorous and comprehensive adjustment to "system properties".'

36 K. Boyle and J. Sheen, *Freedom of Religion and Belief: A World Report* (London: Routledge, 1997), 209.

37 I do not want to suggest an infinite regress, but it is possible to invert this point partly. It is possible to explain some of the ways in which Hinduism and Buddhism evolved as polytheistic religious cultures by saying that, for whatever reason, none of the tribal or ethnic groups that carried particular cults was able to impose itself completely on its neighbours or those whose lands it entered. The absence of deep social divisions and a high degree of cohesion among the settlers then explains polytheism, rather than the other way round.

38 A. Ravitsky, 'The contemporary Lubavitch Hasidic movement', in M. E. Marty and R. S. Appleby (eds), *Accounting for Fundamentalisms* (Chicago: University of Chicago Press, 1994), 303–27.

39 B. B. Keller, 'Millenarianism and resistance: the Xhosa cattle killing', *Journal of Asia and African Studies*, 13 (1978), 95–110.

40 P. Worsley, *The Trumpet Shall Sound: A Study of 'Cargo' Cults in Melanesia* (London: MacGibbon & Kee, 1957).

41 A. D. Smith, 'Ethnic election and national destiny: some religious origins of nationalist ideas', *Nations and Nationalism*, 5 (1999), 335.

42 R. Robinson, *Islam and Muslim History in South Asia* (New Delhi: Oxford University Press, 2000), 196.

43 Quoted in D. Cush and X. Robinson, 'The contemporary construction of Hindu identity: Hindu universalism and Hindu nationalism', *Diskus: An Internet Journal of Religion* (1997).

44 For a depressing catalogue of incidents of communal violence 1997–2001, see 'India: statistics on religion', www.atheism.about. com/religion/atheism/library/irf99/bl_irf_india99.htm.

45 Huntington, *The Clash of Civilizations*, 47–8.

46 The evolution of modern Hinduism is traced in A. T. Embree, 'The function of the Rashtriya Swayamsevak Sangh: to define the Hindu nation', and P. van der Veer, 'Hindu nationalism and the discourse of modernity: the Vishva Hindu Parishad', in Marty and Appleby (eds), *Accounting for Fundamentalisms*, 617–52, 653–68.

47 P. Nitzova, 'Islam in Bulgaria', *Religion, State and Society*, 22 (1994), 9.

48 Of course, nominal Christians have fought as mercenaries all over the globe and nominally Christian nations have united in defence of secular principles. What I mean is that the Crusades represented the last time significant numbers of people from a number of Christian states combined in pursuit of religious goals.

49 For an excellent review of Islamic political history that usefully reminds us that 'Islam and the nation-state are indeed compatible', see J. P. Piscatori, *Islam in a World of Nation-States* (Cambridge: Cambridge University Press, 1986).

50   S. V. R. Nasr, *The Vanguard of the Islamic Revolution: The Jamaʿat-I Islami of Pakistan* (Berkeley and Los Angeles: University of California Press, 1994), 79.
51   Robinson, *Islam and Muslim History in South Asia*, 183.
52   S. Bruce, *Conservative Protestant Politics* (Oxford: Oxford University Press, 1998), ch. 2.
53   S. Bruce, *Choice and Religion: A Critique of Rational Choice Theory* (Oxford: Oxford University Press, 1999), 99–113.
54   H. Hardacre, *Shinto and the State Shinto Shrines, 1868–1988* (Princeton: Princeton University Press, 1991), 148.
55   R. S. O'Fahey, 'The past in the present? The issue of sharia in Sudan', in H. B. Hansen and M. Twaddle (eds), *Religion and Politics in East Africa* (London: James Colley, 1995), 41.
56   For a philosophical and historical discussion, see M. Cook, *Commanding Right and Forbidding Wrong in Islamic Thought* (Cambridge: Cambridge University Press, 2001).
57   *Guardian*, 17 Dec. 2001.
58   Halliday, *Nation and Religion in the Near East*, 132.
59   This parallels the Lubavitcher criticism of Zionism: concentration on change in the material world will distract people from the more important goal of changing their spiritual condition.
60   H. Marcuse, *One Dimensional Man: Studies in the Ideology of Advanced Industrial Society* (New York: Beacon Press, 1992).
61   M. Foucault, *Discipline and Punish: The Birth of the Prison* (Harmondsworth: Penguin, 1991).
62   T. Abdul-Raheem, 'Islamist bigots: the case of Safiya Hussaini', *Jenda: The Journal of Culture and African Women's Studies*, 1 (2001), 2.
63   J. Sproxton, *Violence and Religion: Attitudes towards Militancy in the French Civil Wars and the English Revolution* (London: Routledge, 1995), 98.
64   Quoted in Robinson, *Islam and Muslim History in South Asia*, 185.
65   T. Ali, 'Mullahs and heretics', *London Review of Books*, 24/3, 7 Feb. 2002, p. 13.
66   F. Halliday, 'Islam and the West', *Prospect* (Nov. 2001), 17.
67   R. H. Dekmejian, *Islam in Revolution: Fundamentalism in the Arab World* (Syracuse, NY: Syracuse University Press), 76.
68   L. Stenberg, 'The revealed word and the struggle for authority: interpretation and use of Islamic terminology among Algerian Islamists' in D. Westerlund (ed.), *Questioning the Secular State: The Worldwide Resurgence of Religion in Politics* (London: Hurst, 1996), 146.
69   A. Mahmoud, 'The discourse of the Ikhwan of Sudan and Secularism' in Westerlund (ed.), *Questioning the Secular State*, 171.
70   Quoted in C. Bennett, 'Islamic imperialism: politics, religion, minorities and war in the Muslim world', paper presented at World 2000 conference, Austin, Texas, Feb. 2000; http://www.geocities.com/clintonbennett/IslamicImperialism.html.

71   B. Lewis, 'Islam and liberal democracy', *Atlantic Monthly* (Feb. 1993), 8.

72   Ibid.

73   A full explanation of secularization can be found in S. Bruce, *Religion in the Modern World: From Cathedrals to Cults* (Oxford: Oxford University Press, 1996), and *God is Dead: Secularization in the West* (Oxford: Blackwell, 2002).

74   I must apologize to that tiny band of people who know my previous works well; they will recognize what follows. Unfortunately, as I have not changed my mind about the matters in hand and have spent a long time finding clear and succinct ways of expressing them, I could present my thoughts in a very different form only by making the presentation less effective.

75   M. Weber, *The Protestant Ethic and the Spirit of Capitalism* (London: George Allen & Unwin, 1976). Weber spawned an industry of imitation and criticism. For an excellent sympathetic summary and elaboration, see G. Marshall, *In Search of the Spirit of Capitalism* (London: Hutchinson, 1982).

76   Some Marxists of a nostalgic bent see the narrowing of class domination, from the complex web of reciprocal obligations characteristic of feudalism to the contract and 'wage slavery' of modern capitalism as a bad thing. My case is that it was an important expansion of individual liberty.

77   Shortage of space requires me to tell the story in terms of extremes. Pre-Reformation there were guilds and societies and associations. The craftsmen and merchants of the cities and towns were a long way from the fatalism and inertia of the feudal serf. But the basic contrast stands.

78   D. Martin, *Tongues of Fire: The Explosion of Protestantism in Latin America* (Oxford: Blackwell, 1994).

79   A. Thomson, *Historical Sketch of the Origins of the Secession Church* (Edinburgh: Fullarton, 1848), 164.

80   I. Green, *Print and Protestantism in Early Modern England* (Oxford: Oxford University Press, 2000).

81   P. Gifford, *Christianity and Politics in Doe's Liberia* (Cambridge: Cambridge University Press, 1992), 55.

82   Robinson, *Islam and Muslim History in South East Asia*, 77.

83   Confusingly, this was not Cyrillic. That came later and was named after Cyril rather than being invented by him.

84   There is an alternative: the creation of insulated sectarian subcultures in which one particular faith can regain the domination enjoyed by the pre-Reformation church. As I argued in the second half of chapter 5, such subcultures are viable only where it is possible to create genuinely distinct subsocieties: a circumstance that prevailed in the USA and was largely absent elsewhere.

85   R. Inglehart, *Modernization and Postmodernization: Cultural, Political and Economic Change in 43 Countries* (Princeton: Princeton University Press, 1997).

INDEX